MICROSOFT®
EXCEL 2002
VISUAL BASIC®

FOR APPLICATIONS
STEP BY STEP

Reed Jacobson

PUBLISHED BY
Microsoft Press
A Division of Microsoft Corporation
One Microsoft Way
Redmond, Washington 98052-6399

Copyright © 2001 by Reed Jacobson

Library of Congress Cataloging-in-Publication Data
Jacobson, Reed.
    Microsoft Excel 2002 Visual Basic for Applications Step by Step / Reed Jacobson.
        p. cm.
    Includes index.
    ISBN 0-7356-1359-1
    1. BASIC (Computer program language)   2. Microsoft Visual Basic.   3. Microsoft
Excel (Computer file)   I. Title.

    QA76.73.B3 J339   2002
    005.26'8--dc21   2001042734

Printed and bound in the United States of America.

1 2 3 4 5 6 7 8 9   QWT   6 5 4 3 2 1

Distributed in Canada by Penguin Books Canada Limited.

A CIP catalogue record for this book is available from the British Library.

Microsoft Press books are available through booksellers and distributors worldwide. For further informa-
tion about international editions, contact your local Microsoft Corporation office or contact Microsoft
Press International directly at fax (425) 706-7329. Visit our Web site at www.microsoft.com/mspress.
Send comments to *mspinput@microsoft.com*.

ActiveX, Microsoft, Microsoft Press, MS-DOS, PivotChart, PivotTable, Visio, Visual Basic, Windows,
and Windows NT are either registered trademarks or trademarks of Microsoft Corporation in the United
States and/or other countries. Other product and company names mentioned herein may be the trademarks
of their respective owners.

The example companies, organizations, products, domain names, e-mail addresses, logos, people, places,
and events depicted herein are fictitious. No association with any real company, organization, product,
domain name, e-mail address, logo, person, place, or event is intended or should be inferred.

Acquisitions Editor: Kong Cheung
Project Editor: Jean Cockburn
Technical Editor: Dail Magee, Jr.

Body Part No. X08-04878

Contents

Part 1   Automating Everyday Tasks

1:   Make a Macro Do Simple Tasks   1

2:   Make a Macro Do Complex Tasks   24

Part 2   Exploring Objects

3:   Explore Workbooks and Worksheets   50

11: Create a Custom Form 224

12: Create an Enterprise Information System 254

Index 295

Introduction

Microsoft Excel is a powerful tool for analyzing and presenting information. One of the strengths of Excel has always been its macro language. Since Excel first appeared, it has always had the most extensive and flexible macro language of any spreadsheet program. Visual Basic for Applications (VBA) first appeared as part of Excel in version 5. In fact, Excel was the first major application to include this exciting new architecture. Starting with Excel 97, VBA became a complete development environment, consistent with the standalone version of Visual Basic and shared by all Microsoft Office applications.

When you first start writing macros in Excel, you need to learn two different skills. First, you need to learn how to work with VBA. Everything you learn about VBA will be true not only for Excel, but also for other applications that incorporate VBA. Second, you need to learn how to control Excel. The more you know about Excel as a spreadsheet application, the more effective you can be at developing macros that control Excel. While this book focuses on VBA as Excel's development environment, much of what you will learn will help you be more effective using spreadsheets as well.

Microsoft Excel 2002 Visual Basic for Applications Step By Step walks you through tasks one at a time, keeping you on track with clear instructions and frequent pictures of what you should see on your screen. In each section, you'll become familiar with another important aspect of Excel or VBA.

You'll notice some changes as soon as you start Microsoft Excel 2002. The toolbars and menu bar have a new look, and there's a new task pane on the right side of your screen. But the features that are new or greatly improved in this version of Excel go beyond just changes in appearance. Some changes won't be apparent to you until you start using the program.

For more information about the Excel product, see *http://www.microsoft.com/excel*.

Getting Help

This book is designed for Excel users who are starting to write macros and for programmers familiar with another programming system (such as Visual Basic or COBOL) who want to use Excel as a platform for developing applications. You'll get the most out of this book if you're already familiar with the basic capabilities of Excel, such as entering values and formulas into worksheets.

Learning about VBA and about how Excel works with VBA can seem overwhelming. That's why you need this book. It starts with simple, practical tasks and then takes you on to advanced concepts and powerful applications.

Every effort has been made to ensure the accuracy of this book and the contents of its CD-ROM. If you do run into problems, please contact the appropriate source for help and assistance.

Getting Help with This Book and Its CD-ROM

If your question or issue concerns the content of this book or its companion CD-ROM, please first search the online Microsoft Knowledge Base, which provides support information for known errors in or corrections to this book, at the following Web site:

http://mspress.microsoft.com/support/search.htm

If you do not find your answer at the online Knowledge Base, send your comments or questions to Microsoft Press Technical Support at:

mspinput@microsoft.com

Getting Help with Microsoft Excel 2002

If your question is about a Microsoft software product, including Excel, and not about the content of this Microsoft Press book, please search the Microsoft Knowledge Base at:

http://support.microsoft.com/directory/

In the United States, Microsoft software product support issues not covered by the Microsoft Knowledge Base are addressed by Microsoft Product Support Services. The Microsoft software support options available from Microsoft Product Support Services are listed at:

http://support.microsoft.com/directory/

Outside the United States, for support information specific to your location, please refer to the Worldwide Support menu on the Microsoft Product Support Services Web site for the site specific to your country:

http://support.microsoft.com/directory/

Using the Book's CD-ROM

The CD-ROM inside the back cover of this book contains all the practice files you'll use as you work through the exercises in this book. By using practice files, you won't waste time creating samples and typing spreadsheet data—instead, you can jump right in and concentrate on learning how to use Excel 2002.

Important

The CD-ROM does not contain the Excel 2002 software. You should purchase and install that program before using this book.

Important

Before you break the seal on the CD package, be sure that this book matches your version of the software. This book is designed for use with Microsoft Excel 2002 (version 10) or Microsoft Office XP Professional, Professional Special Edition, or Developer for the Windows 98, Windows NT, Windows 2000, Windows Me, or Windows XP operating systems. To find out what software you're running, you can check the product package or you can start the software, and then on the Help menu click About Microsoft Excel. If your program is not compatible with this book, a *Step by Step* or *Fundamentals* book matching your software is probably available. Please visit our World Wide Web site at *http://www.microsoft.com/mspress* or call 1-800-MSPRESS for more information.

System Requirements

To use this book, you will need:

- Microsoft Windows 98, Windows NT 4, Windows Millennium Edition, Windows 2000, or Windows XP
- Microsoft Excel 2002

Installing the Practice Files

You need to install the practice files on your hard disk before you use them in the chapters' exercises. Follow these steps to prepare the CD's files for your use:

1 Insert the CD-ROM into the CD-ROM drive of your computer.

A StartCD screen appears.

Important

If the menu screen does not appear, start Windows Explorer. In the left pane, locate the icon for your CD-ROM and click the icon. In the right pane, double-click the file StartCd.exe.

2 Click Install Practice Files.

3 Click the Continue button to install the practice files.

4   After the practice files have been installed, click ok.

A folder will be installed on your hard disk: C:\Excel VBA Practice Files. Within that folder are subfolders for each chapter.

Using the Practice Files

Each chapter's introduction lists the files that are needed for that chapter and explains any file preparation that you need to take care of before you start working through the chapter.

Each chapter explains how and when to use any practice files. The file or files that you'll need are indicated in the margin at the beginning of the chapter above the CD icon:

FileName

The following table lists each chapter's practice files.

Chapter	File Names
Chapter 1: Make a Macro Do Simple Tasks	Budget.xls
Chapter 2: Make a Macro Do Complex Tasks	Nov2002.txt Orders.dbf
Chapter 3: Explore Workbooks and Worksheets	-
Chapter 4: Explore Graphical Objects	Graphics.xls
Chapter 5: Explore Range Objects	Ranges.xls
Chapter 6: Explore PivotTable Objects	Orders.dbf
Chapter 7: Control Visual Basic	Orders.dbf Flow.xls
Chapter 8: Extend Excel and Visual Basic	Function.xls
Chapter 9: Launch Macros with Events	Events.xls
Chapter 10: Use Dialog Box Controls on a Worksheet	Loan.xls
Chapter 11: Create a Custom Form	Budget.xls

Chapter	File Names
Chapter 12: Create an Enterprise Information System	Finished\Chapter12.xls
	Map.wmf
	Oders.dbf
	Orders.mdb
	Code12A.txt
	Code12B.txt
	Code12C.txt
	Code12D.txt
	Code12E.txt
	Code12F.txt
	Code12G.txt

Uninstalling the Practice Files

After you finish working through this book, you can uninstall the practice files to free up hard disk space.

Tip

If you saved any files outside the Practice Files folder, they will not be deleted by the following uninstall process. You'll have to manually delete them.

To uninstall the practice files, follow these steps:

1 On the Windows task bar, click the Start button, point to Settings, and then click Control Panel.

2 Double-click the Add/Remove Programs icon.

3 Click the Microsoft Excel 2002 VBA SBS files to remove, and click Add/Remove. (If you're using Windows 2000 Professional, click the Remove or Change/Remove button.)

4 Click Yes when the confirmation dialog box appears.

Important

If you need additional help installing or uninstalling the practice files, please see the section "Getting Help" earlier in this book. Microsoft's product support does not provide support for this book or its CD-ROM.

Checking Your Configuration

Microsoft Excel allows you to customize your work environment to a remarkable degree. You can decide which toolbars are visible, which commands are on a toolbar, how the gridlines are displayed, and countless other customizations. In fact, you might have customized your working environment so that some of the exercises in this book work differently from the way they're described.

In general, this book assumes that your environment matches the default settings for Excel. If you find that your copy of Excel or the Microsoft Visual Basic Editor doesn't behave the way the book describes, compare your custom settings with those described here.

Excel Environment

The settings for Excel are separate from the settings in the Visual Basic Editor.

Windows

- The workbook window is maximized.
- The Excel window can either be maximized or resizable.

Toolbars

- The Standard and Formatting toolbars are visible.
- After Chapter 1, the Visual Basic toolbar is visible.
- The menus and all toolbars contain default commands.

To control which toolbars are visible, click Customize on the Tools menu, click the Toolbars tab, and then put a check mark next to only those toolbars that you want to see.

To reset the toolbars, click Customize on the Tools menu and then click the Toolbars tab. Select a toolbar or menu name, and then click the Reset button.

Add-Ins

This book doesn't require that any add-ins be installed. For the most part, installing or removing the add-ins that come with Excel shouldn't affect any exercises in this book (except that if you've installed the AutoSave add-in, you might occasionally be prompted to save the open workbooks). If you're uncertain whether an add-in might be affecting the way the exercises in this book are working, you can safely disable any add-in you've installed.

To disable an add-in, click Add-Ins on the Tools menu, select the add-in name, and remove the check box next to the name.

View Options

This book assumes that the following View options are set. View options that aren't mentioned don't matter.

- Show Formula Bar is turned on.
- Show Status Bar is turned on.
- Objects Show All is turned on.
- Formulas is turned off.
- Gridlines is turned on.
- Gridlines Color is Automatic.
- Row & Column Headers is turned on.
- Horizontal Scroll Bar is turned on.
- Vertical Scroll Bar is turned on.
- Sheet Tabs is turned on.

To set the View options, click Options on the Tools menu, click the View tab in the dialog box, and select the desired options.

Calculations Options

This book assumes that the following Calculations options are set. Calculations options that aren't mentioned don't matter.

- In the Calculation group, Automatic is selected.
- In the Workbook Options group, Accept Labels In Formulas is selected.

To set the Calculations options, click Options on the Tools menu, click the View tab in the dialog box, and select the desired options.

General Options

This book assumes that the following General options are set. General options that aren't mentioned don't matter.

- R1C1 Reference Style is turned off.
- Sheets In New Workbook is 3.
- User Name is set to your name.

To set the General options, click Options on the Tools menu, click the General tab in the dialog box, and then select the desired options.

Visual Basic Editor Environment

The Visual Basic Editor Environment has customization settings that are independent of Excel. To display the Visual Basic Editor, click the Visual Basic Editor button on the Visual Basic toolbar in Excel.

Windows

- All windows are closed except the code window.
- The code window is maximized.

Toolbars

- The Standard toolbar is visible.
- The menu and toolbars contain the default commands.

To control which toolbars are visible, click Customize on the Toolbars submenu of the View menu, click the Toolbars tab, and then put a check mark next to only the Standard toolbar.

To reset the toolbars, click Customize on the Toolbars submenu of the View menu, and then click the Toolbars tab. Select a toolbar or menu name, and then click the Reset button.

Editor Options

This book assumes that the following Editor options are set. Editor options that aren't mentioned don't matter.

- Auto Syntax Check is turned on.
- Require Variable Declaration is turned off (until possibly after Chapter 8).
- Auto List Members is turned on.
- Auto Quick Info is turned on.
- Auto Data Tips is turned on.
- Auto Indent is turned on.
- Default To Full Module View is turned on.
- Procedure Separator is turned on.

To set the Editor options, click Options on the Tools menu, click the Editor tab in the dialog box, and select the desired options.

Editor Format Options

This book assumes that the following Editor Format options are set. Editor Format options that aren't mentioned don't matter.

- Normal Text has Auto for Foreground, Background, and Indicator.
- Execution Point Text has Auto for Foreground and is yellow for Background and Indicator.
- Breakpoint Text is dark red for Foreground, and Auto for Background and Indicator.
- Comment Text is dark green for Foreground, and Auto for Background and Indicator.
- The Margin Indicator Bar is turned on.

To set the Editor Format Options, click Options on the Tools menu and click the Editor Format tab in the dialog box. Select the desired type of text, and choose the options you want.

Docking Options

This book assumes that the following Docking options are set. Docking options that aren't mentioned don't matter. (These window settings don't affect the way anything in the book works, but they might make your screens appear different than the captured screens in the text.)

All windows are dockable. (The Object Browser is dockable after Chapter 3.)

To set the Docking options, click Options on the Tools menu, click the Docking tab in the dialog box, and select the desired options.

Conventions and Features

You can save time when you use this book by understanding how the Step by Step series shows special instructions, keys to press, buttons to click, and so on.

Convention	Meaning
1 **2**	Numbered steps guide you through hands-on exercises in each topic.
●	A round bullet indicates an exercise that has only one step.
Filename.doc  (CD icon)	This icon at the beginning of a chapter lists the files that the lesson will use and explains any file preparation that needs to take place before starting the lesson. Practice files that you'll need to use in a topic's procedure are shown above the CD icon.
Tip	This section provides a helpful hint or shortcut that makes working through a task easier.
Important	This section points out information that you need to know to complete the procedure.
Troubleshooting	This section shows you how to fix a common problem.
Save  (Save button icon)	When a button is referenced in a topic, a picture of the button appears in the margin area with a label.
Alt+Tab	A plus sign (+) between two key names means that you must press those keys at the same time. For example, "Press Alt+Tab" means that you hold down the Alt key while you press Tab.
Blue boldface type	Text that you are supposed to type appears in **blue boldface type** in the procedures.

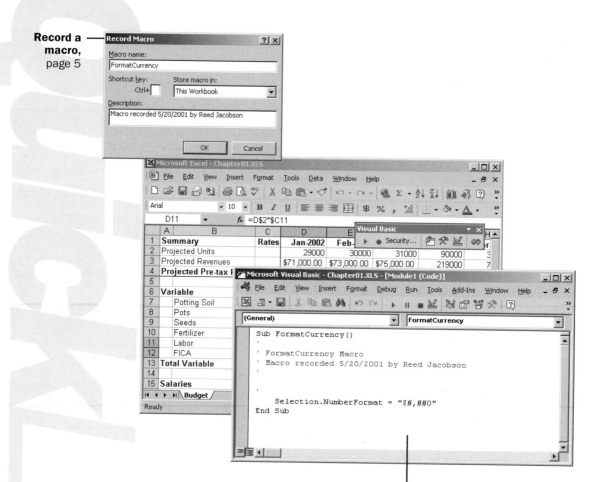

Record a macro, page 5

Learn how to read a macro, page 8

Chapter 1
Make a Macro
Do Simple Tasks

After completing this chapter, you will be able to:

✔ **Record and run a macro.**

✔ **Understand and edit simple recorded macros.**

✔ **Run a macro by using a shortcut key.**

Last month, I lost the remote control to my VCR. It was awful. I wanted to set the machine to record a "Gilligan's Island" rerun at 3:00 A.M. one night, but I couldn't do it because all the scheduling features were built into the remote control. Fortunately, after about two weeks, my roommate detected a bulge in the cloth backing of the recliner and retrieved the precious controller. I'm so happy that I can again record classic television. Someday I might even watch some of the shows.

Microsoft Visual Basic for Applications (VBA) is the remote control for Microsoft Excel 2000. Sure, you can use Excel without ever using VBA, but the VBA "remote control" can make Excel more convenient to use and allow you to take advantage of features that can't be accessed with the standard "front-panel" controls. Once you become acquainted with Excel's remote control, you'll wonder how you ever got along without it.

How Visual Basic for Applications Talks to Excel

The first spreadsheet macro languages mimicked the user interface. For example, if you typed **R** (for "Range"), **N** (for "Name"), and **C** (for "Create") in the user interface, you would enter **RNC** into the macro to automate the process. This approach had inherent weaknesses. Not only were keystroke macros difficult to read, but they also didn't adapt well to the graphical user interface. What keystrokes would you use to represent dragging a rectangle with the mouse?

To solve these problems, the early versions of Excel contained a new type of macro language that made the macro commands independent of the user interface. For example, in Excel version 4 you could copy a range at least three different ways: press Ctrl+C, click the Copy toolbar button, or click Copy on the Edit menu. All those user interface sequences translated to a single macro function, =COPY( ). These function-based macros had two major drawbacks: First, Excel macros were very specific to Excel; the language couldn't be adapted to other applications. Second, the number of functions kept increasing with each new version, and there was no good way to organize or group the thousands of possibilities.

Excel with VBA incorporates *Automation* (once known as OLE Automation), a powerful way of automating applications. Excel was the first major application to take advantage of this concept. In this approach, VBA acts as a general-purpose language that's independent of the application. Suddenly, anyone who knows how to work with any version of Visual Basic has a big head start in automating Excel, and anyone who learns how to write Excel macros in VBA can transfer that knowledge to other types of Visual Basic programming.

Important

VBA is a version of Visual Basic that's hosted by an application, such as Microsoft Excel. A VBA macro can't run independently of its host application. VBA and the stand-alone version of Visual Basic both use the same language engine, editor, and most supporting tools. In this book, I'll use "VBA" to refer specifically to the macro language in Excel, and "Visual Basic" to refer to anything that's shared by all versions of Visual Basic.

Even though Excel hosts VBA, VBA doesn't have any special hooks into the internals of Excel. Rather, Excel exposes its capabilities to VBA by means of a special set of commands known as an *object library*. VBA talks to the Excel object library.

VBA can control not only Excel, but also any application that provides an object library. All Microsoft Office applications provide object libraries, and several other Microsoft and non-Microsoft applications also do.

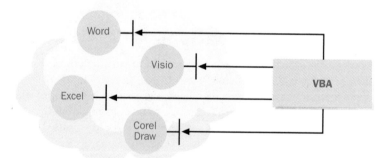

The VBA that comes with Excel isn't the only language that can communicate with the object library. Any language that supports Automation can control Excel. You can control Excel not only with the VBA hosted by Excel, but also with a VBA project hosted by Microsoft Word, with the stand-alone version of Visual Basic, or even with C++ or Inprise Corporation's Delphi program.

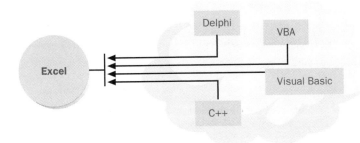

Excel Objects and You

Not only does the object library expose Excel's capabilities to VBA, but more importantly, it also exposes Excel's capabilities to you. Once you know how to read and interpret an object library, you can discover new features and quickly figure out how to put them to work. The best way to learn how VBA communicates with Excel objects is to record some simple macros. Eventually, however, you'll want to move beyond the limitations of the macro recorder.

If you work through this book sequentially, you'll first learn how to record and modify simple macros. Then you'll learn how to use the VBA tools for exploring objects as you learn how to use some of the most important objects in Excel. Next you'll learn how to use VBA features to make your applications more powerful. And finally you'll learn how to make a macro easy to use.

Budget.xls

This chapter uses the practice file Budget.xls that you installed from the book's CD-ROM. For details about installing the practice files, see "Using the Book's CD-ROM" at the beginning of this book.

Getting Started

1   Start Excel.

Open

2   On the Standard toolbar, click the Open button, and then in the Open dialog box, click the Favorites button.

3   Double-click the folder that contains the practice files installed from the companion CD, and then double-click the Budget workbook.

4   Save the Budget file as **Chapter01**.

The Chapter01 workbook contains a single worksheet, named Budget. This worksheet includes a projected month-to-month budget for the year 2002.

Creating a Simple Macro

Excel has a large collection of convenience tools readily available as shortcut keys and as buttons on toolbars. Sometimes, however, a built-in convenience tool doesn't work quite the way you want. Enhancing a built-in tool is a good first macro to create.

Show the Visual Basic Toolbar

Before you start creating the macros, take one small step that will make your work with macros much easier.

1   Point to any toolbar, and click the right mouse button. (This is called *right-clicking*.) The toolbar shortcut menu appears, showing most of the available toolbars.

2   Select Visual Basic from the toolbar list. The Visual Basic toolbar appears. You can change the location and shape of this toolbar just as you can any other Excel toolbar.

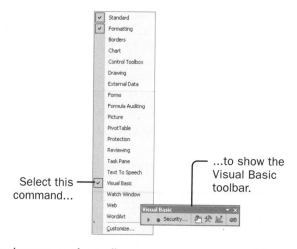

Select this command...

...to show the Visual Basic toolbar.

The buttons on the toolbar are supposed to resemble controls on a VCR. When you're ready to record a macro, click the circle on the toolbar—the "record" button. Then, when you're ready to run a macro, click the triangle—the "play" button.

Format Currency with a Built-In Tool

On the Formatting toolbar, Excel has a button that formats the current selection as currency: the Currency Style button.

1   In the Chapter01 workbook, select cells D3:F4 on the Budget worksheet.

Currency Style

2   Click the Currency Style button on the Formatting toolbar. Excel reformats the selected cells as currency.

Click here to format the
selection as currency.

The currency format that Excel applies when you click the Currency Style button has two decimal places. In your checkbook, you might want to display currency with two decimal places. But your budget contains estimates, and displaying values to the penny seems silly. You want to create a macro that formats selected cells as currency with no decimal places.

Record a Macro to Format Currency

1 On the Budget worksheet, select cells D7:F8.

Record Macro

2 On the Visual Basic toolbar, click the Record Macro button.

3 Replace the default macro name with **FormatCurrency**, and then click OK. A macro name must begin with a letter, and it can contain uppercase and lowercase letters, numbers, and underscores, but no spaces or other special characters.

Type the name of the
new macro here.

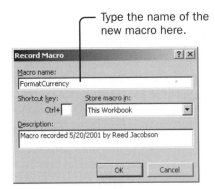

The word *Recording* appears in the status bar, and a Stop Recording toolbar appears. You're recording.

4 On the Format menu, click the Cells command. If necessary, click the Number tab in the Format Cells dialog box.

5 Select Currency from the Category list.

6 Replace the value in the Decimal Places box with a zero.

Select Currency...

...and specify zero decimal places.

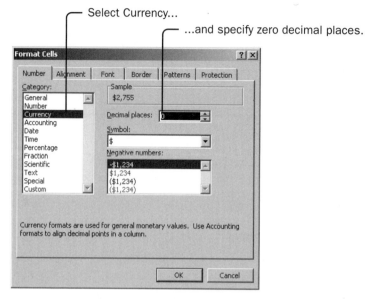

7 Select Custom from the Category list, and look in the Type text box. The characters $#,##0 represent a currency format with no decimal places. This is the format that gets applied to the selected cells. (To learn more about format strings, type "number format codes" in the Excel Help box.)

8 Click OK to format the selected cells as currency without decimal places.

Stop Recording

9 Click the Stop Recording button, and save the Chapter01 workbook.

That's it. You recorded a macro to format a selection with the currency format you want. Now you probably want to try the macro to see how it works.

Run the Macro

1 On the Budget worksheet, select cells D9:F10.

2 On the Visual Basic toolbar, click the Run Macro button.

3 Select the FormatCurrency macro in the list, and click Run.

Your macro applies your customized currency format to the selected cells. Running the macro from the Macro dialog box isn't much easier than directly assigning the number format. To make the macro easy to run, you can use a shortcut key.

Assign a Shortcut Key to the Macro

Run Macro

1 On the Visual Basic toolbar, click the Run Macro button.

2 Select the FormatCurrency macro in the list, and then click the Options button. The Macro Options dialog box allows you to change the macro's shortcut key assignment and its description. You can also assign a shortcut key at the time you first record a macro.

3 Assign Ctrl+Shift+C as the shortcut key. With the box below the Shortcut Key label selected, press Shift+C.

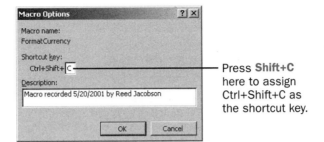

Press **Shift+C** here to assign Ctrl+Shift+C as the shortcut key.

Important

Excel uses many Ctrl key combinations as built-in shortcuts. For example, Ctrl+C is Copy and Ctrl+Z is Undo. If you assign one of these shortcuts to your macro, pressing the shortcut key combination runs your macro rather than the built-in command. If you always use Ctrl+Shift key combinations when you assign shortcut keys to your macros, you'll be much less likely to override a built-in shortcut.

4 Click OK to return to the Macro dialog box, and then click Cancel to get back to the worksheet.

5 Select cells D11:F12, and press Ctrl+Shift+C to run the macro.

6 Save the Chapter01 workbook.

Now you've successfully recorded, run, and enhanced a macro—all without seeing the macro itself. Maybe you'd like to actually see what you created.

Look at the Macro

The macro is hidden away in the workbook, and you need to open the Visual Basic Editor to see it.

Run Macro

1 On the Visual Basic toolbar, click the Run Macro button.

2 Click FormatCurrency, and then click Edit.

The Visual Basic Editor window appears. The Visual Basic Editor appears to be a separate program, but it is "owned" by Excel—that is, if you quit Excel, the editor automatically shuts down. Inside the Visual Basic Editor, a window captioned Module1 appears as well.

3 Maximize the Module1 window so that it fills the Visual Basic Editor, and then resize the Visual Basic Editor window so that you can see the Excel workbook in the background.

4 If any other windows are visible in the Visual Basic Editor, close them now.

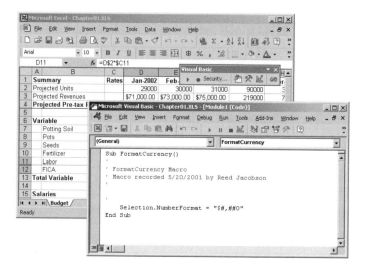

The window has the caption Module1. A *module* is the place where the recorder puts macros. Your macro is in the Module1 module. The macro looks like this:

```
Sub FormatCurrency()
'
' FormatCurrency Macro
' Macro recorded 5/20/2001 by Reed Jacobson
'


'
    Selection.NumberFormat = "$#,##0"
End Sub
```

The five lines that start with apostrophes are *comments*. An apostrophe tells Visual Basic to ignore all remaining text on the line. (The blank line among the comments, without even an apostrophe, is where the recorder would have put the shortcut key combination if you had assigned it when you recorded the macro.) The recorder puts in the comments partly to remind you to add comments as you write a macro. You can add to them, change them, or delete them as you want without changing how the macro runs. Comments appear in green to help you distinguish them from statements. Everything in Visual Basic that is not a comment is a statement. A statement tells Visual Basic what to do.

The first statement in the macro begins with *Sub*, followed by the name of the macro. This statement tells Visual Basic to begin a new macro. Perhaps the word *Sub* is used because a macro is typically hidden, or out of sight, like a *sub*marine. Or maybe *Sub* is used for historical reasons. The last statement of a macro is always *End Sub*. This statement tells Visual Basic to stop running the macro.

All the statements between Sub and End Sub form the *body* of the macro. These are the statements that do the real work. The first (and only) statement in the body of the FormatCurrency macro begins with *Selection.NumberFormat*. The word *Selection* refers to an object—the currently selected range of cells. The word *NumberFormat* refers to an attribute—or *property*—of that object. Whenever the macro recorder creates a statement that contains an equal sign, the word to the left of the equal sign is a property. The property is preceded by an object, and the object and its property are separated by a period. The value to the right of the equal sign is what gets assigned to the property. In this example, the value assigned to the NumberFormat property is the number format code you saw earlier in the Format dialog box. To interpret a Visual Basic statement, read it from right to left. For example, read this statement as, "Let such-and-such be the number format of the selection."

Tip

Some people wonder why *NumberFormat* comes after *Selection* if you read *Selection.NumberFormat* as "number format of the selection." Macro statements in Visual Basic work backward, the same as actions do in an Excel worksheet. In a macro statement, you state what you're going to work on and then you do something to it. The order is similar to the way you interact with cells in an Excel worksheet: You don't specify an action first and then the object. ("Copy these cells. Paste the copy in those cells.") Instead, you select the object first and then perform the action. ("These cells—copy. Those cells—paste.") Selecting the object first makes carrying out multiple actions more efficient.

Changing Multiple Properties at Once

The FormatCurrency macro changes a single property (the number format) of a single object (the currently selected cells). Assigning a value to the property changes the object. Many macro statements assign a value to a property of an object. Sometimes when you record an action, the macro changes multiple properties of one object at the same time.

Merge Text Vertically with a Command

Excel has a toolbar button that can merge and center several cells in a horizontal row: the Merge And Center button. But sometimes you might want to merge cells vertically along the edge of a report. Excel doesn't have a toolbar button that merges cells in a vertical column, but you can record a macro that does.

To better understand what's required, first walk through the steps to create this format using menu commands.

1 Activate the Budget window.

2 Select the range A6:A12. The label Variable is at the top of the selected range.

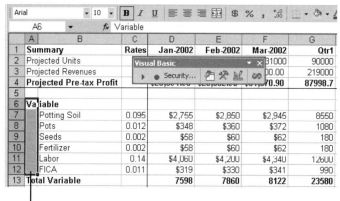

Select the cells you want to merge.

3 On the Format menu, click Cells. In the Format Cells dialog box, click the Alignment tab. The Alignment tab has several controls that control alignment, wrapping, orientation angle, text direction, shrinking, and merging.

4 Click the Merge Cells check box, and drag the red diamond in the orientation control to the top of the arc to set the orientation to 90 degrees.

Select the Merge Cells check box...

...and drag the orientation to 90 degrees...

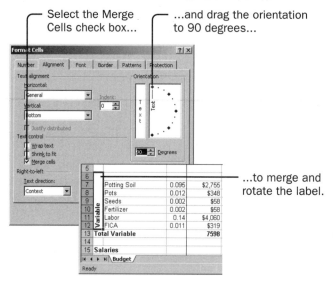

...to merge and rotate the label.

5 Click OK to merge and tilt the label.

Putting a label to the side of a block of cells is extremely powerful. You can make it easy to do by recording a macro.

Record a Macro to Merge Cells Vertically

1 Rearrange your windows as necessary so that you can see both the Module1 window and the Excel window.

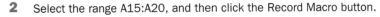

Tip

To rearrange the windows, minimize all the applications you have open except Excel and the Visual Basic Editor, and activate Excel. Then right-click the taskbar, and on the shortcut menu, click Tile Windows Horizontally.

Record Macro

2 Select the range A15:A20, and then click the Record Macro button.

3 In the Record Macro dialog box, replace the default macro name with **MergeVertical**, replace the default description with **Merge cells vertically**, and set Ctrl+Shift+M as the shortcut key.

Important

If you assign the same shortcut key to two macros, the one that appears first in the Run Macro list is the one that runs. A shortcut key is valid only while the workbook containing the macro is open.

4 Click OK. In the module window, you can see that the recorder immediately puts the comment lines, the keyboard shortcut, and the Sub and End Sub lines into the macro.

Tip

The first time you record a macro, Excel creates a new module. Each time you record an additional macro, Excel adds the new macro to the end of the same module. When you close and reopen the workbook, the macro recorder starts recording macros into a new module. There is no way for you to control where the recorder puts a new macro. Having macros in multiple modules shouldn't be a problem. When you use the Macro dialog box to select and edit a macro, it automatically takes you to the appropriate module.

5 On the Format menu in the Excel window, click Cells. In the Format Cells dialog box on the Alignment tab, select the Merge Cells check box, set the orientation to 90 degrees, and click OK. The recorder puts several lines into the macro all at once.

Stop Recording

6 Click the Stop Recording button, and save the Chapter01 workbook.

The new macro in the Module1 window looks like this:

```
Sub MergeVertical()
'
' MergeVertical Macro
' Merge cells vertically
'
' Keyboard Shortcut: Ctrl+Shift+M
'
    With Selection
        .HorizontalAlignment = xlGeneral
        .VerticalAlignment = xlBottom
        .WrapText = False
        .Orientation = 90
```

(continued)

```
            .AddIndent = False
            .IndentLevel = 0
            .ShrinkToFit = False
            .ReadingOrder = xlContext
            .MergeCells = True
        End With
    End Sub
```

The macro shows nine different properties that relate to cell alignment. Each property name is followed by an equal sign. These properties correspond to the controls you saw on the Alignment tab of the Format Cells dialog box.

All these properties pertain to the same object—the currently selected cells, as does the NumberFormat property in the FormatCurrency macro. In the FormatCurrency macro, however, the object directly precedes the property, separated only by a period. In this MergeVertical macro, however, each property name just hangs there, preceded only by a dangling period.

The object for all these properties appears in a statement that begins with the word *With*. The group of statements from With to End With is called a *With structure*. Whenever a property inside a With structure is preceded by a dangling period with no object, you simply pretend that the object from the With statement is there. With structures make the code easier to read because you can tell instantly that all the properties relate to the same object—the current selection in this case. You'll often see With structures in macros that you record.

Eliminate Unnecessary Lines from the Macro

In many dialog boxes, the macro recorder records all the possible properties, even though you might change the values of only one or two of them. You can make your macro easier to understand if you eliminate unnecessary property assignments.

In the MergeVertical macro, you need to change the values of only the Orientation and MergeCells properties. You can therefore delete the other statements from the With structure.

1 Activate the Visual Basic Editor window, and click as far to the left of the HorizontalAlignment statement as you can within the Editor window. (Your mouse pointer should turn into a right-pointing arrow before you click.)

This action selects the entire line, including the indent that precedes the text.

Tip

If you see a red circle in the margin after you click, you clicked too far into the gray area. Click in the red circle to remove it, and try again.

2 Press the Delete key.

3 Repeat steps 1 and 2 for each property except Orientation and MergeCells. If you delete too much, click the Undo button to restore what you deleted. The simplified macro (ignoring the comment lines, which you can delete if you want) should look like this:

```
Sub MergeVertical()
    With Selection
        .Orientation = 90
        .MergeCells = True
    End With
End Sub
```

4 Activate the Excel window, and select cells A25:A30.

5 Press Ctrl+Shift+M. The macro adjusts the label.

6 Save the Chapter01 workbook.

Now you've not only recorded a macro, but you've also deleted parts of it—and it still works. Next you'll record a macro and make additions to it.

Editing a Recorded Macro

A typical Excel worksheet has light gray gridlines that mark the boundaries of the cells. Sometimes, you might want to remove the gridlines. First walk through the process to remove the gridlines with menu commands, and then record a macro to make the change.

Remove Gridlines with a Command

1 On the Tools menu, click Options, and then, if necessary, click the View tab.

2 Clear the Gridlines check box at the bottom of the Window Options group.

3 Click OK. The gridlines disappear.

4 Repeat step 1, select the Gridlines check box to turn the gridlines back on, and then click OK.

Gridlines are a property of the window. You can select the Gridlines check box so that the value of the property is *True* and the window displays the gridlines, or you can clear the check box so that the value of the property is *False* and the window doesn't display the gridlines. Now see how the recorder turns off the gridlines.

Record a Macro to Remove Gridlines

Record Macro

1 Click the Record Macro button.

2 Replace the default macro name with **RemoveGrid**, and click OK. The recorder puts the shell of the macro (the comments and the Sub and End Sub lines) into the module.

3 On the Tools menu, click Options, clear the Gridlines check box on the View tab, and then click OK. The gridlines disappear.

Stop Recording

4 Click the Stop Recording button, and then save the Chapter01 workbook.

Run Macro

5 Click the Run Macro button, select RemoveGrid, and then click Edit to look at the resulting code. Ignoring the comment lines, here's what it looks like:

```
Sub RemoveGrid()
    ActiveWindow.DisplayGridlines = False
End Sub
```

This macro is similar to the FormatCurrency macro. You can read it as "Let 'False' be the Display Gridlines state of the active window." This time you're not changing the selected cells but rather the active window. In both cases, you're changing an *object*, an Excel element that you can control with macros. However, this time the object isn't a range of cells, but a window.

Run the Macro from the Visual Basic Editor

You can easily change the macro to make it restore the gridlines.

1 In the RemoveGrid macro, replace *False* with **True**.

You can't use a shortcut key while you're in the Visual Basic Editor, but the Visual Basic Editor has its own shortcut for running whatever macro you're currently editing.

2 Press F5 to run the macro. The gridlines reappear in the current Excel worksheet. Pressing F5 from the Visual Basic Editor is a fast way to run a macro while you're testing it.

Tip

If you're in VBA and want to display the Macro dialog box so that you can select a macro, click outside any macro before you press F5.

Toggle the Value of a Property with a Macro

You could create one macro to turn the gridlines off and a second macro to turn them on; but somehow, letting a single macro toggle the value of the property seems more natural. To toggle the value of a property, you first ask Excel for the current value, which you can store in a special container called a *variable*. You then change the value as you assign the variable back to the property. Here's how:

1 Insert a new blank line after the comments.

2 Select *ActiveWindow.DisplayGridlines*, and press and hold the Ctrl key as you drag it up to the blank line. This makes a copy of the expression.

3 Type **myGrid =** at the beginning of the new line; the resulting statement is *myGrid = ActiveWindow.DisplayGridlines*. This statement stores the current value of DisplayGridlines, whether True or False, in the variable *myGrid*.

Important

Variable names follow the same rules as macro names: begin with a letter, and use only letters, numbers, and underscores. You should also avoid names already used by Excel or Visual Basic. If you add a prefix such as *my* to the variable name, you'll most likely avoid any conflict.

4 Double-click *True* in the original statement, and replace it with **Not myGrid**. The VBA keyword *Not* turns the value *True* into *False* and *False* into *True*.

5 Change the name *RemoveGrid* to **ToggleGrid** to better reflect the macro's new capabilities. This is what the macro should look like now:

```
Sub ToggleGrid()
    myGrid = ActiveWindow.DisplayGridlines
    ActiveWindow.DisplayGridlines = Not myGrid
End Sub
```

Important

If *Option Explicit* appears at the top of the module, delete it before running this macro.

6 Click the Save button in the Visual Basic Editor. This saves the workbook that contains the macros.

7 Click within the ToggleGrid macro, and then press F5 several times to test the macro.

The macro reads the old value of the property, changes it to the opposite with the keyword *Not*, and assigns the newly inverted value back to the property. By now, you should see a pattern to creating a simple convenience macro: First try out an action interactively. Once you know how to do the task, start the recorder. Do the task with the recorder on. Then stop the recorder and edit the recorded macro if necessary.

Recording Actions in a Macro

So far, all the macros you've recorded have changed the value of one or more properties of an object. Some actions that you can record don't change the value of a property. Let's see what a macro looks like when it doesn't change a property.

Suppose you want to freeze the formulas of some cells in the Budget worksheet at their current values. First change the formulas to values using menu commands, and then create a macro that can change any formula to a value.

Convert a Formula to a Value Using Menu Commands

1 Activate the Budget window, and then select cell D4.

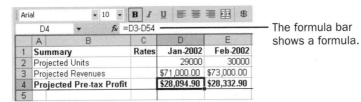

The formula bar shows a formula.

Notice the formula in the formula bar: =D3-D54.

2 On the Edit menu, click the Copy command.

3 Don't change the selection. On the Edit menu, click the Paste Special command. The Paste Special dialog box appears. The Paste Special dialog box has two option groups—Paste and Operation—and two check boxes—Skip Blanks and Transpose. You can choose only one option within a group, and only one state for a check box, so you have four distinct options you can choose within the Paste Special dialog box.

4 Select the Values option from the Paste group, and click OK. Excel pastes the value from the cell over the top of the existing cell, eliminating the formula that was in it. The moving border is still visible around the cell, indicating that you could paste the value again somewhere else.

5 Press the Esc key to get out of copy mode and clear the moving border. In the formula bar, cell D4 now contains the value 28094.9.

Copying selected cells is an action. Pasting the values of selected cells is a different action. When you execute the Copy command, you don't see a dialog box. Excel simply puts a moving border around the cells and a message in the status bar; you don't tell Excel how to do the copying. When you execute the Paste Special command, on the other hand, you do see a dialog box. Excel needs additional information about exactly how you want the paste to behave. Some actions in Excel require additional information about how to carry out the action, and some don't.

Convert a Formula to a Value with a Macro

Record a macro to convert formulas to values. Compare how the macro recorder handles actions that display a dialog box to how it handles actions that don't.

1 On the Budget worksheet, select cell E4. Notice the formula in the formula bar: =E3-E54.

Record Macro

2 On the VBA Toolbar, click Record Macro, replace the default name with **ConvertToValues**, set the shortcut key to Ctrl+Shift+V, and click OK.

3 On the Edit menu, click Copy.

4 On the Edit menu, click Paste Special, click the Values option, and click OK.

5 Press the Esc key to get rid of the moving border.

Stop Recording

6 Click the Stop Recording button, and save the Chapter01 workbook. In the formula bar, cell E4 now contains the value 28332.9.

7 Switch to VBA to look at the recorded macro. Ignoring comments, the macro looks like this:

```
Sub ConvertToValues()
    Selection.Copy
    Selection.PasteSpecial Paste:=xlPasteValues, Operation:=xlNone, _
        SkipBlanks:=False, Transpose:=False
    Application.CutCopyMode = False
End Sub
```

The basic structure of this macro is the same as that of the other macros you've seen in this chapter. The last statement in the body of the macro, for example, sets the value of the CutCopyMode property in much the same way that the ToggleGrid macro changed the value of the DisplayGridlines property of the active window. The two statements that begin with *Selection*, however, are something new. Neither has a simple equal sign in it.

Selection.Copy looks similar to Selection.NumberFormat from the FormatCurrency macro. In that macro, NumberFormat was a property of the selection and you were assigning a new value to the NumberFormat property. Copy, however, isn't a property. That's why it doesn't have an equal sign after it. You don't assign anything to Copy; you just do it. Actions that don't use an equal sign to set the value of a property—that is, actions like Copy—are called *methods*. Like the names of properties, the names of methods are recorded by Excel and displayed at the end of the object's name.

When you use the Copy command from the menu, Excel doesn't ask you for any extra information. In the same way, when you use the Copy method in a macro, you don't give any extra information to the method.

The next statement begins with Selection.PasteSpecial. Similar to Copy, PasteSpecial is a method, not a property. Similar to Copy, PasteSpecial does not have an equal sign after it. When you execute the Paste Special command in Excel, you see a dialog box that lets you give extra information to the command. When you execute the PasteSpecial method in a macro, you need to give the same extra information to the method. The extra pieces of information you give to a method are called *arguments*.

Using a method with an object is like giving instructions to your nine-year-old son. With some instructions—like, "Come eat"—you don't have to give any extra information. With other instructions—like, "Go to the store for me"—you have to tell what to buy (milk), how to get there (on your bike), and when to come home (immediately). Giving these extra pieces of information to your son is like giving arguments to an Excel method. (You call them arguments because whenever you tell your son how to do something, you end up with one.)

The four arguments you give to PasteSpecial correspond exactly to the four option groups in the Paste Special dialog box. Each argument consists of a name for the argument (for example, *Paste*) joined to the argument value (for example, *xlPasteValues*) by a colon and an equal sign (:=).

Don't confuse an *argument* with a *property*. When you assign a new value to a property, you separate the value from the property with an equal sign, as in this statement:

```
ActiveWindow.DisplayGridlines = False
```

You read this statement as "Let 'False' be the DisplayGridlines state of the active window."

Assigning a value to a property is superficially similar to using a named argument with a method. There is an equal sign involved in each case. When you assign a value to a property, you separate the property name from the property value with an equal sign (=). When you use a named argument with a method, you separate the argument name from the argument value with a colon plus an equal sign (:=). Confusing an equal sign with a colon plus equal sign is like confusing beer with root beer. Another difference is that the equal sign used with a property always has spaces on both sides, whereas the colon plus equal sign used with a named argument never has space on either side.

You separate the method name from the argument name with a space, and when you have more than one argument, separate each one from the next with a comma and a space, as in this statement:

```
Selection.PasteSpecial Paste:=xlValues, Operation:=xlNone
```

An argument looks a lot like a property, but a property is followed by an equal sign, while an argument is followed by a colon and an equal sign. Also, an argument follows a method, while a property follows an object. With a property, assigning the value to the property is what carries out the action, while an argument simply affects the way the method does its job.

Make a Long Statement More Readable

When a statement in a macro gets to be longer than about 70 characters, the macro recorder puts a space and an underscore (_) after a convenient word and continues the statement on the next line. The underscore tells the macro that it should treat the second line as part of the same statement. You can manually break long statements into several lines, as long as you break the line after a space. You can also indent related lines with tabs to make the macro easier to read.

1 In the ConvertToValues macro, put each argument of the PasteSpecial statement on a separate line, using a space and an underscore character at the end of each line except the last.

```
Sub ConvertToValues()
    Selection.Copy
    Selection.PasteSpecial _
        Paste:=xlValues, _
        Operation:=xlNone, _
        SkipBlanks:=False, _
        Transpose:=False
    Application.CutCopyMode = False
End Sub
```

Splitting a statement into several lines doesn't change the way the macro runs; it just makes it easier to read.

2 In Excel, select cell F4 and press Ctrl+Shift+V to run the macro. Look at the formula bar to make sure the formula changed to a value.

3 Save the Chapter01 workbook.

Most of the macros in this chapter change the settings of object properties, but this macro executes object methods. Both properties and methods are separated from objects by periods, and both allow you to carry out actions. However, you assign a value to a property to carry out the action, whereas you simply execute a method, sometimes giving it arguments along the way.

Signing Personal Macros

Excel protects you from workbooks containing macro viruses that can harm your computer. It also prevents you from running your own macros. If you haven't changed the default security setting, whenever you open a workbook that contains a macro, Excel displays a message stating that it won't enable macros from unsigned workbooks, including workbooks you've created yourself.

One way to avoid this warning message is to change Excel's security level to Medium or Low, but then you have to either reassure Excel that you don't need the security each time you open your own workbook or forgo the protection from macro viruses.

You can enable your own macros without a warning message by adding a digital signature to your VBA project. Before you can sign a project, you need to obtain a digital signature. You can obtain a digital signature in one of three ways: you can request one from your company if you work for a company that can issue digital signatures; you can obtain one from a certificate authority such as VeriSign or Thawte; or you can create a self-signature for your own macros.

Tip

For information about how to obtain a digital certificate from an official certificate authority, type *digital signature* into the Help box.

Create a Personal Digital Signature

Included with your Microsoft Office XP CD is a program you can use to create a personal signature. If you already have a digital signature from your company or a certifying agency, do not create a personal signature, but use the official one you already have.

1   Run the Microsoft Office Setup program. On the Features To Install screen, expand the Office Shared Features folder. Click the arrow next to Digital Signature For VBA Projects, click Run From My Computer, and then click Update.

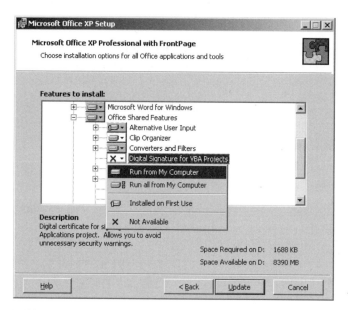

2 In Windows Explorer, search the drive that contains Microsoft Office programs for the file **selfcert**, and run the program.

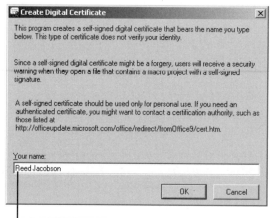

Enter your name to create a certificate
for your personal use.

3 In the Your Name box, type your name and click OK. Click OK to close the confirmation box.

Important

A self-signed certificate can be forged. If you have concerns that someone may attempt to forge your signature in order to inflict a virus on you, you should obtain a signature from an official certifying agency.

4   If open, close the Search Results window.

You've now created a personal signature that you can use to sign your macro projects.

Add a Signature to Your Project

You add a signature to the VBA project part of your workbook. If a virus—or anything else—changes the VBA project, the signature becomes invalid. The signature applies only to the VBA project, not to the workbook data, so anyone can change the worksheets without invalidating the signature.

1   With the Chapter01 workbook open, activate the Visual Basic Editor, and on the Tools menu, click Digital Signature.

2   In the Digital Signature dialog box, click Choose.

3   In the Select Certificate dialog box, select the certificate with your name and click OK.

4   Click OK to close the dialog box. Switch to Excel, and save and close the workbook.

The project in the Chapter01 workbook is now signed. If you need to modify a macro, as long as you do it on the machine that contains your digital signature, VBA automatically reapplies the signature. But no one else can reapply your signature to the project.

Trust a Signature

Now that you have a workbook containing a signed project, you can tell Excel to trust workbooks that contain macros you have signed.

1 Open the Chapter01 workbook.

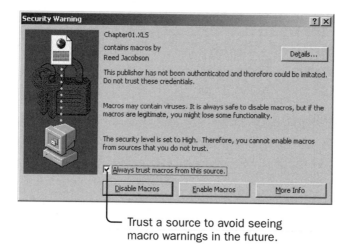

Trust a source to avoid seeing macro warnings in the future.

A message asks whether you want to enable macros, and also whether you want to trust macros from this source in the future.

Tip

When you create your own digital signature, Excel can't be certain that the signature is authentic, so it displays a warning message. If you obtain your signature from a certifying agency, no caution message appears.

2 Select the Always Trust Macros From This Source check box, and click the Enable Macros button.

3 Close the Chapter01 workbook, and then reopen it. No warning message appears. Excel recognizes you as a trusted source for macros.

Security is important when you create any programs, including macros. Security is especially important when you share applications with others. If you create macros for others to use, you'll probably want to obtain a properly authenticated digital signature to protect your work.

Chapter Wrap-Up

● Close the Chapter01 workbook, and quit Excel.

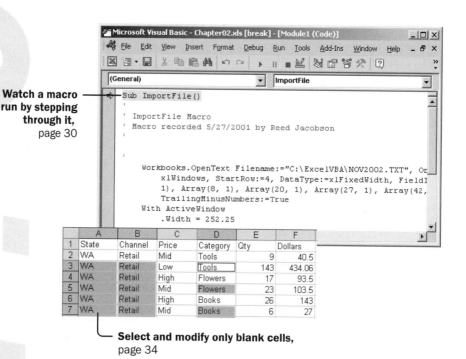

Watch a macro run by stepping through it, page 30

Select and modify only blank cells, page 34

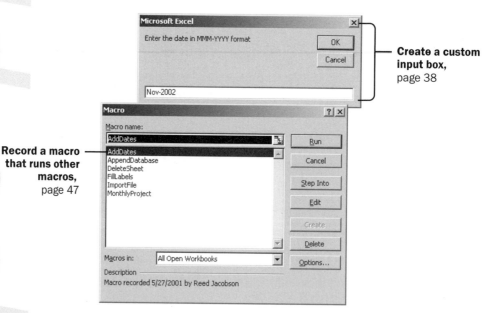

Create a custom input box, page 38

Record a macro that runs other macros, page 47

Chapter 2
Make a Macro Do Complex Tasks

After completing this chapter, you will be able to:

- ✔ **Break a complex project into manageable pieces.**
- ✔ **Watch a macro run one statement at a time.**
- ✔ **Enter values into a macro while it's running.**
- ✔ **Record movements relative to the active cell.**
- ✔ **Create a macro that runs other macros.**

Rube Goldberg was famous for inventing intricate contraptions with hundreds of parts that made what should have been a simple device appear wildly complex. For example, his cat "alarm clock" drops a ball into a bucket and the weight of the bucket lifts a lever that releases a spring that wakes up a cat. Milton Bradley has been successful for years with the Mousetrap game, which is based on a Rube Goldberg concept. Rube Goldberg contraptions are fun to look at. Boston's Logan International Airport has two massive, perpetually working Rube Goldberg contraptions in the lobby that entertain travelers for hours.

Entertainment is one thing. Getting your job done is another. Sometimes the steps you go through to get out a monthly report are as complicated as a Rube Goldberg invention. First you import the monthly order file and add new columns to it. Then you sort it and print it and sort it, a different way, and print it again. Then you paste it at the end of the cumulative order-history file, and so forth. Each step has to be completed just right before the next one is started. Pretty soon, you start scheduling your vacations around the project because you don't want to train someone else to do it all correctly. Right?

One good use for macros is putting together numerous steps and turning a cumbersome Rube Goldberg monthly report into a mouse click. This chapter will help you learn how to do that.

Orders.dbf
Nov2002.txt

This chapter uses the practice files Orders.dbf and Nov2002.txt that you installed from the book's CD-ROM. For details about installing the practice files, see "Using the Book's CD-ROM" at the beginning of this book.

Getting Started

Save

- Start Microsoft Excel, and save a blank workbook as Chapter02 in the folder that contains the practice files for this book. (If you installed the practice files using the default settings, click the Save button on the toolbar, select the Favorites group, double-click the Excel VBA Practice folder, type **Chapter02** as the filename, and click Save.)

Divide and Conquer

The secret to creating a macro capable of handling a long, intricate project is to break the project into small pieces, create a macro for each piece, and then glue the pieces together. If you just turn on the recorder, carry out 400 steps, and cross your fingers hoping for the best, you have about a 1-in-400 chance of having your macro work properly. Let's look at a hypothetical example.

As the bookkeeper at The Garden Company, you have an elaborate month-end project you'd like to automate so that you can delegate it to subordinates when you go on vacation. You get a monthly summary report of orders for the previous month from the order-processing system.

```
                    Company Confidential
               Order Summary for November 2002

State     Channel      Price  Category        Qty    Dollars
========  ==========   ====== =============   ====== ==========
WA        Retail       Mid    Tools              9       40.50
                       Low                      143      434.06
                       High   Flowers            17       93.50
                       Mid                       23      103.50
                       High   Books              26      143.00
                       Mid                        6       27.00
                       Low                         4      14.00
                       High   Nuts               13       71.50
                       Mid                         7      31.50
                       Low                       25       87.50
                       Mid    Herbs              22       99.00
                       Low                       22       77.00
                       Mid    Shrubs            143      554.32
                       Low                       13       45.50
                       Mid    Fruits             35      157.50
                       Low                       40      140.00
          Wholesale    Mid    Tools              30       67.50
                       Low                       10       17.50
                       High   Flowers           410    1,062.13
                       Mid                      900    1,848.48
                       High   Books              25       68.75
                       Mid                       30       67.50
                       Low                         5       8.75
                       High   Nuts              910    2,134.83
                       Mid                       60      135.00
                       Low                      405      687.60
                       Mid    Herbs             660    1,401.08
                       Low                      345      586.60
                       Sh                               146.25
```

The report shows sales information for each combination of state, channel, price range, and category. The order-processing system exports the report as a text file. You prepare the file and add the new month's orders to a cumulative order-history database.

This chapter shows you how to record the tasks that make up this large, complex project and then combine these small macros into one comprehensive macro. Along the way, you might learn some useful techniques for completing everyday tasks as well.

Task One: Opening the Report File

The orders for the most recent month, November 2002, are in the text file Nov2002.txt. The first task is to open the file, splitting it into columns as you do, and move the file into the workbook with the macro.

Open a Text File

Tip
You might want to carry out steps 3 through 6 as a dry run before recording the macro.

Restore
Window

1   If the Chapter02 workbook window is maximized, click the Restore Window button (for the workbook, not for the Excel application).

Record Macro

2   On the Visual Basic toolbar, click the Record Macro button, type ImportFile as the macro name, and then click OK.

If the Visual Basic toolbar is not visible, right-click any toolbar and click Visual Basic.

Open

3   Click the Open button.

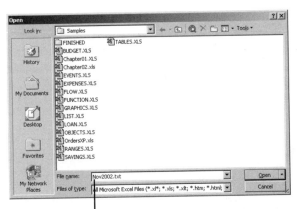

└─ Type the file name here, even though the file is not an Excel file.

4   Type **Nov2002.txt** in the File Name box, and then click Open. Step 1 of the Text Import Wizard appears.

Change this number to skip
rows at the top of the file.

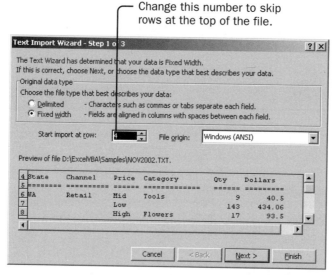

5 The first three rows of the file contain the report title and a blank line. You want to skip the first three rows, so change the Start Import At Row value to **4**. Accept all the other default options in the Text Import Wizard, and click Finish.

The text file opens, with the columns split into Excel columns.

6 Drag up the bottom of the new window so that you can see the tabs at the bottom of the Chapter02 workbook. Then drag the tab for the Nov2002 worksheet down in front of the Sheet1 tab of the Chapter02 workbook.

Drag the Nov2002 tab from here...

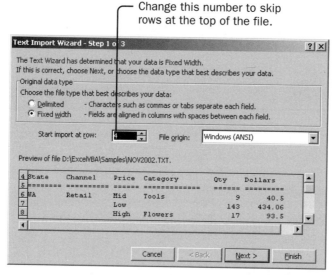

...to here to move the sheet to the
Chapter02 workbook.

The Nov2002 worksheet moves to the Chapter02 workbook, and the Nov2002.txt workbook disappears (because it lost its only worksheet, and a workbook can't exist without at least one sheet).

Tip

You'll have several copies of the Nov2002 worksheet after you test this macro several times. Multiple copies will be useful as you develop the macros for the later project tasks. Once you have a worksheet named Nov2002 in the workbook, new copies are automatically named Nov2002 (2), Nov2002 (3), and so forth.

7 Row 2 contains equal signs that you don't need. Select cell A2, choose the Edit menu and click the Delete command, select the Entire Row option in the Delete dialog box, and then click OK.

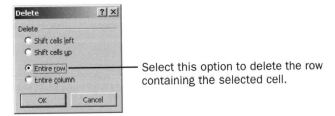

Select this option to delete the row containing the selected cell.

Stop Recording

8 Select cell A1, and click the Stop Recording button to stop the recorder.

9 Save the Chapter02 workbook.

You should now have the imported file split into columns and stripped of extraneous rows.

Watch a Macro Run by Stepping Through It

Rather than merely read a macro, you can step through it. This allows you to both read and test the macro as you watch it work. As you step through the macro, make notes of minor changes you might want to make to it.

When you step through a macro, the Visual Basic Editor window appears over the top of the workbook. The Visual Basic window displays the selected macro and allows you to see which statement will execute next.

Run Macro

1 Click the Run Macro button, select ImportFile from the Macro Name list, and click Step Into.

The Visual Basic window appears on top of the workbook, with your recorded macro visible in the module. The statement that is ready to execute is highlighted in yellow, with a yellow arrow in the left margin.

The arrow shows which statement will execute next.

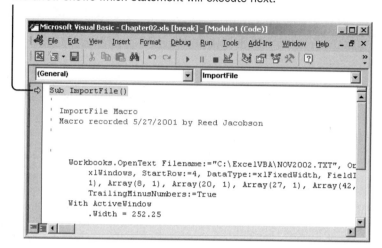

The highlighted statement, which is the first statement in the macro, contains the macro name. In your recorded macro, the line divisions will differ from those in this example.

```
Sub ImportFile()
```

2 Press F8 to highlight the first statement in the body of the macro.

```
Workbooks.OpenText _
    FileName:="C:\ExcelVBA\Nov2002.txt", _
    Origin:=xlWindows, _
    StartRow:=4, _
    DataType:=xlFixedWidth, _
    FieldInfo:=Array(Array(0, 1), Array(8, 1), _
        Array(20, 1), Array(27, 1), Array(42, 1), _
        Array(49, 1)), _
    TrailingMinusNumbers:=True
```

This long statement opens the text file. You can probably identify the argument that spec-ifies the file name. The *Origin* and *DataType* arguments were default values in the first step of the Text Import Wizard. The *StartRow* argument is where you specified the number of rows to skip. The *FieldInfo* argument specifies how to split the text file into columns. Be grateful that the macro recorder can create this statement so that you don't have to!

The macro recorder divides this long statement into several lines by putting a space and an underscore at the end of each partial line. However, it doesn't divide the statement at the most logical places. When you edit the macro, you should redivide the statement into meaningful lines. You can use the way the statement is divided in the preceding OpenText statement as a model.

This month, you opened the Nov2002.txt file. Next month, you'll open the Dec2002.txt file. Make a note to change the macro statement to let you select the file you want to open. You'll learn how to generalize your macro in the next section.

3   Press F8 to open the file and highlight the next statement, which is the first line of this With structure:

```
With ActiveWindow
    .Width = 452.25
    .Height = 254.25
End With
```

These four statements were added when you moved the window out of the way. (Your Width and Height properties might have different values, and if you moved the window, there will be statements that change the Top and Left properties as well.) When you edit the macro, you'll be able to delete these statements without harming the macro.

4   Press F8 to step through any statements that move or resize the window. Make a note to delete all of them. The next statement is now highlighted:

```
Sheets("Nov2002").Select
```

This statement makes the Nov2002 sheet into the active sheet, even though it was already the active sheet. (Macro recorders can't be too cautious.) You'll be able to delete this statement later also.

Tip

You can edit many statements while stepping through the macro. For example, you could delete the Select statement. Some changes, however, would force you to restart the macro. For example, you can't delete a With structure without restarting the macro (although you can delete individual statements inside a With structure). Visual Basic warns you if you try to make a change that would require you to restart the macro.

5   Press F8 to highlight the next statement:

```
Sheets("Nov2002").Move _
    Before:=Workbooks("Chapter02.xls").Sheets(1)
```

This statement moves the new sheet into the Chapter02 workbook. But when you run this macro next month, the sheet won't be named Nov2002. It will be Dec2002. Make a note to change *Sheets("Nov2002")* to *ActiveSheet* in the macro so that it will work every month.

6   Press F8 to move the worksheet and highlight the next statement:

```
Range("A2").Select
```

This statement selects cell A2 of the worksheet.

7   Press F8 to select cell A2 and highlight the next statement:

```
Selection.EntireRow.Delete
```

Because the selected cell is A2 and this statement deletes the entire row of the selected cell, this statement deletes row 2.

8   Press F8 to delete the row and highlight the next statement:

```
Range("A1").Select
```

This statement selects cell A1.

9   Press F8 to select cell A1 and highlight the final statement of the macro:

```
End Sub
```

10 Press F8 to end the macro.

In summary, this is how you want to modify the macro:

- Allow the user to decide which file to open.
- Delete unnecessary statements.
- Make the macro work with any month's file.

The next section shows you how to make these changes.

Select a File While Running a Macro

Excel provides a method that prompts the user to open a file, but Excel doesn't actually open the file. Instead it returns the name of the file, which you can turn over to the OpenText method.

1 Make the statement that begins with *Workbooks.Open* easier to read by dividing it into meaningful lines. Put a space and an underscore at the end of each partial line. Follow the ImportFile macro example in the "Watch a Macro Run by Stepping Through It" section earlier in this chapter.

Important

If *Option Explicit* appears at the top of your module sheet, delete it before continuing.

2 Insert a new line immediately before the *Workbooks.OpenText* statement, and enter this statement:

```
myFile = Application.GetOpenFilename("Text Files,*.txt")
```

As soon as you type the period after *Application*, Visual Basic displays a list of all the methods and properties that can be used with an Application object. This feature is called *Auto List Members*. (The word *Members* refers to both methods and properties.) When you type the letter G, the list scrolls to show methods and properties that begin with that letter. At that point, you can press the Down Arrow key to select GetOpenFilename and press the Tab key to enter the method name into the macro.

When you type the opening parentheses, Visual Basic displays the possible arguments for the GetOpenFilename method. This feature is called *Auto Quick Info*. You can ignore it for now. Just type the words in parentheses as they appear at the beginning of this step.

The Application.GetOpenFilename method displays the Open dialog box, just as if you had clicked the Open toolbar button. The words in parentheses tell the method to display only text files—files ending with the *.txt* extension. (Be careful to type the quotation marks just as they appear at the beginning of this step.) The word *myFile* at the beginning of the statement is a variable for storing the selected filename.

3 In the Workbooks.OpenText statement, select the entire file name, including the quotation marks, and delete it. In its place, type **myFile.** The first part of the statement should look like this when you finish:

```
Workbooks.OpenText _
    Filename:=myFile, _
    Origin:=xlWindows, _
    StartRow:=4, _
```

By the time this statement executes, the variable *myFile* will contain the name of the file.

4 Delete the statements that resize the window and also the statement that selects the Nov2002 sheet.

5 Change the words *Sheets("Nov2002").Move* to **ActiveSheet.Move**. When you're finished, the macro should look like this:

```
Sub ImportFile()
    myFile = Application.GetOpenFilename("Text Files,*.txt")
    Workbooks.OpenText _
        FileName:=myFile, _
        Origin:=xlWindows, _
        StartRow:=4, _
        DataType:=xlFixedWidth, _
        FieldInfo:=Array(Array(0, 1), Array(8, 1), _
            Array(20, 1), Array(27, 1), Array(42, 1), _
            Array(49, 1)), _
        TrailingMinusNumbers:=True
    ActiveSheet.Move _
        Before:=Workbooks("Chapter02.xls").Sheets(1)
    Range("A2").Select
    Selection.EntireRow.Delete
    Range("A1").Select
End Sub
```

6 Save the Chapter02 workbook.

7 Press F5 to run the macro and make sure it works. It should display the Open dialog box (displaying only text files), and then it should open the file that you select and move the worksheet to the Chapter02 workbook.

That concludes the macro for the first task of your month-end processing project. By now, you should have several copies of the Nov2002 worksheet in the Chapter02 workbook. You're ready to move on to the next task.

Task Two: Filling in Missing Labels

When the order-processing system produces a summary report, it enters a label in a column only the first time that label appears. Leaving out duplicate labels is one way to make a report easier for a human being to read, but for the computer to sort and summarize the data properly, you need to fill in the missing labels.

	A	B	C	D	E	F
1	State	Channel	Price	Category	Qty	Dollars
2	WA	Retail	Mid	Tools	9	40.5
3			Low		143	434.06
4			High	Flowers	17	93.5
5			Mid		23	103.5
6			High	Books	26	143
7			Mid		6	27

Fill the blank cells with the label from the cell above.

You might assume that you need to write a complex macro to examine each cell and determine whether it's empty, and if so, what value it needs. In fact, you can use Excel's built-in capabilities to do most of the work for you. Because this part of the project introduces some powerful worksheet features, you'll go through the steps before recording the macro.

Select Only the Blank Cells

Look at the places where you want to fill in missing labels. What value do you want in each empty cell? You want each empty cell to contain the value from the first nonempty cell above it. In fact, if you were to select each empty cell in turn and put into it a formula pointing at the cell immediately above it, you would have the result you want. The range of empty cells is an irregular shape, however, which makes the prospect of filling all the cells with a formula daunting. Fortunately, Excel has a built-in tool for selecting an irregular range of blank cells.

1 In a copy of the Nov2002 worksheet in the Chapter02 workbook, select cell A1.

2 Choose the Edit menu, and click the Go To command. The Go To dialog box appears.

Tip

You also can press Ctrl+Shift+* to select the current region. Press and hold the Ctrl key while pressing * on the numeric keypad or Shift+8 on the regular keyboard.

3 In the Go To dialog box, click Special.

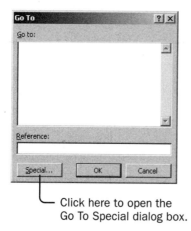

Click here to open the
Go To Special dialog box.

4 In the Go To Special dialog box, click the Current Region option and then click OK.

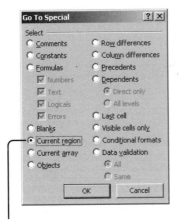

Click here to select the current region.

Excel selects the *current region*—the rectangle of cells including the active cell that is surrounded by blank cells or worksheet borders.

5 Choose the Edit menu, click Go To, and then click Special.

6 In the Go To Special dialog box, click the Blanks option, and then click OK. Excel subselects only the blank cells from the selection. These are the cells that need new values.

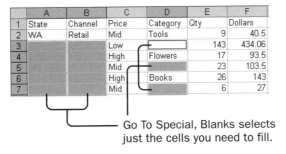

Go To Special, Blanks selects
just the cells you need to fill.

Excel's built-in Go To Special feature can save you—and your macro—a lot of work.

Fill the Selection with Values

You now want to fill each of the selected cells with a formula that points at the cell above. Normally when you enter a formula, Excel puts the formula into only the active cell. You can, however, if you ask politely, have Excel put a formula into all the selected cells at once.

1 With the blank cells selected and D3 as the active cell, type an equal sign (=) and then press the Up Arrow key to point at cell D2. The cell reference D2—when found in cell D3—actually means "one cell above me in the same column."

2 Press Ctrl+Enter to fill the formula into all the currently selected cells. When more than one cell is selected, if you type a formula and press Ctrl+Enter, the formula is copied into all the cells of the selection. (If you press the Enter key without pressing and holding the

Ctrl key, the formula goes into only the one active cell.) Each cell with the new formula points to the cell above it.

	A	B	C	D	E	F
1	State	Channel	Price	Category	Qty	Dollars
2	WA	Retail	Mid	Tools	9	40.5
3	WA	Retail	Low	Tools	143	434.06
4	WA	Retail	High	Flowers	17	93.5
5	WA	Retail	Mid	Flowers	23	103.5
6	WA	Retail	High	Books	26	143
7	WA	Retail	Mid	Books	6	27

Use Ctrl+Enter to fill all the selected cells.

3   Press Ctrl+Shift+* to select the current region.

4   Choose the Edit menu, and click Copy. Then choose the Edit menu, click Paste Special, click the Values option, and then click OK.

5   Press the Esc key to get out of copy mode, and then select cell A1.

Now the block of cells contains all the missing-label cells as values, so the contents won't change if you happen to re-sort the summary data. In the next section, you'll select a different copy of the imported worksheet and follow the same steps, but with the macro recorder turned on.

Record Filling the Missing Values

1   Select a copy of the Nov2002 worksheet (one that doesn't have the labels filled in), or run the ImportFile macro again.

Record Macro

2   Click the Record Macro button, type **FillLabels** as the name of the macro, and then click OK.

3   Select cell A1 (even if it's already selected), press Ctrl+Shift+*, choose the Edit menu, click Go To, click the Special button, click the Blanks option, and then click OK.

4   Type =, press the Up Arrow key, and press Ctrl+Enter.

5   Press Ctrl+Shift+*.

6   Choose the Edit menu, and click Copy. Next choose the Edit menu, click Paste Special, click the Values option, and then click OK.

7   Press the Esc key to get out of copy mode, and then select cell A1.

Stop Recording

8   Click the Stop Recording button, and save the Chapter02 workbook.

You've finished creating the FillLabels macro. Read it while you step through the macro.

Watch the FillLabels Macro Run

1   Select another copy of the imported worksheet, or run the ImportFile macro again.

Run Macro

2   Click the Run Macro button, select the FillLabels macro, and click Step Into. The Visual Basic window appears, with the header statement of the macro highlighted.

3   Press F8 to move to the first statement in the body of the macro:

```
Range("A1").Select
```

This statement selects cell A1. It doesn't matter how you got to cell A1—whether you clicked the cell, pressed Ctrl+Home, or pressed various arrow keys—because the macro recorder always records just the result of the selection process.

4 Press F8 to select cell A1 and highlight the next statement:

```
Selection.CurrentRegion.Select
```

This statement selects the current region of the original selection.

5 Press F8 to select the current region and move to the next statement:

```
Selection.SpecialCells(xlCellTypeBlanks).Select
```

This statement selects the blank special cells of the original selection. (The word *SpecialCells* refers to cells you selected using the Go To Special dialog box.)

6 Press F8 to select just the blank cells and move to the next statement:

```
Selection.FormulaR1C1 = "=R[-1]C"
```

This statement assigns *–R[-1]C* as the formula for the entire selection. When you entered the formula, the formula you saw was =C2, not =R[-1]C. The formula =C2 really means "get the value from the cell just above me," but only if the active cell happens to be cell C3. The formula =R[-1]C also means "get the value from the cell just above me," but without regard for which cell is active.

Tip

For more information about R1C1 notation, type **R1C1 references** into the Ask A Question box in the Excel window.

You could change this statement to *Selection.Formula = "=C2"* and the macro would work exactly the same—provided that the order file you use when you run the macro is identical to the order file you used when you recorded the macro and that the active cell happens to be cell C3 when the macro runs. If the command that selects blanks produces a different active cell, however, the revised macro will fail. The macro recorder uses R1C1 notation so that your macro will always work correctly.

7 Press F5 to execute the remaining statements in the macro:

```
Selection.CurrentRegion.Select
Selection.Copy
Selection.PasteSpecial Paste:=xlPasteValues, _
    Operation:=xlNone, SkipBlanks:=False, Transpose:=False
Application.CutCopyMode = False
Range("A1").Select
```

These statements select the current region, convert the formulas to values, cancel copy mode, and select cell A1.

You've completed the macro for the second task of your month-end project. Now you can start a new macro to carry out the next task—adding dates.

Task Three: Adding a Column of Dates

The order summary report you're working with doesn't include the date in each row since the text file includes numbers for only a single month. Before you can append these new records to the order-history database, you'll need to add the current month to each record.

Add a Constant Date

First you'll create a macro that fills the range with the date *Nov-2002* by inserting a new column A and putting the date into each row that contains data.

Record Macro

1 Select a worksheet that has the labels filled in, click the Record Macro button, type **AddDates** as the name of the macro, and then click OK.

2 Select cell A1, and then choose the Insert menu and click Columns. Excel inserts a new column A, shifting the other columns to the right.

3 Type **Date** in cell A1, and then press the Enter key.

4 Press Ctrl+Shift+* to select the current region.

5 Choose the Edit menu, click Go To, and click the Special button. Click the Blanks option, and click OK to select only the blank cells. These are the cells that need date values.

6 Type **Nov-2002** and press Ctrl+Enter to fill the date into all the cells. Excel fills the date into all the rows. (Excel displays the date as Nov-02, but it stores the full date.)

Stop Recording

7 Select cell A1, and then click the Stop Recording button to stop the recorder.

Step Through the Macro

1 With cell A1 selected, choose the Edit menu, click Delete, click the Entire Column option, and then click OK.

Run Macro

2 Click the Run Macro button, select the AddDates macro, and then click Step Into. If you ignore the comments, this is what the macro should look like:

```
Sub AddDates()
    Range("A1").Select
    Selection.EntireColumn.Insert
    ActiveCell.FormulaR1C1 = "Date"
    Range("A2").Select
    Selection.CurrentRegion.Select
    Selection.SpecialCells(xlCellTypeBlanks).Select
    Selection.FormulaR1C1 = "Nov-2002"
    Range("A1").Select
End Sub
```

3 Press F8 repeatedly to step through the macro.

This macro is pretty straightforward. Notice that the statement that enters the word *Date* has the word ActiveCell as the object, changing the "formula" of only the active cell, whereas the statement that enters the actual date changes the "formula" of the entire selection uses Selection as the object. When you enter a formula using the Enter key alone, the macro uses the word *ActiveCell*. When you enter a formula using Ctrl+Enter, the macro uses the word *Selection*. (If the selection is only a single cell, *ActiveCell* and *Selection* are equivalent.)

The recorder always records putting a value into a cell by using the Formula R1C1 property—even if you enter a label—just in case you might have entered a formula.

Prompt for the Date

Your recorded macro should work just fine if you always run it using the same month's data file. But the next time you actually use this macro, you'll be working with December orders, not November orders. You need to change the macro so that it asks you for the date when you run it.

1. Insert a new line after the comments in the AddDates macro, and enter this new statement:

```
myDate = InputBox("Enter the date in MMM-YYYY format")
```

InputBox is a Visual Basic function that prompts for information while a macro runs. The words in parentheses are the message it displays. The variable *myDate* stores the date until the macro is ready to use it.

Tip

The InputBox function is a useful tool for making a macro work in slightly changing circumstances.

2. Select and delete the text "*Nov-2002*" in the macro. Be sure to delete the quotation marks.

3. Type **myDate** where the old date used to be. The revised statement should look like this:

```
Selection.FormulaR1C1 = myDate
```

4. Activate a worksheet that needs the date column added. (Delete the old date column, or run the FillLabels macro, as needed.)

5. Click the Run Macro button, select the AddDates macro, and then click Run. The macro prompts for the date.

Important

If you click the Cancel button, the macro leaves the date cells empty. In Chapter 7, you'll learn how to program the macro to determine whether the user clicked the Cancel button.

6 Type **Nov-2002** and click OK. The macro inserts the date into the appropriate cells in column A.

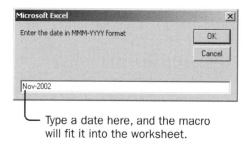

└─ Type a date here, and the macro will fit it into the worksheet.

7 Save the Chapter02 workbook.

This completes your third task. Now you're ready to append the new data to the database.

Task Four: Appending to the Database

Now that you've added monthly dates to the imported Nov2002 worksheet, it has the same columns as the order-history database, so you can just copy the worksheet and append it to the first blank row below the database. Of course, you don't want to include the column headings.

Append a Worksheet to a Database

First you'll copy the data (without the headings) from the Nov2002 worksheet. Then you'll open the database, select the first blank cell below the database, rename the database range to include the new rows, and close the database file.

Record Macro

1 Select one of the Nov2002 worksheets that has the labels filled and the dates added, click the Record Macro button, type **AppendDatabase** as the macro name, and then click OK.

2 Select cell A1. Choose the Edit menu, click Delete, click the Entire Row option, and click OK.

This deletes the heading row so that you won't include it in the range you copy to the database.

3 Press Ctrl+Shift+* to select the current region, and then click Copy on the Edit menu.

Open

4 On the toolbar, click the Open button, type **Orders.dbf** in the File Name box, and click Open.

The Orders.dbf database file opens with cell A1 selected. The values in column A appear as number signs because the column is too narrow to display the dates.

5 In the column headings, double-click the border between columns A and B to adjust the width of the Date column. (The dates in the database look different than those in Nov2002 because of formatting differences.)

6 Press Ctrl+Down Arrow to go to the last row of the database.

7 Press the Down Arrow key to select the first cell below the database. (It should be cell A3301.)

	A	B	C	D	E	F	G
3299	10/1/2002	WA	Retail	Mid	Nuts	6	27.00
3300	10/1/2002	WA	Retail	Mid	Books	5	22.50
3301							
3302							
3303							

You want to paste into the first cells
under the database.

8 Choose the Edit menu, click Paste to append the rows you previously copied, and then
press the Esc key to remove the copy message from the status bar.

	A	B	C	D	E	F	G
3299	10/1/2002	WA	Retail	Mid	Nuts	6	27.00
3300	10/1/2002	WA	Retail	Mid	Books	5	22.50
3301	Nov-02	WA	Retail	Mid	Tools	9	40.5
3302	Nov-02	WA	Retail	Low	Tools	143	434.06
3303	Nov-02	WA	Retail	High	Flowers	17	93.5
3304	Nov-02	WA	Retail	Mid	Flowers	20	103.5

9 Press Ctrl+Shift+* to select the entire new database range, including the newly appended
rows.

Important

When you open a dBase file in Excel, the range containing the actual database records is automatically named Database. When you save the updated Orders.dbf file as a dBase file, only
the values within the range named Database are saved. Any other cell values in the file are
discarded. To have the new rows saved with the file, you must enlarge the Database range definition to include them.

10 Choose the Insert menu, choose the Name submenu, and click the Define command.
Type **Database** in the Names In Workbook box, and then click OK.

Important

Don't select Database from the list of names. If you do, the range the name refers to will
remain unchanged.

Type the name here to redefine the database.
Don't select the name from the list.

Define Name dialog box:

- Names in workbook: Database
- List: Database
- Buttons: OK, Close, Add, Delete
- Refers to: =ORDERS!$A$1:$H$3478

Now the entire database, including the new rows, is included in the Database range name and will be saved with the file.

11 Choose the File menu, click Close, and then click No when asked whether you want to save changes. For now, you don't want to save the database with the new records to the Orders.dbf file because you want to first test the macro.

Stop Recording

12 Select cell A1, and then click the Stop Recording button to turn off the recorder.

Step Through the AppendDatabase Macro

Step through the macro to see it work, and note any changes you should make.

1 Activate a worksheet with the labels filled in and the dates added. (Run the ImportFile, FillLabels, and AddDates macros if necessary.)

Run Macro

2 Click the Run Macro button, select the AppendDatabase macro, and click the Step Into button. Look at the first five lines of the macro:

```
Sub AppendDatabase()
    Range("A1").Select
    Selection.EntireRow.Delete
    Selection.CurrentRegion.Select
    Selection.Copy
```

These statements are similar to statements you've seen in earlier macros.

3 Press F8 five times to execute the first five statements in the macro. In the Visual Basic window, the statement that opens the database should be highlighted:

```
Workbooks.Open Filename:="C:\ExcelVBA\Orders.dbf"
```

This statement opens the database.

Tip

If you remove everything except Orders.dbf from the file name, the macro looks for the file in the current folder. That would be useful if you move the project to a new folder.

4 Press F8 to execute the statement containing the Open method and move to the next statement:

```
Columns("A:A").EntireColumn.AutoFit
```

This statement makes column A wide enough to show all the values.

5 Press F8 to resize the column and move to the next statement:

```
Selection.End(xlDown).Select
```

This statement is equivalent to pressing Ctrl+Down Arrow. It starts with the active cell, searches down to the last nonblank cell, and selects that cell.

6 Press F8 to select the last cell in the database and move to the next statement:

```
Range("A3301").Select
```

This statement selects cell A3301. That is the first cell below the database this month, but next month it will be wrong. This is the statement the recorder created when you pressed the Down Arrow key. What you wanted was a statement that moves one cell down from the active cell. You'll need to fix this statement. Make a note to do so.

7 Press F8 to select cell A3301 and move to the next statement. The next two statements work together:

```
ActiveSheet.Paste
Application.CutCopyMode = False
```

These statements paste the new rows into the database and remove the status bar message.

8 Press F8 twice. The next two statements redefine the Database range:

```
Selection.CurrentRegion.Select
ActiveWorkbook.Names.Add Name:="Database", RefersToR1C1:= _
    "=Orders!R1C1:R3478C7"
```

The first statement selects the current region, which is the correct range for the new database range. The second statement gives the name Database to the specific range R1C1:R3478C7 (A1:G3478). This isn't what you want. You want the name Database to be assigned to whatever selection is current at the time the statement executes. You'll also need to fix this statement. Make a note to do so.

9 Press F8 twice to move to the statement that closes the workbook file:

```
ActiveWorkbook.Close
```

This statement closes the active workbook. If you've made changes to the workbook, it also prompts you to save the changes. You can program the macro to always save changes or (while testing) to never save changes. (See the "Choose Whether to Save Changes While Closing a File" section later in this chapter.)

10 Press F8 to close the database workbook. Click No when asked whether you want to save changes. Only two statements remain in the macro:

```
Range("A1").Select
End Sub
```

11 Press F8 twice to end the macro.

The macro works now only because you're running it under circumstances identical to those when you recorded it, with the same current month file and the same database file. Here's a recap of the changes you'll need to make:

- Select the first row under the database.
- Give the name Database to the current selection.
- Don't prompt when closing the database.

Record a Relative Movement

Take a closer look at the two statements in *AppendDatabase* that find the first blank cell under the database. Imagine what will happen when you run this next month, when the database has more rows. The statement

```
Selection.End(xlDown).Select
```

will select the bottom row, but then the statement

```
Range("A3301").Select
```

will always select the absolute cell A3301 anyway.

When you select a cell, the macro recorder doesn't know whether you want the absolute cell you selected or a cell relative to where you started. For example, when you select a cell in row 1 to change the label of a column title, you always want the same absolute cell, without regard to where you started. But when you select the first blank cell at the bottom of a database, you want the macro to select a cell relative to where you started.

The macro recorder can't automatically know whether you want to record absolute cell addresses or relative movements, but you can tell the recorder which kind of selection you want. Use the recorder to record a new statement that you can use to replace the offending statement. You'll record the new statement in a new, temporary macro, and then copy the statement and delete the temporary macro.

1 Click the Record Macro button, type **TempMacro** as the macro name, and click OK.

2 On the Stop Recording toolbar, click the Relative Reference button.

Relative
Reference

When this button is activated, the recorder makes all new cell selections relative to the original selection. Now you need to replace the statement that selects cell A3301 with one that makes a relative movement.

You want to record the action of moving down one cell so that you can record the macro from any cell, on any worksheet.

3 Press the Down Arrow key once to record a relative movement.

Stop Recording

4 Click the Relative Reference button to deselect it, and then click the Stop Recording button.

5 Edit the TempMacro macro and look at the change. The new statement you recorded should look like this:

```
ActiveCell.Offset(1,0).Range("A1").Select
```

This statement means, "Select the cell below the active cell." It really does. At this point, you don't need to understand everything about how this statement works. Just trust the recorder. But you might wonder why the statement includes the words *Range("A1")* when it has nothing to do with cell A1. This statement calculates a new single-cell range shifted down one cell from the original active cell. The macro treats that new range as if it were the upper left corner of an entire "virtual" worksheet and selects cell A1 of that imaginary worksheet!

6 Select the new statement, and copy it.

7 Open the Procedure drop-down list (below the toolbars on the right side of the Module window), and select AppendDatabase.

8 Select *Range("A3301").Select*, delete it, and paste the new statement in its place.

9 Select the TempMacro macro from the Procedure drop-down list.

10 Delete the TempMacro macro by first selecting all the statements from *Sub TempMacro* to *End Sub* and then pressing the Delete key.

With the Relative Reference button, you can control whether selections are absolute or relative to the current active cell. You can turn the Relative Reference button on and off as many times as you need while you're recording a macro.

Name the Current Selection

The statement in the AppendDatabase macro that defines the Database range name contains a potentially serious problem.

```
ActiveWorkbook.Names.Add Name:="Database", RefersToR1C1:= _
    "=Orders!R1C1:R3478C9"
```

This statement sets the name Database to the range that the database occupies at the end of this month. If you don't change this statement before next month, December orders will be discarded from the database when you save it. This is a case where the macro recorder generates a complicated statement when a simple one would work better.

1 Delete the entire recorded statement.

2 In its place, type

```
Selection.Name = "Database"
```

Name is a property of a range. By simply assigning a word in quotation marks as the value of the Name property, you can name the range.

Choose Whether to Save Changes While Closing a File

The statement that closes the database file looks like this:

```
ActiveWorkbook.Close
```

This statement triggers a prompt that asks whether you want to save changes to the file, because you've made changes to it since you opened it. Sometimes when you automate a process, you know that you always will (or won't) want to save changes. The Close method has an optional argument that allows you to specify whether to save changes. For now, while you're testing the macro, set the statement to *not* save the changes.

1 Change the statement that closes the workbook to this:

```
ActiveWorkbook.Close SaveChanges:=False
```

The *SaveChanges* argument answers the dialog box's question before it even gets asked.

2 Save the Chapter02 workbook. Then run and test the AppendDatabase macro yourself.

3 Once you've finished testing the macro and are ready to use it regularly, change the word *False* to **True**.

Tip

Technically, since the active workbook happens to be a dBase file, setting the *SaveChanges* argument to *True* prevents Excel from asking whether you want to save the changes, but Excel still displays a dialog box to ensure that you want to save the file as a dBase file. If the active workbook is a native Excel workbook, however, the *SaveChanges* argument causes Excel to save it quietly.

Here's the final version of the AppendDatabase macro:

```
Sub AppendDatabase()
    Range("A1").Select
    Selection.EntireRow.Delete
    Selection.CurrentRegion.Select
    Selection.Copy
    Workbooks.Open Filename:="C:\Excel VBA Practice\Orders.dbf"
    Columns("A:A").EntireColumn.AutoFit
    Selection.End(xlDown).Select
    ActiveCell.Offset(1, 0).Range("A1").Select
    ActiveSheet.Paste
    Application.CutCopyMode = False
    Selection.CurrentRegion.Select
    Selection.Name = "Database"
    ActiveWorkbook.Close SaveChanges:=True
    Range("A1").Select
End Sub
```

If you want, you can run the macro again now. It will work the same as it did before, but it's also ready for next month, when the database will have more records.

You're almost finished. The only task left is to get rid of the imported worksheet.

Task Five: Deleting the Worksheet

You imported the text file worksheet so that you could fill in the labels and add a column of dates before appending the data to the database. Once the data is safely appended, you don't need the imported worksheet any more.

Create a Macro to Delete the Active Worksheet

Record Macro

1 Activate an expendable worksheet, click the Record Macro button, type **DeleteSheet** as the macro name, and then click OK.

2 Choose the Edit menu, click Delete Sheet, and then click Delete when asked to confirm.

Stop Recording

3 Click the Stop Recording button to turn off the recorder.

4 Select another expendable worksheet, and step through the DeleteSheet macro:

```
Sub DeleteSheet()
    ActiveWindow.SelectedSheets.Delete
End Sub
```

5 Click Delete when asked to confirm the deletion.

The recorded statement refers to the "selected sheets of the active window" because it's possible to select and delete multiple sheets at the same time. (Press and hold the Ctrl key as you click several sheet tabs to see how you can select multiple sheets. Then click an unselected sheet without using the Ctrl key to deselect the sheets.) Because you're deleting only one sheet, you could change the statement to *ActiveSheet.Delete* if you wanted, but that isn't necessary.

The only problem with this macro is that it asks for confirmation each time you run it. When the macro deletes the imported sheet as part of the larger project, you would prefer not to be prompted.

Make the Macro Operate Quietly

The Delete method does not have an optional argument that eliminates the confirmation prompt. You must add a new statement to turn off the warning.

Run Macro

1 Click the Run Macro button, select the DeleteSheet macro, and click Edit.

2 Insert a new line after the comments following the statement *Sub DeleteSheet()* and then enter this statement:

```
Application.DisplayAlerts = False
```

DisplayAlerts is a property of the Excel application. When you set the value of Display-Alerts to *False*, any confirmation prompts that you would normally see are treated as if you had selected the default answer. The DisplayAlerts setting lasts only until the macro finishes running; you don't need to set it back to *True*. However, you do need to be careful not to run this macro when the active sheet is something you care about. You should also, naturally, save your work often.

Tip

The Auto List Members feature will help you type the words *DisplayAlerts* and *False*. When you select a word in the list, press the Tab key to finish entering the word into the statement.

3 Save the Chapter02 workbook.

4 Select an expendable worksheet, and run the DeleteSheet macro.

Assembling the Pieces

You have all the subordinate task macros ready for carrying out your complex monthly project:

- ImportFile opens and parses the text file.
- FillLabels makes the file look like a database.
- AddDates distinguishes one month from another in the database.
- AppendDatabase adds the new rows to the bottom of the saved database.
- DeleteSheet cleans up the temporary worksheet.

Each piece is prepared and tested. Now you get to put them all together.

Record a Macro that Runs Other Macros

The easiest way to glue macros together is to record a macro that runs other macros.

Record Macro

1 Click the Record Macro button, type **MonthlyProject** as the macro name, and click OK.

Run Macro

2 Click the Run Macro button, click ImportFile, and then click Run.

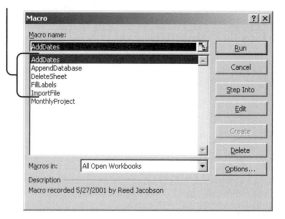

3 Select the text file you want to import, and then click Open.

4 Click the Run Macro button, click FillLabels, and then click Run.

5 Click the Run Macro button, click AddDates, and then click Run.

6 Type an appropriate date, and click OK.

7 Click the Run Macro button, click AppendDatabase, and then click Run.

8 Click the Run Macro button, click DeleteSheet, and then click Run.

Stop Recording

9 Click the Stop Recording button.

Now you can look at what you created. Click the Run Macro button, select the MonthlyProject macro, and click Edit. After deleting the standard comments, here's what the macro to run other macros looks like:

```
Sub MonthlyProject()
    Application.Run Chapter02.xls!ImportFile"
    Application.Run Chapter02.xls!FillLabels"
    Application.Run Chapter02.xls!AddDates"
    Application.Run Chapter02.xls!AppendDatabase"
    Application.Run Chapter02.xls!DeleteSheet"
End Sub
```

The MonthlyProject macro runs each of the subordinate macros in turn. The subordinate macros are known as *subroutines*. (By the way, this is the reason you start macros with the word *Sub*, so that you can turn them into subroutines simply by running them from another macro.)

Simplify the Subroutine Statements

The statement that the macro recorder creates for running a subroutine is somewhat unwieldy. You can simplify the statement, making it easier to read and faster to run.

1   Delete everything from each recorded subroutine statement except the name of the macro itself. Here's what the macro should look like when you're done:

```
Sub MonthlyProject()
    ImportFile
    FillLabels
    AddDates
    AppendDatabase
    DeleteSheet
End Sub
```

2   Save the Chapter02 workbook.

3   Press F5 to test the MonthlyProject macro. (You might also want to try pressing F8 to step through the main macro and each of the subroutines.)

You now have an automated process for importing each new month's data. You've worked hard and deserve a rest. Take the rest of the day off.

Create a new workbook, page 55

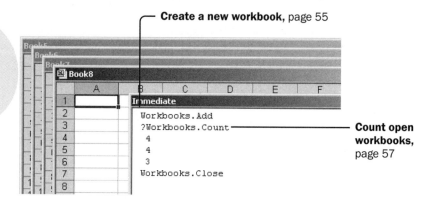

Count open workbooks, page 57

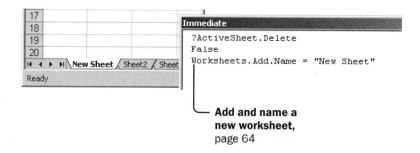

Add and name a new worksheet, page 64

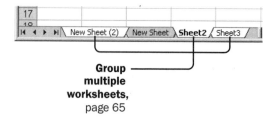

Group multiple worksheets, page 65

QuickLook

Chapter 3
Explore Workbooks and Worksheets

After completing this chapter, you will be able to:

✔ **Manipulate collections of workbooks and worksheets.**

✔ **Manipulate individual workbook and worksheet items.**

✔ **Use the Immediate window to execute individual statements.**

Think back on your third-grade classroom. Your wooden frame desk, decorated with decades of crudely carved names, was fourth from the front, over in the last row next to the windows. Remember those big stairs down to the main floor, with that magnificent banister you would always watch for a chance to slide down? The main hallway was papered with drawings clustered around each classroom door. Each door led to a classroom, and each classroom was filled with kids.

A Microsoft Excel workbook is a lot like a school. The cells in a worksheet appear in rows and columns like students in a classroom. Worksheets are grouped into workbooks like classrooms in a school. And Excel can have several open workbooks, just as a city can have several schools. Just as you were able to move around freely in the rooms and halls of your old elementary school, you will soon be able to move around freely in Excel objects with your macros. Microsoft Visual Basic interacts with Excel by working with Excel objects. Everything in Excel that Visual Basic can control—workbooks, worksheets, cells, menus, text box controls—are objects. To control Excel from Visual Basic effectively, you must understand what objects are and how they work in Excel.

Getting Started

1 Open Excel with a clean, blank workbook. If you have other workbooks open, such as the Personal Macro Workbook, close them. (To find any hidden workbooks, click Unhide on the Window menu.)

2 Restore the Excel workbook window (not the Excel application window) so that it is not maximized.

3 If the Visual Basic toolbar is not visible, use the right mouse button to click any toolbar and click Visual Basic on the shortcut menu.

What Is an Object?

The easiest way to understand objects in Excel is to compare them to objects in the real world. In the real world, cities, schools, classrooms, and students are all objects. A city is dotted with schools, a school is lined with classrooms, a classroom is packed with students—and all the students are arranged in tidy rows of tidy desks, smiling happily and listening attentively to the kind, wise, and firm but patient teacher. Well, maybe not all the desks are tidy.

Objects Come in Collections

Look around you. The world consists of objects in collections, which are in turn objects in other collections: rooms in apartments in buildings in complexes, flowers in beds in yards in neighborhoods, rocks on crags on mountains in ranges, children in households in extended families in clans. Each object—each city, each student, each flower, each mountain, and each family—is an individual item, yet each also belongs to a collection of similar objects, and each collection of objects is itself an individual item within a larger collection.

If you're a city official thinking about the collection of School objects, you might refer to the collection of schools as a group: "All the schools have asbestos problems." Or you might refer to an individual school: "We need to replace the light fixtures at Jefferson Elementary School." When you do refer to an individual school, you might refer to the school by name: "Jefferson Elementary School, as you may know, was named for the esteemed author of the Declaration of Independence." Or you might refer to it by its position in the collection: "The first school built in our city, back in 1887, is the one I attended as a child." Or (if you are conducting a driving tour) you might refer to the individual school by pointing: "Notice the classic architecture of this magnificent school building."

An Excel workbook is like a school. Just as you can have more than one school in a city, you can have more than one workbook open in Excel. Each workbook is individual and unique, yet each is a Workbook object. You can refer to the entire collection of open workbooks as a group ("Close all the open workbooks"), or you can refer to individual workbooks. If you refer to an individual workbook, you can specify the workbook by name ("Open the Chapter 3 workbook"), by position ("What is the first workbook in the list of recently opened files?"), or by pointing ("Save the active workbook").

A worksheet in a workbook is like a classroom in a school, and worksheet cells are like students in a classroom, arranged in neat little rows and columns. Excel also has other collections of objects: menu items in menus in menu bars, columns in a series in a group in a chart, items in fields in rows in a PivotTable. You can refer to each collection, whether in Excel or in the natural world, as a whole or you can refer to a single item within the collection. When you refer to a single item within the collection, you can refer to it by name, by position, or by pointing.

Objects Have Properties

Do you see that little boy in Mrs. Middlefield's class—the one in the third row, in the fourth seat over? He's about four feet seven inches tall. His hair is short. The color of his shirt is blue. His name is Jared. And his eyes are closed.

The boy's height, hair length, shirt color, name, and eye state are properties of that one particular Student object. The little girl sitting behind him also has Height, HairLength,

ShirtColor, Name, and EyeState properties, but the values of her properties are different. The boy is a different object than the girl, but each is a Student object.

The boy's desk is also an object, a Desk object. A Desk object has a Height property, as does a Student object, but a Desk object does not have a HairLength property. Likewise, a Student object does not have a ManufacturerName property, as a Desk object does. Because the boy and the desk have different lists of properties, they are different types, or classes, of objects. Because the boy and girl share the same list of properties—even though they have different values for the properties—they both belong to the same class of object. They both belong to the Student *object class*. Sharing the same list of properties is what makes two objects belong to the same object class.

Just as Jared is an object—a Student object—Mrs. Middlefield's entire collection of students is also an object—a Students object. The Students collection has its own properties; the properties of the collection are not the same as the properties of the individual objects contained within it. For example, you don't really care about a HairLength property of the entire collection of students. (Would that be total hair length or average hair length?) But a collection object does have properties of its own. For example, the number of students in the collection (the Count) is a property of the Students object. Because Mrs. Middlefield's collection of students has a different list of properties than Jared's property list, Students is a different object class from Student. But because Mr. Osgood's Students collection and Mrs. Middlefield's Students collection have the same list of properties—even though they might have different values for the properties—both collections belong to the same Students object class. The Students object class is different than the Student object class because the two object classes have different lists of properties.

Some properties are easy to change. You could perhaps change Jared's EyeState property with a good, sharp rap with a ruler on his desk. (And of course, he can change the property right back after you look the other way.) You might even change Jared's name to Gerard temporarily for French language instruction. But changing Jared's height, weight, eye color, or gender probably falls outside the scope of a normal school activity.

Excel objects have properties also. A workbook has an author. A worksheet has a name. A cell has a width, a height, and a value. A menu has a caption. A collection of worksheets has a count of the worksheets in the collection. Changing some of the properties—such as the name of a worksheet or the height of a cell—is easy. Changing other properties—such as the count of cells on a worksheet—probably falls outside the scope of a normal macro activity.

Objects Have Methods

Look, Mrs. Middlefield is telling the class to stand up. She's leading them in a stirring rendition of "Row, Row, Row Your Boat." Student objects can sing songs. Singing a song is an activity. Student objects also do other activities. Student objects eat. Student objects draw pictures. One student might sing, or eat, or draw well; another student might sing, or eat, or draw badly; but they both share the ability to do the action. Desk objects, on the other hand, do not sing, eat, or draw. Desk objects might squeak, whereas Student objects generally don't. In the same way that different classes of objects have different lists of properties, they also have different lists of activities they can do. The activities an object can do are called *methods*. Objects that belong to the same class can all do the same methods.

A collection object has a list of methods separate from the list of methods that belongs to the individual items in it. One of the most important methods for most collections is adding a new item to the collection. When a new student moves into the class, you are executing the Add method on the Students object, not on an individual Student object. When the construction bond passes and the school gets a new wing, you are executing the Add method on the Classrooms object. You don't add the new classroom to an individual classroom; you add it to the collection of classrooms.

Most Excel collection objects have an Add method for adding a new item to the collection, and they all have an Item property for establishing a link, or a reference, to an individual item in the collection. Excel worksheet objects also have a Calculate method for causing all the cells to recalculate, and Excel charts have a ChartWizard method that quickly changes various attributes of a chart.

Sometimes the distinction between a method and a property is vague. When Jared opens his eyes, is he carrying out the OpenEyes method (an action), or is he assigning a new value to his EyeState property? Here are some concepts that might help:

- **Methods can change properties** Some methods do change properties. When Jared carries out the Fingerpaint method, the action happens to change his ShirtColor property. When he goes home and carries out the WashClothes method, the Shirt-Color property changes back (with perhaps a few residual stains). Likewise, in Excel, the ChartWizard method can change several properties of the chart.

- **Properties can involve actions** Setting a property usually involves some kind of action. When you change the classroom's WallColor property, you do get out the paint rollers and the ladders and start working, but you are more concerned about the finished attribute of the wall than about the action that changed the attribute. In Excel, hiding a worksheet is an example of setting a property (because the worksheet is still there and you might want to change the property back). But closing a file is a method because there's no trace of the file left in memory after you're done.

Tip

Most of the time, you don't need to worry about the difference between properties and methods. Excel has online tools to help you find the methods and properties for objects, and you might not need to know which is which. For example, you can turn on the macro recorder, carry out a task, and then modify the code that the macro recorder produced—without ever really knowing whether Excel used a property or a method for any given action.

In summary, an individual item is an object from one object class, while a collection of those items is an object from a different object class. A single item from one collection can contain an entire collection of other objects. For example, a single school from the district's collection of schools can contain an entire collection of classrooms. Each object belongs to an object class that has a unique list of properties and methods. Many different individual objects (Student objects) can belong to a single object class (the Student object class), in which case they all share the same list of properties and methods while each retains its individuality. In this chapter, you'll learn how to work with many kinds of Excel objects.

Understanding Workbooks

Workbooks are the major structural unit in Excel. You can learn much about how objects and collections work in Excel by experimenting with workbooks.

Excel also has a powerful tool to help you experiment with objects, properties, and methods: the Immediate window of the Visual Basic Editor. You can use the Immediate window to explore Workbook objects. The Immediate window is a place to do experiments without writing macros. Everything you do in the Immediate window is lost when you close Excel.

Add a New Workbook

In this section, you'll use a macro statement to create a new workbook. This is equivalent to clicking the New button on the toolbar. The macro statement for creating a new workbook is Workbooks.Add. Rather than put that statement in a macro, you can execute it directly in the Immediate window. Rather than type the statement, you can let the editor help you construct it.

Visual Basic
Editor

1 Click the Visual Basic Editor button on the Visual Basic toolbar. Resize the Visual Basic Editor so that you can see the Excel application.

2 On the View menu, click the Immediate Window command. If the Immediate window is docked within the Visual Basic Editor, double click the caption bar to undock the window. Then resize the Immediate window so that you can see the Excel application.

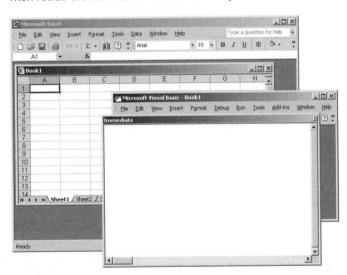

3 With the Immediate window active, point at the Edit menu and click Complete Word.

A list of methods and properties appears. These are the methods and properties that don't need an explicit object.

4 Type **Wo**, the first two letters of the word *Workbooks*. This is enough to select the word in the list. (You could also just type a *W* and point at Workbooks or press the Down Arrow key three times.)

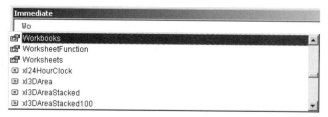

5 Type a period (.) to display a list of methods and properties suitable for the Workbooks object.

You don't need to type the whole word before typing a period. The list that appears is called an AutoList. It contains all the methods and properties that you can use with the preceding object.

6 Type **A**, the first letter of the word *Add*.

The first letter is enough to select the appropriate word.

7 Press Enter to add a new workbook on top of the first workbook.

The Add method added a new workbook to the collection, and you watched it happen.

Executing the Add method
of the Workbooks object...

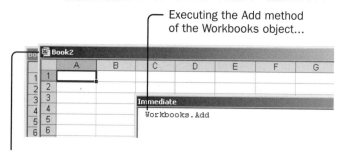

...adds a new workbook to the collection.

In the Immediate window, you can type macro statements and see the effect immediately. The Immediate window is an effective tool for finding out what a statement does. You can use it when planning how to create a new macro or when debugging an existing macro.

8 Press the Up Arrow key to put the insertion point back in the Workbooks.Add statement, and press Enter. The Add method adds another Workbook object. Whenever you want to reexecute a statement in the Immediate window, simply put the insertion point anywhere in the line and press Enter.

The word *Workbooks* refers to the Workbooks object—the collection of workbooks currently open in Excel. The word *Add* is a method of the Workbooks object that adds a new item to the collection. A method follows an object, separated by a single period (object.method). Most collections in Excel have an Add method for adding a new item to the collection.

Dockable Views

The windows in the Visual Basic Editor can be confusing. You might find it easier to understand how they work if you compare them to windows in the Excel environment.

In Excel, each workbook you open has its own window. A workbook window can be either maximized to fill Excel's entire work area or resized to have more than one window visible at a time. A worksheet window can never move outside the boundary of the Excel application. It's completely owned by the main Excel window. This kind of window is a *child* window.

A toolbar, on the other hand, can be either docked or floating. A toolbar can be docked to the top, bottom, left side, or right side of Excel's main window. To undock a toolbar, you drag the toolbar away from the docking position. A floating toolbar can be placed anywhere; it doesn't have to remain inside Excel's main window. A toolbar is actually a kind of window—a *dockable* window.

The Visual Basic environment has both dockable and child windows. A module window is a child window. It can be minimized, restored, or maximized, but it can never move outside the boundaries of the main Visual Basic window.

The Immediate window is by default a dockable window, as are toolbars in Excel. You can dock the Immediate window to the top, bottom, left side, or right side of the Visual Basic window, or you can make it float by dragging it away from a docking position. You can also prevent the window from docking by pressing and holding the Ctrl key as you move the window.

Visual Basic has six dockable windows: the Locals window, the Immediate window, the Watch window, the Project Explorer window, the Properties window, and the Object Browser window. You can display any of these windows by choosing the appropriate command from the View menu.

To change a Visual Basic dockable window into a child window, right-click the window and then click the Dockable command to turn off the check mark. With the dockable setting turned off, the window behaves just like any child window; you can minimize, maximize, restore, cascade, or tile it, but you can't move it outside the main window, and it can't float above another active window.

I usually make all windows dockable but undocked. I move, hide, and unhide windows as necessary. I also maximize the module window and keep it relatively small so that I can see the Excel window in the background.

Count the Workbooks

You have now used a method—the Add method—with a Workbooks object. The Workbooks object also has properties. One of the properties—the Count property—tells you how many items are in the collection. The Count property returns a value that you can display in the Immediate window.

1 In the Immediate window, type **?Workbooks.Count** and press Enter. (After typing the question mark, you can use the Complete Word command on the Edit menu to help you construct the rest of the statement.)

The number 3 (or however many workbooks are currently open) appears. In the Immediate window, when you type a question mark followed by anything that returns a value, that value appears on the next line. Because the Count property returns a number value, you can display that value by using the question mark.

2 Press the Up Arrow key to get back to the Workbooks.Add statement, press Enter to add a new workbook, and then press Enter again in the ?Workbooks.Count statement to see the new count of workbooks.

The count should now be 4 (or one greater than whatever it was before).

The word *Count* is a property. You attach the Count property to its object with a period in the same way that you attach the Add method to the object.

When you execute the Add method, you don't put a question mark in front of it because the Add method does not return a simple value. You can see the effect of the Add method by looking at the Excel application window. When you use the Count property, you want to find out the value of the property. You can't change the number of workbooks by changing the Count property; you must use the Add method to add a new workbook to the collection. A property whose value you can look at but cannot change is called a read-only property.

Close the Workbooks

The Add method works on the Workbooks object by adding one item to it. The Workbooks object has an additional method—the Close method—that can close the entire collection.

1 Type **Workbooks.Close** and press Enter. Click No if asked to save changes.

All the open workbooks disappear. Using the Close method on the Workbooks object closes the entire collection. The Close method closes everything so fast that you might want to see it work again.

2 Reexecute the *Workbooks.Add* statement three or four times to create a few new workbooks.

3 Reexecute the *?Workbooks.Count* statement to see how many workbooks are in the collection.

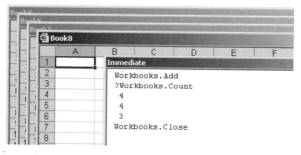

4 Reexecute the *Workbooks.Close* statement to close all the workbooks. (Doesn't that give you a great sense of power? With one keystroke, all those workbooks are annihilated!)

5 Reexecute the *?Workbooks.Count* statement to see how many workbooks are in the collection. The number 0 appears because you destroyed all the workbooks.

Add and Close are both methods of the Workbooks object. Count is a property of the Workbooks object. The Add and Close methods indirectly change the value of the Count property—they are, in fact, the only ways you can change the read-only Count property.

Refer to a Single Workbook

Closing the entire Workbooks collection all at once is a powerful experience, and might even possibly, occasionally, be useful, but usually you want more control over which workbooks disappear. To close a single workbook, you need to specify a single item out of the Workbooks collection.

1 Run the *Workbooks.Add* statement at the top of the Immediate window several times to create a few new workbooks.

2 Scroll to the bottom of the Immediate window. (You can press Ctrl+End to scroll quickly to the bottom of the Immediate window.)

3 Type **?Workbooks.Item(1).Name** and press Enter.

The name of the first workbook—the first of the current set of workbooks to be opened (probably something like Book9)—appears. Reading from right to left, you could paraphrase this statement as: "The name of the first item in the Workbooks collection is what?"

```
Immediate
Workbooks.Close
?Workbooks.Item(1).Name
Book9
```

- *Name* is a property of a single workbook. Because Name is a property that returns a value, you can display its value by putting a question mark at the beginning of the statement. The Name property is not available for a Workbooks object because a collection of workbooks doesn't have a name.

- *Item* is a property of a collection. Like the teacher establishing a communication link by addressing an individual student, the Item property creates a reference to an individual item in a collection. The Item property requires a single argument: in this case, the position number of the item you want.

- *Workbooks* establishes a reference to the entire collection of workbooks—the Workbooks object. Once you have a reference to the Workbooks object, the word *Item(1)* switches the reference to the specified item within the collection—a *Workbook* object. Once you have a reference to the Workbook object, the Name property returns the name of that object.

Tip

Retrieving a single item from a collection is so common that you can leave out the word *Item* (and its accompanying period) and put the parentheses right after the name of the collection. The statement *?Workbooks(1).Name* achieves the same result as *?Workbooks.Item(1).Name*. The macro recorder, Excel's Help files, and most people all use the shorter form. However, if you find that you consistently forget to use a plural for the collection method name, you might want to explicitly use the Item property for a while.

4 Type **Workbooks(1).Close** and press Enter. The first workbook disappears.

5 Reexecute the *?Workbooks.Item(1).Name* statement.

The name of the first workbook appears. (If the first workbook was Book9 before, the new first workbook is probably Book10.)

6 Reexecute the *Workbooks(1).Close* statement to close the newly promoted first workbook in the collection.

The word *Workbooks* has two meanings in Excel. On one hand, Workbooks is the name of an object class—the Workbooks object class; it is a noun, a "thing." On the other hand, Workbooks is also the name of a property that establishes a reference to the collection of open workbooks; it is a verb, an "action." You cannot put the actual Workbooks object (or thing) into your macro. (The Workbooks object is inside Excel; you can see it on your computer screen.) What you put into your macro is the Workbook property that establishes a reference to the Workbooks thing.

Once the Workbooks property establishes a reference to the Workbooks object, you can "talk" to the object using methods and properties from the list that a Workbooks object understands. You can use the Count property to look at the number of items in the collection. You can use the Add method to add a new workbook to the collection. You can use the Close method to close the entire collection of workbooks. *Count*, *Add*, and *Close* are three of the words that a Workbook object can understand.

A Workbooks object can also understand the Item property. The Item property establishes a reference to an individual Workbook thing. Excel doesn't have a Workbook property to link to a single Workbook object. You use the Item property of the Workbooks object (the shortcut form) to establish a reference to an individual object.

Once the Item property establishes a reference to an individual Workbook object, you can talk to the object by using methods and properties that a Workbook object understands. You can use the Name property to look at the workbook's name. And you can use the Close method to close the workbook.

As a general rule, each collection object in Excel shares the same name as the property that establishes a reference to that object. The Workbooks object shares its name with the Workbooks property. The Workbooks property establishes a reference with the Workbooks object. As you learn more about objects, you will see that this pattern holds—the Windows object shares its name with the Windows property, the Charts object shares its name with the Charts property, and so forth.

In Visual Basic code, you never refer to an individual item from a collection by leaving the letter *s* off the name of the collection. For example, you never refer to an individual workbook in a macro by using the word *Workbook*. Every collection object class has an Item property that you use to establish a reference to an individual item in the collection.

Refer to a Workbook by Name

So far when you have used the Item property to establish a reference to an individual workbook, you have specified the workbook you want by number—by indicating its position in the collection. Another way you can refer to an item in a collection is by its name.

If you use the name, you must put it in quotation marks. If you use the position number, you do not use quotation marks.

1 If you are running out of workbooks, scroll to the top of the Immediate window and execute the *Workbooks.Add* statement a few more times.

2 Scroll to the bottom of the Immediate window (press Ctrl+End). Pick the name of one of the workbooks, preferably one in the middle of the stack, perhaps a workbook named Book14.

3 Type **Workbooks("Book14").Activate** and press Enter. The workbook you specified moves to the top of the stack of workbooks. The word *Activate* is a method that a single Workbook object understands. Because Book14 is the name of the workbook, it appears in quotation marks.

4 Type **Workbooks("Book14").Close** and press Enter to close the workbook.

5 Reexecute the *Workbooks("Book14").Close* statement.

Excel displays an error message because the workbook with that name no longer exists. When you refer to an item in a collection by name, you always get the same item—as long as it still exists.

6 Click OK to remove the error message.

You can use either the name or the position number to refer to an item in a collection. If you use the position number, you might get a different item each time you use the Item property; if you use the name, you'll get an error if the item no longer exists.

Refer to a Workbook by Pointing

Suppose you want to refer to the top workbook on the stack but you don't know its name or its position number. Because the top workbook is the active workbook, you can refer to it by pointing.

● On a blank row at the bottom of the Immediate window, type **ActiveWorkbook.Close** and press Enter. The top workbook in the stack disappears.

The word *ActiveWorkbook* in this statement establishes a reference directly to the active workbook, bypassing the Workbooks object. If the first workbook opened happens to be the active workbook, you could substitute *Workbooks(1)* to establish a reference to the same workbook object as ActiveWorkbook. Once you have a reference to the workbook, you can look up its name or close it. Once you have a reference to an object, the process by which you established that reference is not important.

Change a Workbook Property Value

Both the Count property of the Workbooks object and the Name property of a Workbook object are read-only properties. You can look at the value returned by the property, but you cannot change it. A workbook has other properties, read-write properties, whose values you can change as well as look at.

1 In the Immediate window, type **?ActiveWorkbook.Saved** and press Enter.

The word *True* appears because the workbook hasn't had any changes made to it. When you close a workbook, Excel uses the value of the Saved property to decide whether to prompt you to save changes. If the value of the Saved property is *True*, Excel does not prompt you; if it is *False*, Excel does prompt you. Normally, you change the Saved property to *False* by changing the contents of a cell, and you change the Saved property to *True* by saving the workbook. You can, however, change the Saved property directly.

2 Type **ActiveWorkbook.Saved = False** and press Enter.

Nothing seems to happen, but you just changed the value of the property.

3 Reexecute the *?ActiveWorkbook.Saved* statement to see the new value for the property.

The word *False* appears. Now Excel thinks the workbook has unsaved changes in it.

4 Reexecute the *ActiveWorkbook.Close* statement.

Because you set the Saved property to *False*, Excel asks if you want to save changes.

5 Click the Cancel button to leave the workbook open.

6 At the bottom of the Immediate window, type **ActiveWorkbook.Saved = True** and press Enter.

7 Reexecute the *ActiveWorkbook.Close* statement.

The workbook closes without a whisper.

If you write a macro that modifies a workbook and you want to close the workbook without saving changes (and without displaying a warning prompt), make the macro change the Saved property of the workbook to *True*.

The Saved property is a read-write property. You can display its current value, and you can also change its value.

Understanding Worksheets

Worksheets come in collections just as workbooks do. By manipulating worksheets in the Immediate window, you will see some similarities—and some differences—between different collection classes.

Add a New Worksheet

1 In Excel, close all but one workbook.

The one workbook should have three sheets, named Sheet1, Sheet2, and Sheet3, with Sheet1 as the active sheet.

2 Switch to the Visual Basic Editor. In the Immediate window, type **Worksheets.Add** and press Enter. A new worksheet named Sheet4 appears before the original active sheet.

You add a new worksheet to the current workbook the same way you add a new workbook to Excel: by using the Add method.

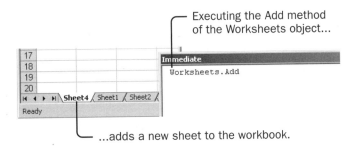

Executing the Add method
of the Worksheets object...

...adds a new sheet to the workbook.

Rename and Delete a Worksheet

A worksheet is an object with properties and methods of its own. You can use those methods and properties to manipulate a worksheet. As you work with worksheets, you will notice that the AutoList of methods and properties will not always appear after you type a period. Later in this chapter, you will learn how to get an AutoList to always appear with a worksheet object.

1 Type **?Worksheets(1).Name** and press Enter to display the name of the first worksheet (probably Sheet4).

In the same way that you use the Item property (in either its long form or its short form) on a Workbooks object to establish a reference to a single Workbook object, you use the Item property on a Worksheets object to establish a reference to a single Worksheet object. Once you have a reference to a Worksheet object, you can use Worksheet object properties, such as Name.

Important

The name of a workbook is a read-only property; you have to save a file to change its name. The name of a worksheet, however, is a read-write property; you can change the name directly.

2 Type **Worksheets(1).Name = "Input Values"** and press Enter.

The name of the worksheet changes.

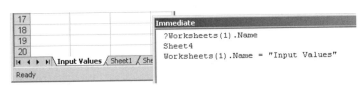

3 Type **Worksheets("Sheet1").Activate** and press Enter.

The worksheet named Sheet1 becomes the active sheet.

4 Type **ActiveSheet.Delete** and press Enter. Click Delete when warned that the sheet might contain values.

5 Type **Worksheets("Input Values").Activate** and press Enter.

As with workbooks, you can refer to a single worksheet by number, by name, or by pointing. With the first worksheet named Input Values and activated, the expressions *Worksheets("Input Values")*, *Worksheets(1)*, and *ActiveSheet* all establish a reference to the same Worksheet object.

Look at the Return Value of the Delete Method

Normally, you execute a method and you change or retrieve the value of a property. Methods do, however, return values, and you might want to see the value that a method returns. For example, when you use the Delete method on a worksheet, the effect of the method is to close the worksheet, but the method also returns a value to the macro.

1 Type **?ActiveSheet.Delete** and press Enter. Click Delete when warned about the sheet containing data.

The active sheet disappears, and the word *True* appears after the statement. When the Delete method carries out its task, it returns the value *True* if it completes the task successfully. The deleting of the worksheet is the effect of the method. The word *True* that appears in the Immediate window is the *return value* of the method.

2 Type **?ActiveSheet.Delete** and press Enter. This time, click Cancel when warned.

The word *False* appears after the statement. The Delete method did not complete the task of deleting the worksheet, so it returns the value *False*. You can often look at a method's return value to find out whether it completed its task.

Most methods return something. Some methods (like Delete) return either *True* or *False*, depending on whether they were successful at their task.

Look at the Result of the Add Method

The Delete method of the Worksheet object returns either *True* or *False*, depending on whether it achieves the desired effect. The Add method also has an effect—it creates a new item in the collection. But the Add method does not return *True* or *False*. Rather, the Add method returns a reference to the newly created object. You can use that reference the same way you can use the reference created by the Item property or by the ActiveSheet property.

1 In the Immediate window, type **Worksheets.Add.Name = "New Sheet"** and press Enter.

A new worksheet appears in the workbook, with the name New Sheet.

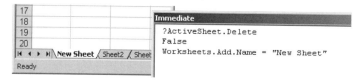

2 Type **Worksheets.Add.Delete** and press Enter. When the confirmation dialog box appears, you can see the new worksheet in Excel. Click Delete, and watch the worksheet disappear.

This example is bizarre because it deletes the worksheet in the same statement that creates it. It does, however, illustrate how the Add method returns a reference to the newly created object.

The Add method has an effect—it creates a new worksheet. In addition, it returns a reference to the new object. If you don't use the reference immediately—as part of the same statement—the reference is discarded. If you then want to communicate with the new worksheet, you must establish a new reference using the ActiveSheet property or the Item property. Usually, you don't bother using the reference returned by Worksheets.Add because using ActiveSheet to establish a new reference is as easy as shouting "Jared" to get a slumbering student's attention.

Copy a Worksheet

Another useful method for a worksheet allows you to make a copy of the worksheet. You can copy the worksheet either to a new workbook or to the same workbook.

1 In the Immediate window, type **Worksheets("New Sheet").Copy** and press Enter.

This statement creates a new workbook that includes the copy.

2 Type **ActiveWorkbook.Close SaveChange:=False** and press Enter to delete the new workbook.

3 Type **Worksheets("New Sheet").Copy Before:=Worksheets(1)** and press Enter.

This statement copies the worksheet before the specified worksheet. You must give a reference to a worksheet as the Before argument. If you want to copy a worksheet to the end of the workbook, the Copy method has an After argument you can use instead of the Before argument.

The Copy method is a convenient way to clone a worksheet. The Copy method does not return a reference to the new worksheet; if you need to refer to it, you must use ActiveSheet or some other method or property.

Manipulate Multiple Worksheets

When you work with collections, you typically work with the entire collection (as when you closed all the workbooks at the same time using the statement *Workbooks.Close*), or you work with a single item from the collection (as when you closed a single workbook by using the statement *Workbooks(1).Close*.) With worksheets, however, you sometimes need to create a subcollection—a new collection that includes some, but not all, the worksheets in the collection.

1 Type **Worksheets(3).Select** and press Enter to select the third worksheet in the workbook, the Sheet2 worksheet.

The Select method allows you to select a new worksheet within the workbook.

2 Type **Worksheets(Array(1,3,4)).Select** and press Enter to select the first, third, and fourth worksheets.

Array is a function that lets you treat multiple values as one. With the Array function, you can select more than one worksheet at the same time. (When you are not in a macro, you select multiple worksheets by holding down the Ctrl key and clicking the sheet tabs.)

3 Type **Worksheets(3).Activate** and press Enter to activate the third worksheet in the work-book, the Sheet2 worksheet, while leaving all three worksheets selected.

When you select more than one worksheet, one of the worksheets is on top as the active worksheet. All three worksheets are selected, but only one is active. You use the Activate method to specify which worksheet should be the active worksheet. If only one worksheet is selected, the Select method and the Activate method act the same: they select and activate a single worksheet. You can execute methods or assign values to properties for the entire subcollection of worksheets at once.

4 Type **Worksheets(2).Activate** and press Enter to select only the second worksheet.

When you activate a worksheet that is not selected, the selection changes to include only the newly activated worksheet.

5 Type **?Worksheets(Array(1,3,4)).Count** and press Enter.

The number 3 appears. When you select items from a collection with the Array function, the selected items form a new collection.

Declare Variables to Enable Auto Lists

In a Visual Basic statement, when you type **ActiveWorkbook** and follow it with a period, an Auto List of methods and properties appropriate for a workbook appear. When you type **ActiveSheet** and follow it with a period, no Auto List appears. The Auto List does not appear because a workbook can contain different types of sheets: The active sheet could be a chart sheet as well as a worksheet. In the context of a macro, you can get the Auto List to appear by creating an appropriate variable for the object reference.

1 Close the Immediate Window, point at the Insert menu, and click Module.

2 In the module, type **Sub Test** and press Enter. This creates a new macro.

3 Type **mySheet** and then type a period. No Auto List appears.

The word *mySheet* acts as a variable. When you create a new word and use it as a variable, Visual Basic makes it Variant. *Variant* means that you can assign anything you want to the variable and it will change from Integer to String to Workbook to Range as fast as you can assign different values or objects to it. Visual Basic can't display the Auto List because it really doesn't know what type of value or object will be assigned to the variable at any given moment. You can, however, promise Visual Basic that you'll never, ever assign anything other than a Worksheet object to the *mySheet* variable.

4 Delete the period you just typed. At the top of the macro, just below the Sub Test statement, enter this statement: **Dim mySheet As Worksheet.**

This statement *declares* the variable to Visual Basic—that is, you declare to Visual Basic that *mySheet* is a variable and that the only thing you'll ever assign to it is a reference to a Worksheet object. (*Dim* is an archaic term. It's short for *Dimension* and has to do with telling the computer how much space you'll need for the variable.)

5   Position the cursor at the end of the statement beginning with mySheet, and type a period.

Sure enough, the Auto List appears. Type **N** to select the Name property.

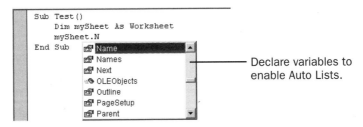

Declare variables to enable Auto Lists.

6   Press Space, and then type **= "Test Sheet"**.

The final statement should be **mySheet.Name = "Test Sheet"**. The problem with the macro is that even though you promised that *mySheet* would contain only a worksheet, you still haven't assigned a worksheet reference to it.

7   After the Dim statement, add the statement **Set mySheet = ActiveSheet**.

The Set statement assigns a reference to the ActiveSheet object to the *mySheet* variable.

8   Press F8 repeatedly to run the macro.

The macro first assigns the active sheet object to the variable and then changes the name of that sheet.

You can create a variable "on the fly" simply by assigning a value or an object to it, but if you use Dim to declare how you intend to use the variable, Visual Basic can display Auto Lists that make code much easier to write and less likely to contain errors.

Add a shape to your worksheet, page 72

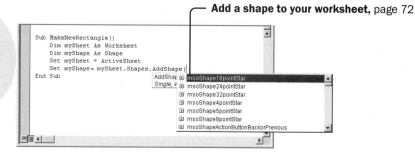

Modify a chart programmatically, page 82

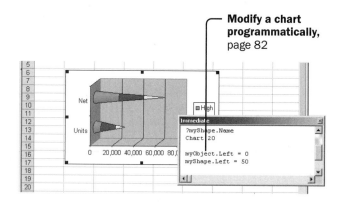

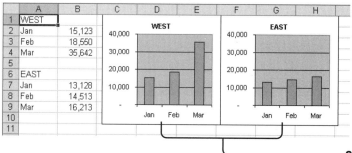

Synchronize multiple charts, page 85

Chapter 4
Explore Graphical Objects

After completing this chapter, you will be able to:

✔ **Manipulate drawing objects on a worksheet.**

✔ **Manipulate chart objects.**

✔ **Use the macro recorder as a reference tool.**

On a warm summer day, nothing beats lying on your back in a grassy field, watching clouds float across the sky. Trees, mountains, and buildings just sit there, attached firmly to the ground. But clouds move. Clouds change shape. They change color. Clouds can come in layers, too, with closer clouds drifting in front of the clouds in back.

On a worksheet, ranges with their formulas and formats are attached firmly to the worksheet, just as buildings are attached firmly to the ground. Cell A1 will always be in the upper left corner of the worksheet. Drawing objects, however, are like clouds. They float freely above the worksheet. They can disappear and reappear. They can change color and shape.

Drawing objects—including not only shapes such as rectangles, ovals, and lines, but also charts, list box controls, and spinner controls—add interest, information, and functionality to a worksheet. In this chapter, you'll learn how to use Microsoft Visual Basic for Applications macros to control drawing objects.

Graphics.xls

This chapter uses the practice file Graphics.xls that you installed from the book's CD-ROM. For details about installing the practice files, see "Using the Book's CD-ROM" at the beginning of this book.

Getting Started

1 Start Microsoft Excel, and change to the folder containing the practice files for this book.

2 Open the Graphics workbook, and save it as **Chapter04**.

Exploring Graphical Objects

Some people think of the macro recorder as a tool for beginners—and it is. You can use the macro recorder to build finished macros without having to understand much about how Excel objects really work. But the macro recorder is also a powerful reference tool for advanced developers. In this chapter, you'll see how you can use the macro recorder as a reference tool for learning how to work with Excel objects.

Record a Macro to Create a Rectangle

Graphical objects such as rectangles, ovals, text boxes, and charts can make your worksheets appealing and understandable. Microsoft Office includes an amazing collection of graphical objects. The macro recorder is an excellent tool for learning how to work with these graphical objects. Record creating a rectangle, and see how much you can learn from a simple recorded macro.

Drawing

1 Select the Shapes worksheet in the Chapter04 workbook, and click the Drawing button on the Standard toolbar to display the Drawing toolbar.

— The Drawing toolbar

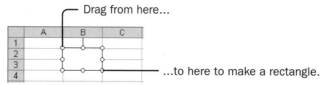

Record Macro

2 Click the Record Macro button on the Visual Basic toolbar, replace the default macro name with **MakeRectangle**, and then click OK.

Rectangle

3 Click the Rectangle button on the Drawing toolbar, and then click the upper left corner of cell B2 and drag to the lower right corner of cell B3.

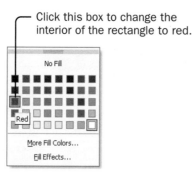

— Drag from here...

...to here to make a rectangle.

Fill Color

4 Click the arrow next to the Fill Color button on the Drawing toolbar, and then click the third box down in the first column.

The interior of the rectangle changes to red.

— Click this box to change the interior of the rectangle to red.

Stop Recording

5 Click the Stop Recording button, and edit the macro.

The numeric values might be different and the line continuation marker in your macro might be in a different place than in the following code sample.

```
Sub MakeRectangle()
    ActiveSheet.Shapes.AddShape(msoShapeRectangle, _
        48#, 13, 48#, 25.5).Select
    Selection.ShapeRange.Fill.ForeColor.SchemeColor = 10
    Selection.ShapeRange.Fill.Visible = msoTrue
    Selection.ShapeRange.Fill.Solid
End Sub
```

This macro is short, but it does a lot. Look at the second statement:

```
ActiveSheet.Shapes.AddShape(msoShapeRectangle, _
    48#, 13, 48#, 25.5).Select
```

The statement starts by pointing at the active sheet and ends by selecting something. *Shapes* is a plural noun, so it might be a collection. To add a new item to most collections, you use the Add method, but *Shapes* is followed by the word *AddShape*. *AddShape* is followed by a list of arguments in parentheses. (The numbers in your list might differ somewhat. You can ignore the symbols after some numbers. The recorder adds them, but they're not necessary.) The first argument seems to indicate what kind of shape you created, and the numbers seem to have something to do with the location and size of the rectangle, since nothing else in the macro sets the location.

The remaining statements set the fill color of the rectangle. The SchemaColor property allows you to select one of the colors from the fill color palette. You can assign any value between 0 and 56 to the SchemaColor property. The Visible property determines whether the fill of the object is transparent or visible, and the Solid method makes the pattern of the fill solid. The default fill for a new shape is to be solid and visible, so these statements are not really necessary.

These recorded statements give you several clues about how to create a new rectangle. Now you can build a macro on your own, using information from the recorder coupled with the Auto Lists that Visual Basic displays.

Write a Macro to Create a Rectangle

1 Under the recorded macro, type **Sub MakeNewRectangle** and press the Enter key.

Visual Basic adds the closing parentheses and the End Sub statement. For Visual Basic to display an Auto List of methods and properties for an object, it must know for sure which object's list to use. The properties ActiveSheet and Selection are too general: either one can refer to any of several types of objects. The best way to let Visual Basic know what kind of object you're using is to assign the object to a variable and declare its type.

2 Type the following three statements to declare the variables and assign the active sheet to a variable:

```
Dim mySheet As Worksheet
Dim myShape As Shape
Set mySheet = ActiveSheet
```

All drawing objects belong to the Shape class. By declaring the variables, you give Visual Basic the information it needs to help you as you enter statements.

3 Type **Set myShape = mySheet.Shapes.** (including the period).

Visual Basic displays the methods and
properties of the Shapes collection.

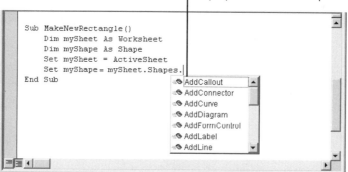

```
Sub MakeNewRectangle()
    Dim mySheet As Worksheet
    Dim myShape As Shape
    Set mySheet = ActiveSheet
    Set myShape = mySheet.Shapes.
End Sub
                                AddCallout
                                AddConnector
                                AddCurve
                                AddDiagram
                                AddFormControl
                                AddLabel
                                AddLine
```

As soon as you type the period, Visual Basic shows the list of methods and properties for
the Shapes collection. Apparently, you can add a lot more than just a Shape object. You
can add Callouts, Curves, Connectors, and other items. That's why the Shapes collection
doesn't just use a simple Add method. You know from the recorded macro that you want
to use the AddShape method to add a rectangle.

4 Type (or select) **AddShape(** and then press the Down Arrow key.

You can create more than 100
different types of shapes.

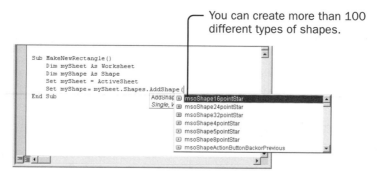

```
Sub MakeNewRectangle()
    Dim mySheet As Worksheet
    Dim myShape As Shape
    Set mySheet = ActiveSheet
    Set myShape = mySheet.Shapes.AddShape(
End Sub
        AddShap        msoShape16pointStar
        Single,        msoShape24pointStar
                       msoShape32pointStar
                       msoShape4pointStar
                       msoShape5pointStar
                       msoShape8pointStar
                       msoShapeActionButtonBackorPrevious
```

As soon as you type the opening parenthesis, Visual Basic shows you the list of possible
values for the first argument. You can add well over 100 different types of shapes. You
know from the recorded macro that you want the *msoShapeRectangle* option. (You can
experiment with others later.)

5 Type (or select) **msoShapeRectangle,**.

When you type the comma, you see that the remaining arguments are *Left*, *Top*, *Width*,
and *Height*. You specify each of these values in *points*. A point is a unit of measurement
originally used by graphic designers to lay out text for publishing. It equals 1/72 inch.

Specify the location and size
of the object using points
(1/72 inch per point).

```
    Set myShape= mySheet.Shapes.AddShape(msoShapeRectangle,
End Sub
                                AddShape(Type As MsoAutoShapeType, Left As Single,
                                Top As Single, Width As Single, Height As Single) As Shape
```

6 For the remaining arguments, type **72** for *Left*, **36** for *Top*, **72** for *Width*, and **36** for *Height*. Then type a closing parenthesis and press the Enter key.

The statement in the recorded macro ended with the Select method. When you assign an object to a variable, you don't put a Select method at the end of the statement.

7 Type **myShape.Fill.ForeColor.SchemeColor = 10** and then press the Enter key. This statement is straight out of the recorded macro.

Each time you type a period, Visual Basic helps with a list of possible methods and properties. If you hadn't assigned the rectangle to a variable—if instead you'd used Select and Selection the way the recorded macro does—Visual Basic wouldn't be able to display the Auto Lists.

Tip

A Shape object uses many subobjects to group formatting options. The Fill property returns a FillFormat object. (The object class name is different than the property name because, for chart objects, the Fill property returns a ChartFillFormat object.) A FillFormat object controls the formatting of the interior of the object. The ForeColor property returns a ColorFormat object. (This time, the object class name is different from the property name because a ColorFormat object can be returned by either the ForeColor property or the BackColor property.) Click any property name, and press F1 to see the Help topic for the property and, if applicable, for its related object.

8 Press F8 repeatedly to step through the macro.

A new rectangle appears on the worksheet. Depending on your screen size and resolution, the rectangle is about ½ inch high and 1 inch wide and is located about half an inch from the top and an inch from the left margin. The rectangle never has selection handles around its border because you never select it. You just assign a reference to a variable.

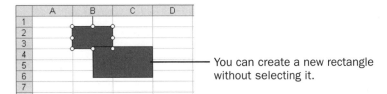

You can create a new rectangle without selecting it.

In this example, you were able to create a rectangle by following the pattern given by the recorder, and you also saw how Visual Basic Auto Lists can help you create variations of the recorded macro.

Modify an Existing Shape

Sometimes you'll want to modify one or more shapes that already exist on the worksheet. The macro recorder can help you see how to select a shape, and then you can use what you know about objects to convert the selection into an object variable.

1 Select the Shapes worksheet in the Chapter04 workbook, and click in cell A1. Show the Drawing toolbar, and start recording a macro named **SelectShapes**.

Select Objects

2 On the Drawing toolbar, click the Select Objects button, and then click the first, smaller rectangle you created.

3 Next drag a rectangle to encompass both rectangles.

73

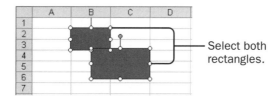

Select both rectangles.

Fill Color

4 Click the arrow next to the Fill Color toolbar button, and click More Fill Colors. Select the purple color at the far right edge of the hexagon, and click OK.

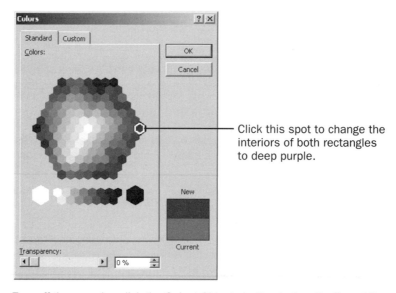

Click this spot to change the interiors of both rectangles to deep purple.

5 Turn off the recorder, click the Select Objects button to turn it off, and then select cell A1.

6 Click the Run Macro button, select the SelectShapes macro, and click Edit. The macro should look something like the following code. (The names in quotation marks might be different in your macro, depending on how many rectangles you created and how you selected them.)

```
Sub SelectShapes()
    ActiveSheet.Shapes("Rectangle 2").Select
    ActiveSheet.Shapes.Range(Array _
        ("Rectangle 2", "Rectangle 3")).Select
    Selection.ShapeRange.Fill.Visible = True
    Selection.ShapeRange.Fill.ForeColor.RGB = RGB(102, 0, 102)
    Selection.ShapeRange.Fill.Solid
End Sub
```

The Shapes property returns a collection of all the Shape objects on a worksheet. You must specify the sheet that contains the shapes. To select a single shape, you simply select a single item from the Shapes collection, using the name or number of the item, the same as you would when selecting an item from any other collection. This action returns a Shape (singular) object, which you can select or assign to a variable.

When you need to refer to more than one Shape object, Excel has a different collection—the ShapeRange collection. A ShapeRange object is like a Shape object, except that a

ShapeRange object can include more than one shape. To create a ShapeRange object from a Shapes collection, you use the Range property with the Visual Basic Array function. The Array function allows you to group a list of items. When you modify the properties of one or more shapes, you always modify the ShapeRange object.

The RGB property is similar to the SchemaColor property, except that the SchemaColor property allows you to specify one of the 56 colors on the Fill Color palette, while the RGB property—which stands for red, green, and blue, the three primary colors for light—allows you to specify any of the billions of colors available by combining 256 levels each of red, green, and blue components.

Tip

Visual Basic includes eight built-in color constants suitable for use with the RGB property. The constants (with their respective red, green, and blue components in parentheses) are as follows: *vbBlack* (0, 0, 0), *vbRed* (255, 0, 0), *vbGreen* (0, 255, 0), *vbBlue* (0, 0, 255), *vbYellow* (255, 255, 0), *vbMagenta* (255, 0, 255), *vbCyan* (0, 255, 255), and *vbWhite* (255, 255, 255).

1 Delete the statements containing the Visible property and the Solid method. They do not change the behavior of the macro.

2 At the top of the macro, insert these two declaration statements:

```
Dim myShape As Shape
Dim myShapeRange As ShapeRange
```

3 Convert the first selection to assign the object to the *myShape* variable rather than select the object. Don't change the name inside the quotation marks. The resulting statement should look something like this:

```
Set myShape = ActiveSheet.Shapes("Rectangle 2")
```

4 Insert a statement to change the RGB value of the foreground color of the fill of the shape to yellow. The final statement should look like the code shown below. (You could also use RGB(255, 255, 0) in place of *vbYellow*.)

```
myShape.Fill.ForeColor.RGB = vbYellow
```

5 Convert the second selection to assign the ShapeRange object to the *myShape* variable rather than select the object, and change it to include the sunburst shape—with the name Shape 3—rather than the Rectangle 2 shape. The resulting statement should look like this, with the possible exception of the names inside quotation marks:

```
Set myShapeRange = ActiveSheet.Shapes.Range(Array _
    ("Rectangle 3", "Shape 3"))
```

6 Convert the final statement to change the RGB value of the foreground color of the fill of the shape range to blue. The resulting statement should look like the code below. (You could also use RGB(0, 0, 255) in place of *vbBlue*.)

```
myShapeRange.Fill.ForeColor.RGB = vbBlue
```

7 Step through the macro, watching the objects change color.

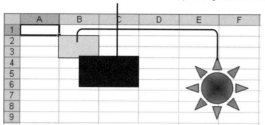

A ShapeRange object lets you change the color of multiple objects at one time.

Shapes allow you to create extremely powerful graphical effects. But keeping the different types of objects straight can be a bit confusing at first.

- **Shapes collection** Use the Shapes collection object for selecting all the shapes or a single shape, and use it for adding new shapes. You cannot use the Shapes collection object to format multiple objects.
- **Shape object** Use the Shape object for formatting a single shape.
- **ShapeRange collection** Use the ShapeRange collection for formatting multiple objects at the same time.

Rename Shapes

When you create a new shape on the worksheet, Excel gives it a default name, usually something like Rectangle 2 or Oval 5. When you record a macro that refers to the shape, the recorder puts that same name into the macro. You'll make your macros easier to read and less likely to have errors if you change the shape names to something meaningful.

Shapes and DrawingObjects

Shapes are a relatively new feature for Excel. Shapes are shared by all Microsoft Office applications and replace the earlier graphical objects that Excel used. Earlier graphical objects belonged to an object class called DrawingObjects, and you can still see some relics of DrawingObjects in Excel today.

For example, Shape objects format the interior of an object using the Fill property. DrawingObjects referred to the interior of an object using the Interior property. Shape objects refer to colors that represent the red, green, and blue components of the color using the RGB property. DrawingObjects referred to the same type of color using the Color property. Shape objects refer to colors from a palette using the SchemeColor property, whereas DrawingObjects used the ColorIndex property. As you might recognize, the Range object still uses all the formatting properties that the old DrawingObjects used: Interior, Color, and ColorIndex.

To maintain backward compatibility, Excel didn't remove the old DrawingObjects. They're still there, but they're hidden. Occasionally, you might see vestiges of these old graphical objects.

1 On the Excel worksheet, click the first, smaller rectangle you created. It has a name like Rectangle 2. You can see the name in the Name box to the left of the formula bar.

This box shows the name of...

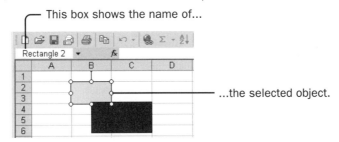

...the selected object.

2 Click in the Name box, and type **Box** as a new name for the rectangle. Press the Enter key, or Excel won't recognize that you've changed the name.

Type the new name here, and press the Enter key.

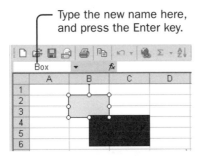

3 Click the second, larger rectangle you created, and give it the name **BigBox**. Then give the sun shape the name **Sun**. Be sure to press the Enter key after typing each name in the Name box.

4 In the SelectShapes macro, change *Rectangle 2* to **Box**, *Rectangle 3* to **BigBox**, and *Shape 3* to **Sun**.

5 Change the colors in the macro from *vbYellow* to **vbGreen** and from *vbBlue* to **vbMagenta**, and then run the macro to test it. Here's what the final macro should look like:

```
Sub SelectShapes()
    Dim myShape As Shape
    Dim myShapeRange As ShapeRange
    Set myShape = ActiveSheet.Shapes("Box")
    MyShape.Fill.ForeColor.RGB = vbGreen
    Set myShapeRange = ActiveSheet.Shapes.Range(Array _
        ("BigBox", "Sun"))
    MyShapeRange.Fill.ForeColor.RGB = vbMagenta
End Sub
```

In the same way that you can give worksheets meaningful names (rather than keeping the default Sheet1, Sheet2, and so forth), you can give meaningful names to shapes on the worksheet, even though these names are less noticeable. Your macros will thank you for it.

Excel can create hundreds of different types of shapes. All these shapes work in much the same way that rectangles do. Embedded charts are also shapes in Excel. You add, manipulate, and delete Chart objects in much the same way you do rectangles. Chart objects, of course, have additional properties that are unique to charts; the macro recorder is an effective tool for finding out what they are.

Exploring Chart Objects

Chart objects have hundreds of properties and methods. Many attributes of a chart are themselves separate objects. Because charts have so many objects and properties, learning how to create and manipulate charts by reading a reference manual is difficult. But creating and manipulating a chart is easy to record, and even though you might see many new methods, properties, and objects, the new objects work according to the same principles as other objects in Excel.

Record a Macro That Creates a Chart

1 Activate the ChartData worksheet in the Chapter04 workbook, and select cell A1.

	A	B	C	D
1	Price	Units	Net	
2	High	6,443	22,600	
3	Mid	12,599	22,800	
4	Low	8,670	19,401	
5				

Record Macro

2 Click the Record Macro button on the Visual Basic toolbar, type **MakeChart** as the name for the macro, and then click OK.

Chart Wizard

3 Click the ChartWizard button on the Standard toolbar, and then click the Finish button to create the default chart.

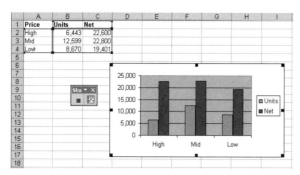

Stop Recording

4 Click the Stop Recording button, delete the chart, and then edit the recorded macro. The following code shows what the macro looks like. (Continuation characters shown here might be in different locations than in your macro.)

```
Sub MakeChart()
    Charts.Add
    ActiveChart.ChartType = xlColumnClustered
    ActiveChart.SetSourceData _
        Source:=Sheets("ChartData").Range("A1:C4")
    ActiveChart.Location _
```

```
        Where:=xlLocationAsObject, _
        Name:="ChartData"
End Sub
```

The macro creates an embedded chart in four steps. First it uses the Add method to create a new, blank chart (as a stand-alone sheet). Second it uses the ChartType property to set the type of the chart. Third it uses the SetSourceData method to assign a data range to the chart. And finally it uses the Location method to move the chart onto the worksheet.

Modify the Macro That Creates a Chart

Once you've recorded the macro to create a chart, you can make modifications to it to instantly create exactly the type of chart you want.

1 Click the word *xlColumnClustered* in the macro. This is one of an enumerated list of values that can be assigned to the ChartType property.

2 Click the Edit menu and the List Constants command. Excel displays the entire list of possible chart types.

Select the chart type from the list.

Tip

Visual Basic is able to display the list of possible values because it knows that ActiveChart can return only a Chart object. Visual Basic doesn't display the list of methods and properties when ActiveSheet or Selection is the object because Visual Basic can't be sure what kind of object is currently selected. If you declare an object variable and assign the object to the variable, Visual Basic will be able to display the helpful lists.

3 Select *xlConeBarStacked* from the list, and double-click it to insert it into the code.

4 At the end of the statement that sets the source data, type a comma, a space, and an underscore. Then press the Enter key to create a new line.

5 Add **PlotBy:=xlRows** as an additional argument to the statement to make the column headings into the category labels. Here's what the revised macro looks like:

```
Sub MakeChart()
    Charts.Add
    ActiveChart.ChartType = xlConeBarStacked
    ActiveChart.SetSourceData _
        Source:=Sheets("ChartData").Range("A1:C4"), _
        PlotBy:=xlRows
    ActiveChart.Location
        Where:=xlLocationAsObject, _
        Name:="ChartData"
End Sub
```

79

6 Press F8 repeatedly to step through the modified macro. Watch how Excel creates the chart as a separate sheet first, adds the data, and finally moves it onto the worksheet.

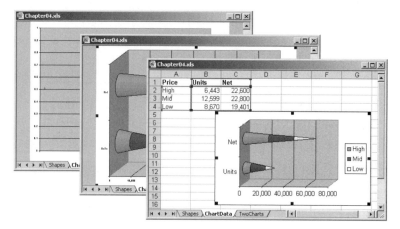

An Excel chart can exist in either of two locations. It can exist as a separate sheet in the workbook, or it can be embedded in a worksheet. Regardless of where a chart is located, it behaves the same way. There are some differences, however, in how you refer to each type of chart.

Refer to an Existing Embedded Chart

When you create a new chart, Excel selects the chart, so you can use ActiveChart to refer to it. If a chart already exists, you have to refer to it differently. A chart that's on a separate sheet is easy to refer to; simply select a single item from the Charts collection. Referring to a chart that's embedded on a worksheet, however, can be confusing. This section, however, will make it all clear.

1 In Excel, if the Chart is selected, press the Esc key to deselect the chart. (If you had selected an object inside the chart, you may need to press the Esc key more than once.)

2 In Visual Basic, at the bottom of the open module, type **Sub SelectChart** and press the Enter key. Add these three declaration statements to the top of the macro:

```
Dim myShape As Shape
Dim myObject As ChartObject
Dim myChart As Chart
```

You'll assign objects to these variables to see how Excel handles charts embedded on a worksheet.

3 Press F8 twice to step down to the End Sub statement in the new macro. From the View menu, click the Immediate Window command to display the Immediate window.

4 In the Immediate window, type **Set myShape = ActiveSheet.Shapes(1)** and press the Enter key to assign a reference to the chart's container to the *myShape* variable.

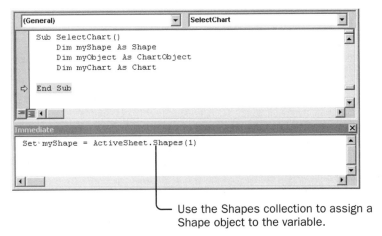

— Use the Shapes collection to assign a
  Shape object to the variable.

5   In the Immediate window, type **Set myObject = ActiveSheet.ChartObjects(1)** and press
the Enter key to assign a reference to the chart's container to the *myObject* variable. (Both
myShape and *myObject* refer to the same chart container object, but *myShape* refers to
the chart as a Shape object, and *myObject* refers to the chart as a ChartObject object.)

6   In the Immediate window, type **?myObject.Name** and press the Enter key. The name of
the chart appears.

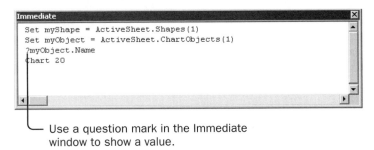

— Use a question mark in the Immediate
  window to show a value.

Tip

In the Immediate window, if you type a question mark in front of an expression that returns a
value and then press the Enter key, you'll see the value displayed immediately.

7   In the Immediate window, type **?myShape.Name** and press the Enter key.

The same name appears again. Both *myObject* and *myShape* refer to the same object.

Both the ChartObject object and the
Shape object refer to the same chart.

```
Immediate
    ?myObject.Name
    Chart 20
    ?myShape.Name
    Chart 20
```

8 In the Immediate window, type **myObject.Left = 0** and press the Enter key. Then type **myShape.Left = 50** and press the Enter key.

In each case, the chart shifts. You can use either container object to move and resize the chart.

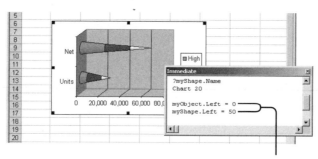

```
Immediate
    ?myShape.Name
    Chart 20

    myObject.Left = 0
    myShape.Left = 50
```

Both the ChartObject and the Shape
can move the container box.

9 In the Immediate window, type **myObject.Select** and press the Enter key. Then type **myShape.Select** and press the Enter key.

In both cases, the statement works and you see white boxes at the corner of the chart. The white handles show that you selected the container object, and not the chart inside.

When you select the chart container, you
see the white selection handles appear.

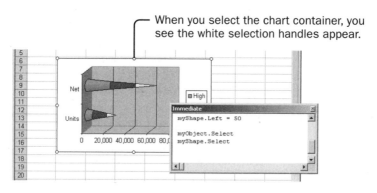

```
Immediate
    myShape.Left = 50

    myObject.Select
    myShape.Select
```

Tip

Interactively, when you click in an embedded chart, you immediately select the portion of the chart that you clicked. For example, if you click around the edge of a chart, you select the Chart Area portion of the chart, which has black handles. To select the container object interactively, you must first click the Select Objects button on the Drawing toolbar. When the container is selected, you can't select any of the chart objects inside.

10 In the Immediate window, type **myObject.Activate** and press the Enter key.

When you activate the ChartObject, you see the boxes at the corners of the chart turn black, indicating that you have now selected the Chart Area inside the chart. As soon as you typed the period, Visual Basic displayed the Activate method in the Auto List, showing that Activate is a method of the ChartObject object.

11 In the Immediate window, type **myShape.Activate** and press the Enter key. (Click OK to close the error message.)

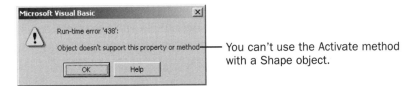 — You can't use the Activate method with a Shape object.

When you try to activate the Shape object, you get an error because the Shape object doesn't have an Activate method. (When Visual Basic displayed the Auto List for the Shape object, the Activate method wasn't in the list.) This is one of the ways in which a new-style Shape object differs from an old-style ChartObject object.

12 In the Immediate window, type **Set myChart = myObject.Chart** and press the Enter key.

In this statement, the Chart property assigns to the variable *myChart* a reference to the chart that is contained in the ChartObject object. In the same way that a Shape object doesn't have an Activate method, a Shape object doesn't have a Chart property either.

Tip

The ChartObjects collection is left over from the old-style Excel drawing objects. It couldn't be hidden like the other old graphical object collections because the Shape object doesn't have an Activate method or a Chart property for working with charts.

13 In the Immediate window, type **myChart.ChartArea.Interior.Color = vbRed** and press the Enter key.

The interior of the chart changes to red. Once you have a reference to the chart, you can manipulate the objects inside it. The Interior and Color properties of a ChartObject object correspond to the Fill and RGB properties of a Shape object.

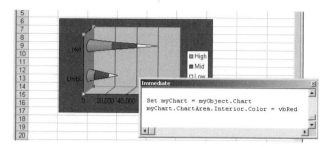

14 Close the Immediate window, and press F8 to finish the macro.

A chart that's embedded in a worksheet consists of two parts: the container box (a ChartObject object) and the chart inside (a Chart object). You can refer to the container box by using either the Shapes collection (which returns a Shape object) or the ChartObjects collection (which returns a ChartObject object), but to get to the chart inside, you must use the ChartObjects collection, not the Shapes collection. For example, you can move and resize the container using either the Shapes collection or the ChartObjects collection, but to change the color of the chart area, you must get to the chart inside using the ChartObjects collection.

Record a Macro That Modifies Chart Attributes

Now that you understand how Excel refers to the chart container and the chart inside, you can record a macro that changes a chart and learn what methods and properties you use to control a chart.

1 On the ChartData worksheet, select cell A1. Start recording a macro named **ChangeChart**.

2 Click the edge of the chart you created in the section "Modify the Macro That Creates a Chart." This activates the chart.

3 Double-click one of the numbers along the bottom of the chart. Doing this selects the value axis and displays the Format Axis dialog box. Select the Scale tab.

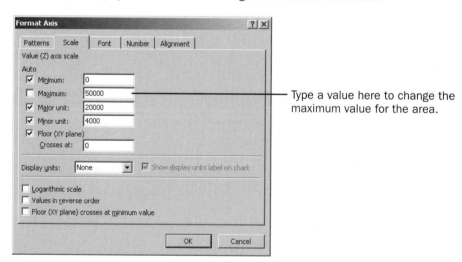

Type a value here to change the maximum value for the area.

4   Change the Maximum value to **50000**. (Entering a value clears the Auto check box.) Click OK.

5   Turn off the recorder, and edit the macro. It looks similar to this, although the chart name inside the quotation marks will probably be different:

```
Sub ChangeChart()
    ActiveSheet.ChartObjects("Chart 20").Activate
    ActiveChart.ChartArea.Select
    ActiveChart.Axes(xlValue).Select
    With ActiveChart.Axes(xlValue)
        .MinimumScaleIsAuto = True
        .MaximumScale = 50000
        .MinorUnitIsAuto = True
        .MajorUnitIsAuto = True
        .Crosses = xlAutomatic
        .ReversePlotOrder = False
        .ScaleType = xlLinear
        .DisplayUnit = xlNone
    End With
End Sub
```

The macro first activates the chart, using the ChartObjects collection. (If you want to refer to the chart inside the embedded container without activating it, you must use the Chart property of the ChartObject object.) The macro then selects the ChartArea object. This statement is superfluous because the statement after it selects the value axis. The macro then sets several properties of the value axis, even though you changed only one in the dialog box.

You could simplify this entire macro to a single statement:

```
ActiveSheet.ChartObjects("Chart 20").Chart.Axes(xlValue) _
    .MaximumScale = 50000
```

You can be grateful, however, that the recorder included everything it did because you can learn the names of a lot of properties very quickly. In the next section, we'll put some of those properties to work in a very useful macro.

Write a Macro That Synchronizes Two Charts

The TwoCharts worksheet contains two charts that show total orders for two different regions.

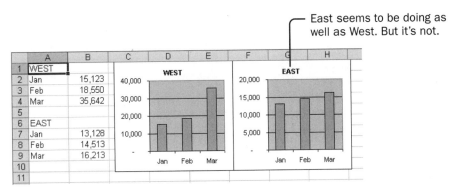

East seems to be doing as well as West. But it's not.

Based on a quick glance at the charts, you might conclude that the performance of the two regions was roughly equal. But that would be wrong. The East region is substantially lower than the West, but Excel automatically scales the axes to fit the data. Let's create a macro that will change the value axis on the East chart to match the axis on the West chart.

Select Objects

1   Name the charts so that you can refer to them by descriptive names. On the Drawing toolbar, click the Select Objects button, click the West chart, and then enter **West** in the Name box. Follow the same steps to give the name **East** to the East chart. Then click the Select Objects button again to deselect it.

2   In Visual Basic, at the bottom of the module, type **Sub SynchronizeCharts** and press the Enter key. Then enter the following two variable declarations:

```
Dim myWest As Chart
Dim myEast As Chart
```

You'll store a reference to a chart in each of these variables.

3   Next enter the following two statements to assign the charts to the variables:

```
Set myWest = ActiveSheet.ChartObjects("West").Chart
Set myEast = ActiveSheet.ChartObjects("East").Chart
```

You must include the Chart property to move from the container to the chart inside. If you hadn't renamed the charts, you'd have to use either the default "Chart 1" and "Chart 2" or the numbers 1 and 2 (and determine which was which by trial and error). Giving the charts explicit, meaningful names makes your code easier to read and less likely to contain errors.

4   Add the following statement to make sure that the value axis on the West chart is automatic:

```
myWest.Axes(xlValue).MaximumScaleIsAuto = True
```

The expression *Axes(xlValue)* was in the recorded macro. That's how you know how to refer to the value axis. The MaximumScaleIsAuto property didn't appear in the recorded macro, but the MinimumScaleIsAuto property did, and you can guess the rest.

5   Add the following statement to make the axes have the same maximum scale:

```
myEast.Axes(xlValue).MaximumScale = _
    myWest.Axes(xlValue).MaximumScale
```

Even though the maximum scale of the West chart is set to automatic, you still can read the current value from it.

6   Press F8 repeatedly to step through the macro.

The difference between the two regions is much more obvious now.

East is now obviously
lower than West.

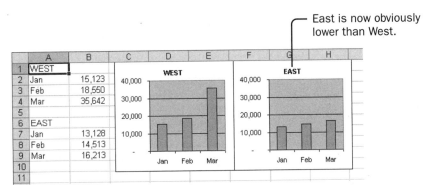

7   On the worksheet, change the March value for the West region to **15,000**. Then run the
SynchronizeCharts macro again.

You could add still other synchronization tasks to this macro as well. For example, you
could make the minimum value for each axis the same. You could make it so that if you
interactively changed the color of the background on the West chart, running the macro
would make the East chart the same color. For each enhancement, you simply record a
macro to learn what you need to change, and then add it to your macro.

Formatting Charts

Charts are an interesting hybrid of Excel's older DrawingObjects and Office's Shapes. Charts
have been around since the first version of Excel, so all the features that can be controlled
with old properties, such as Interior, still use those properties. For example, to set red as the
color of the ChartArea of a chart assigned to the *myChart* variable, you could use the statement *myChart.Interior.Color = vbRed*.

Office Shape objects are newer than Chart objects, but Chart objects can still take advantage
of the fancy formatting that's part of a Shape object. To get to those newer features, you must
use the Fill property. For example, to create a gradient background for the ChartArea, you
could use the statement *myChart.Fill.TwoColorGradient msoGradientHorizontal, 1*.

The formatting properties that can be set using the Interior property can't be set using the Fill
property. For example, you can set the fill color of a shape using the statement
myShape.Fill.ForeColor.RGB = vbRed, but with a chart, the RGB property is read-only. You can
find out the color using the new property, but you have to change it using the old one. Because
the properties and methods of the fill for a chart are somewhat different from those for a
shape, the Fill property for a chart object returns a ChartFillFormat object, whereas the Fill
property for a shape returns a FillFormat object.

Select a single row from a variable-sized list, page 91

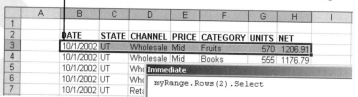

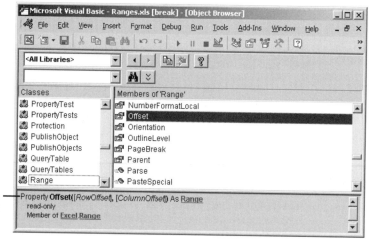

Use the Object Browser to learn about objects, page 100

Add structured formatting to a variable-sized list, page 105

Chapter 5
Explore Range Objects

After completing this chapter, you will be able to:

✔ Use several properties to refer to Range objects from macro statements.

✔ Apply formatting to ranges.

✔ Put values and formulas into cells.

✔ Simplify macros that record selections.

✔ Use the Object Browser to learn about objects, properties, and methods.

The world would be much simpler if everybody were the same size. Cars wouldn't need adjustable seats; heads would never get bumped on door frames; feet would never dangle from a chair. Of course, some new complexities would probably arise. When exchanging that ghastly outfit you received for your birthday, you wouldn't be able to claim it was the wrong size.

In Microsoft Excel 2002, if your worksheets and data files are all the same size, you don't need to worry about Range objects. If you never insert new lines into a budget, if you always put yearly totals in column M, if every month's transaction file has 5 columns and 120 rows, the macro recorder can take care of dealing with ranges for you.

In the real world of humans, however, people are different sizes, and clothes and cars have to adjust to fit them. And in the real world of worksheets, models and data files are also different sizes and you want your macros to fit them. Excel provides many properties for working with Range objects. In this chapter, you'll explore Range objects and in the process learn how the Object Browser can teach you about any unfamiliar object.

Ranges.xls

This chapter uses the practice file Ranges.xls that you installed from the book's CD-ROM. For details about installing the practice files, see "Using the Book's CD-ROM" at the beginning of this book.

Getting Started

1 Start Excel, switch to the folder containing the practice files for this book, and open the Ranges workbook.

2 Save a copy of the workbook as **Chapter05.**

Referring to a Range

A macro that needs to work with ranges of differing sizes must be flexible. In this section, you'll learn various ways to refer to a range. The examples in this section don't *do* anything except reference ranges within a list, but these are all techniques you'll use many times as you work with ranges. Later in the chapter, you'll use these expressions in practical contexts.

Refer to a Range by Using an Address

The Range property is a useful and flexible way of retrieving a reference to a range. The Range property allows you to specify the address of the range you want. You can use the Object Browser to see how to use the Range property.

Visual Basic Editor

1   In the Chapter05 workbook, activate the Data tab. Then click the Visual Basic Editor toolbar button (on the Visual Basic toolbar). Rearrange the Excel and Visual Basic Editor windows so that you can see them side by side.

Object Browser

2   In the Visual Basic Editor, click the Object Browser toolbar button.

The Object Browser appears in the space normally held by the code window. In essence, the Object Browser consists of two lists. The list on the left is a list of object class names. The list on the right is a list of members—methods and properties—available for the currently selected object class. At the top of the list of classes is a special object class named <globals>. The globals class is not a real object class, but it includes in its list of members all the methods and properties you can use without specifying an object. These are the methods and properties you use to start a statement.

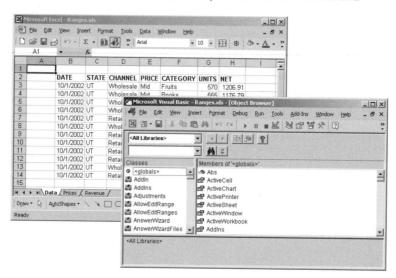

3   In the list of classes, select the <globals> class if it is not already selected. Then click in the list of members and press the letter **R** to scroll to the first member that begins with the letter R. Then select the Range property. The box at the bottom of the Object Browser displays information about the Range property. This property takes two arguments—the second of which is optional—and it returns a reference to a Range object.

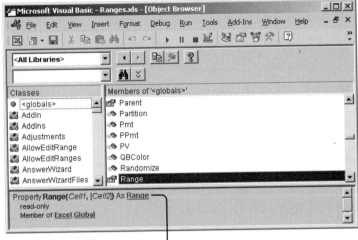

The Range property returns a Range object.

4   Right-click the Range property name in the Members list, and click Copy on the shortcut menu. Then choose the View menu and click Immediate Window. In the Immediate window, choose the Edit menu and click Paste.

5   After the Range property, type an opening parenthesis—Visual Basic will display the argument list—and type **"B2"**, followed by a closing parenthesis and a period. Then type **Select**. The complete statement is *Range("B2").Select*. You need the quotation marks around the range definition because this is the *name* of the range, not the item number of a member of a collection.

6   Press Enter to select cell B2 on the active worksheet.

7   Type **Range("B2:H2").Select** and press Enter. The first argument of the range property can be a multicell range. In fact, it can be anything that Excel recognizes.

	A	B	C	D	E	F	G	H	I
1									
2		DATE	STATE	CHANNEL	PRICE	CATEGORY	UNITS	NET	
3		10/1/2002	UT	Wholesale	Mid	Fruits	570	1206.91	
4		10/1/2002	UT	Wholesale	Mid	Books	555	1176.79	

8   Type **Range("H14").Select** and press Enter to select the lower right corner of the list of values. Then type **Range(Selection, "B2").Select** and press Enter.

This selects the range from cell H14 (the current selection) to cell B2 (the upper left cell of the list). The arguments to the Range property do not have to be strings; they can also be references to range objects. A common use of the two-argument form of the Range property is to select the range that extends from the currently selected range to some fixed point at the top of the worksheet.

The Range property is a flexible way of establishing a link to an arbitrary Range object. You can use either a single text string that contains any valid reference as an argument to the Range property or two arguments that define the end points of a rectangular range.

Refer to a Range as a Collection of Cells

Multiple worksheets can exist in a workbook, and the Worksheets collection is defined as an object class. A Worksheets object has a list of methods and properties that is separate from a Worksheet object.

Similarly, multiple cells exist on a worksheet. You might expect that Excel would have a Cells collection object. But a collection of cells is more complicated than a collection of worksheets because cells come in two dimensions—rows and columns. For example, you can think of the range A1:B3 as a collection of six cells, as a collection of three rows, or as a collection of two columns.

Excel therefore has three properties that look at a range as a collection. The first of these—the Cells property—returns a collection of cells. This is not a separate class, however. The result of the Cells property is still a Range object, and it can use any of the methods or properties of any other Range object.

1 In the Object Browser, with the <globals> object selected in the list of classes, select the Cells property from the list of members. The description at the bottom of the Object Browser indicates that the Cells property returns a Range object.

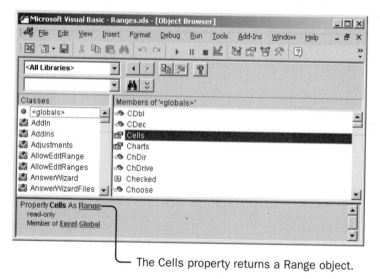

The Cells property returns a Range object.

2 In the Immediate window, type **Cells.Select** and press Enter.

This selects all the cells on the worksheet. This is equivalent to clicking the box at the upper left corner of the worksheet, between the column A heading and the row 1 heading.

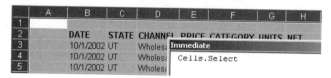

3 Type **Cells.Item(5).Select** and press Enter.

This selects cell E1, the fifth cell in the first row. The Cells property returns the range of all the cells on the worksheet as a collection. An individual item in the collection is a cell.

	A	B	C	D	E	F	G	H
1								
2		DATE	STATE	CHANNEL	PRICE	CATEGORY	UNITS	NET
3		10/1/2002	UT	Wholes				
4		10/1/2002	UT	Wholes				
5		10/1/2002	UT	Wholes				
6		10/1/2002	UT	Wholes				

```
Immediate
Cells.Item(5).Select
```

4 Type **Cells.Item(257).Select** and press Enter.

This selects cell A2, the first cell in the second row. When you use a single number to select an item in the Cells collection, the number wraps at the end of each row. Each row of the worksheet contains 256 cells, so cell 257 is the first cell on the second row.

	A	B	C	D	E	F	G	H
1								
2		DATE	STATE	CHANNEL	PRICE	CATEGORY	UNITS	NET
3		10/1/2002	UT	Wholes				
4		10/1/2002	UT	Wholes				
5		10/1/2002	UT	Wholes				
6		10/1/2002	UT	Wholes				

```
Immediate
Cells.Item(257).Select
```

5 Type **Cells.Item(3,2).Select** and press Enter.

This selects cell B3, the third row and second column in the worksheet. Unlike most other collections, the Cells collection allows you to specify an item by using both the row and column values.

	A	B	C	D	E	F	G	H
1								
2		DATE	STATE	CHANNEL	PRICE	CATEGORY	UNITS	NET
3		10/1/2002	UT	Wholes				
4		10/1/2002	UT	Wholes				
5		10/1/2002	UT	Wholes				
6		10/1/2002	UT	Wholes				

```
Immediate
Cells.Item(3,2).Select
```

6 Type **?Cells.Count** and press Enter.

The number 16777216 appears in the Immediate window. There are 16,777,216 cells in a worksheet.

Tip

Typing a question mark before an expression in the Immediate window allows you to display the value of that expression.

7 Type **Cells.Item(16777216).Select** and press Enter.

This selects cell IV65535, the lower right cell in the worksheet. You could select the same cell by using two arguments with the Cells collection—*Cells.Item(65535,255)*—or by using the Range property—*Range("IV65535")*.

	IR	IS	IT	IU	IV	
65529						
65530						
65531						
65532						
65533						
65534						
65535						
65536						

```
Immediate
    Cells.Item(16777216).Select
```

8   Type **Cells(1).Select** and press Enter. This selects cell A1.

As with other collections, when you use the Cells property to get a collection of cells, you can leave out the Item method, and simply put the argument after the Cells property. The expression *Cells(1)* is equivalent to *Cells.Item(1)*, which is equivalent to *Range("A1")*. All these expressions can be used interchangeably.

Refer to a Range as a Collection of Rows or Columns

In addition to referring to the worksheet range as a collection of cells, you can also think of it as a collection of rows or as a collection of columns. Analogous to the Cells property, the Rows property returns a collection of rows and the Columns property returns a collection of columns. These properties return collections, do not have their own object classes, and return Range objects.

1   In the Object Browser, with the <globals> object selected in the list of classes, select the Columns property in the list of Members.

The description shows that this property, similar to the Range property and the Cells property, returns a Range object.

2   In the Immediate window, type **Columns.Select** and press Enter.

This selects all the cells on the worksheet, exactly the same as Cells.Select. The difference between the two properties appears when you use the Item property to index into a single item in the collection.

3   Type **Columns(3).Select** and press Enter. This selects column C, the third column on the worksheet.

	A	B	C	D	E	F	G	H
1								
2		DATE	STATE	CHANNEL	PRICE	CATEGORY	UNITS	NET
3		10/1/2002	UT	Wholesale	N			
4		10/1/2002	UT	Wholesale	N			
5		10/1/2002	UT	Wholesale	N			

```
Immediate
    Columns(3).Select
```

4   Type **Columns("D").Select** and press Enter. This selects column D. When you specify a column by letter, you are giving the *name* of the item and must enclose it in quotation marks.

```
Immediate
    Columns("D").Select
```

5   Type **Columns("B:H").Select** and press Enter.

This selects the range of columns from B through H. The only way to specify a range of columns within the collection is by using the column letter names.

6   Type **Rows(2).Select** and press Enter.

This selects row 2. With rows, the name of an item is also a number. The expressions *Rows(2)* and *Rows("2")* are functionally equivalent.

7   Type **Rows("3:14").Select** and press Enter.

This selects a range of rows. The only way to specify a range of rows within the collection is by using the row numbers as a name—that is, by enclosing them in quotation marks.

The globals group in the Object Browser includes three properties that return all the cells of a worksheet—Cells, Columns, and Rows. In each case, you get a reference to a Range object, but the properties return that object as a collection of cells, columns, or rows, respectively. There are no object classes for Cells, Columns, and Rows. These are simply different ways of representing the same Range object.

Refer to a Range Based on the Current Selection

Many times when writing a macro you want to refer to a range that is somehow related to the active cell or to the current selection. The macro recorder uses the Selection property to refer to the selected range and the ActiveCell property to refer to the one active cell. A Range object has useful properties that can extend the active cell or the selection to include particularly useful ranges.

1 In the Immediate window, type **Range("B2").Select** and press Enter. This selects the upper left cell of the sample list.

2 In the Object Browser, with the globals group selected in the Classes list, select the ActiveCell property.

The description at the bottom of the Object Browser shows that this property returns a Range object.

3 Activate the Immediate window, choose the Edit menu, and click Complete Word. In the list of members, click ActiveCell.

Tip

At the beginning of a statement—whether in a macro or in the Immediate window—when you use the Complete Word command, the Auto List displays all the members of the globals group.

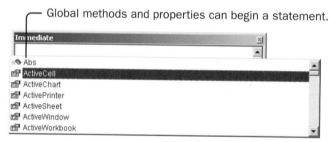

Global methods and properties can begin a statement.

4 Type a period and then **CurrentRegion.Select** to create the statement *ActiveCell.Current Region.Select* and then press Enter.

This selects the entire sample list. The CurrentRegion property selects a rectangular range that includes the original cell and is surrounded by either blank cells or the edge of the worksheet. It is hard to overstate the usefulness of the CurrentRegion property.

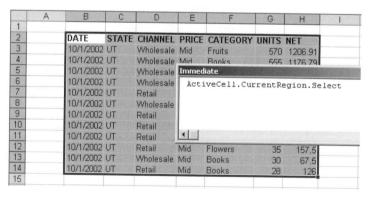

5 Type **ActiveCell.EntireColumn.Select** and press Enter.

This selects all of column B because the active cell was cell B2. Because the starting range was the active cell—not the entire selection—the EntireColumn property returned a reference to only one column.

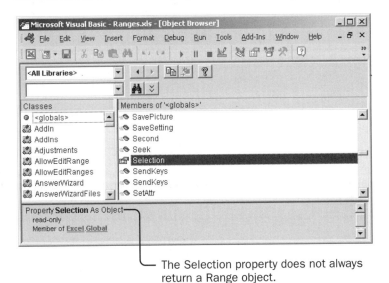

6 In the Object Browser, with the globals group selected, select the Selection property in the list of members. The description at the bottom indicates that the Selection property returns an *object*, not a Range. The Selection property returns a Range object only when cells are selected. If shapes or parts of a chart are selected, this global property returns a different object type. Because the Selection object can return a different object type at different times, it does not display an Auto List the way the ActiveCell property does.

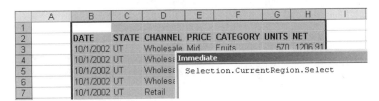

The Selection property does not always return a Range object.

7 In the Immediate window, type **Selection.CurrentRegion.Select** and press Enter. This selects the range B1:H14—the entire sample list plus the one row above it. When you use the CurrentRegion property with a multicell range such as the initial selection in this example, the new range is the current region of the upper left cell of that range.

8 Type **Selection.EntireRow.Select** and press Enter. This selects rows 1 through 14. Because the starting range was a multicell range, the EntireRow property returns the range that extends all the rows of that range.

9 Type **Range("B2").Activate** and press Enter. Because the specified cell is within the selected range, this statement does not change the selection, but it does move the active cell to a new location within the range. If you activate a cell that is not within the current selection, the Activate method behaves the same as Select.

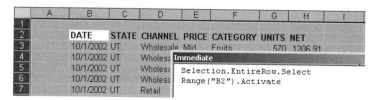

The Selection and ActiveCell properties are useful as starting points for deriving other ranges. The ActiveCell property always returns a reference to a Range object, and therefore displays a convenient Auto List when you are entering a statement. The Selection property returns a reference to a Range object only when a range is actually selected, and thus it does not display an Auto List.

Refer to a Relative Range

When you use one of the range-returning properties from the globals group—Range, Cells, Columns, or Rows—you get a range based on the entire active worksheet. These same properties also exist as properties of a Range object. The easiest way to work with properties of a Range object is to declare a variable as a Range. Then the Auto List can show you the methods and properties as you type a statement, even if you start with a property such as Selection, which does not display an Auto List.

1 In the Visual Basic Editor, choose the Insert menu and click Module. Type **Sub TestRange** and press Enter. Visual Basic adds parentheses and an *End Sub* statement.

2 Type **Dim myRange As Range** and press F8 twice to initialize the variable.

3 In the Immediate window, type **Set myRange = Range("B2")** and press Enter. Then type **myRange.Select** and press Enter. This selects cell B2, confirming that the variable contains a reference to that cell.

Object Browser

4 Click the Object Browser button. In the list of classes, select the Range class. Then in the list of members, select the Range property. This Range property appears very similar to the Range property of the globals group. It behaves, however, *relative* to a starting range.

5 In the Immediate window, type **myRange.Range("A1:G1").Select** and press Enter.

This does not select the range A1:G1. Rather, it selects the range B2:H2. If you think of cell B2 as the upper left cell of an imaginary worksheet, the range A1:G1 of that imaginary worksheet would correspond to the range B2:H2 of the real worksheet.

	A	B	C	D	E	F	G	H	I
1									
2		DATE	STATE	CHANNEL	PRICE	CATEGORY	UNITS	NET	
3		10/1/2002	UT	Wholesale	Mid	Fruits	570	1206.91	
4		10/1/2002	UT	Wholesa	Immediate				
5		10/1/2002	UT	Wholesa	Set myRange = Range("B2")				
6		10/1/2002	UT	Wholesa	myRange.Range("A1:G1").Select				
7		10/1/2002	UT	Retail					

6 Type **Set myRange = Range("B2").CurrentRegion** and press Enter. Then type **myRange. Select** and press Enter. This selects the entire sample list, confirming that the variable contains a reference to the range.

7 Type **myRange.Cells(2,6).Select** and press Enter.

This selects the first value in the Units column—the sixth column of the second row of the list.

	A	B	C	D	E	F	G	H	I
1									
2		DATE	STATE	CHANNEL	PRICE	CATEGORY	UNITS	NET	
3		10/1/2002	UT	Wholesale	Mid	Fruits	570	1206.91	
4		10/1/2002	UT	Wholesale	Mid	Books	555	1176.79	
5		10/1/2002	UT	Wh					
6		10/1/2002	UT	Wh					
7		10/1/2002	UT	Ret					
8		10/1/2002	UT	Wh					

```
Immediate
  Set myRange = Range("B2").CurrentRegion
  myRange.Cells(2,6).Select
```

8 Type **myRange.Rows(2).Select** and press Enter.

This selects the second row of values in the list, even though they exist in row 3 of the worksheet. A single row from the collection referenced by the global Rows property includes the entire row of the worksheet; the Rows property of a Range object includes only the cells within the range.

	A	B	C	D	E	F	G	H	I
1									
2		DATE	STATE	CHANNEL	PRICE	CATEGORY	UNITS	NET	
3		10/1/2002	UT	Wholesale	Mid	Fruits	570	1206.91	
4		10/1/2002	UT	Wholesale	Mid	Books	555	1176.79	
5		10/1/2002	UT	Wh					
6		10/1/2002	UT	Wh					
7		10/1/2002	UT	Ret					

```
Immediate
  myRange.Rows(2).Select
```

9 Type **myRange.Rows(myRange.Rows.Count).Select** and press Enter.

This selects the last row of the list. Because the Rows property returns a collection, you can use the Count property to find the number of items in the collection. That count can serve as an index into the same collection.

10 Type **myRange.Rows(myRange.Rows.Count+1).Select** and press Enter.

With the Cells, Rows, and Columns properties of a Range object, you can actually use an index that does not fit within the limits of the collection. This is a powerful way to select an appropriate range for entering new values or total formulas.

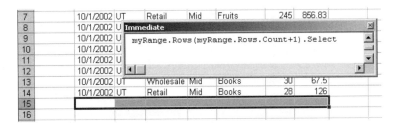

When you use the Range, Cells, Columns, or Rows properties from the global group—or if you use any of these properties with the Application object or a Worksheet object—the addresses are relative to the upper left cell of the worksheet. If you use any of these properties with a Range object, the addresses are relative to the upper left cell of that range.

Refer to Ranges Within the Current Region

Excel has other properties that can calculate a new range based on an existing range. The Offset property references a range shifted down, up, left, or right from a starting range. The Resize property references a range with a different number of rows or columns from a starting range.

1 In the Object Browser, select Range in the Classes list. Then, in the list of members, select the Offset property.

The description indicates that this property has two arguments—both of which are optional—and that it returns a Range object.

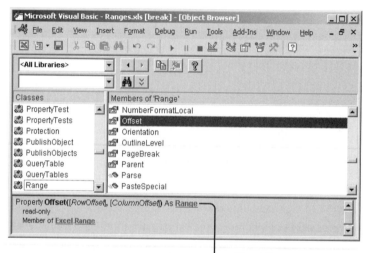

└── The Offset property returns a Range object.

2 In the Immediate window, type **myRange.Offset(1).Select** and press Enter.

This selects a range identical in size and shape to the range stored in the variable, but shifted down by one cell. The first argument to the Offset property indicates the number of rows down to shift the range; the second argument indicates how many columns to the right to shift the range. Omitting an argument is the same as using zero and does not shift the range in that direction.

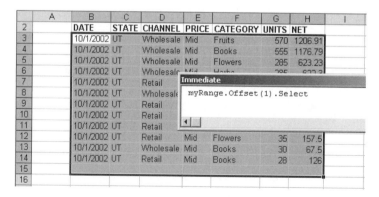

Tip

To understand the Offset property, think of yourself as standing on the upper left cell of the initial range. Face the bottom of the worksheet, and step forward the number of steps specified in the first argument. Zero steps means no movement. Negative steps are backwards. Then face the right side of the worksheet and do the same with the number of steps specified in the second argument. The resulting range is the same size and shape as the original one, but it begins on the cell you end up standing on.

3 In the Object Browser, select Range in the Classes list. Then, in the list of members, select the Resize property.

The description indicates that this property has two arguments—both of which are optional—and that it returns a Range object.

4 In the Immediate window, type **myRange.Offset(1).Resize(5).Select** and press Enter.

This selects the first five rows of data. The Offset property shifts the range down to omit the heading row. The Resize function changes the size of the resulting range. The first argument to the Resize property is the number of rows for the result range; the second is the number of columns for the result range. Omitting an argument is the same as keeping the size of the original range for that direction.

	A	B	C	D	E	F	G	H	I
2		DATE	STATE	CHANNEL	PRICE	CATEGORY	UNITS	NET	
3		10/1/2002	UT	Wholesale	Mid	Fruits	570	1206.91	
4		10/1/2002	UT	Wholesale	Mid	Books	555	1176.79	
5		10/1/2002	UT						
6		10/1/2002	UT						
7		10/1/2002	UT						
8		10/1/2002	UT						

Immediate
```
myRange.Offset(1).Resize(5).Select
```

5 Type **myRange.Offset(1).Resize(myRange.Rows.Count-1).Select** and press Enter.

This selects the range B3:H14, which is the entire list except the heading row. You often need to manipulate the body of a list separately from the heading.

	A	B	C	D	E	F	G	H	I
2		DATE	STATE	CHANNEL	PRICE	CATEGORY	UNITS	NET	
3		10/1/2002	UT	Wholesale	Mid	Fruits	570	1206.91	
4		10/1/2002	UT	Wholesale	Mid	Books	555	1176.79	
11		10/1/2002	UT	Retail	Mid	Books	40	180	
12		10/1/2002	UT	Retail	Mid	Flowers	35	157.5	
13		10/1/2002	UT	Wholesale	Mid	Books	30	67.5	
14		10/1/2002	UT	Retail	Mid	Books	28	126	
15									

Immediate
```
myRange.Offset(1).Resize(myRange.Rows.Count-1).Select
```

6 Type **myRange.Offset(1,5).Resize(1,2).Select** and press Enter.

This selects the range G3:H3, which happens to be the data values in the first row of the body of the list.

	A	B	C	D	E	F	G	H	I
2		DATE	STATE	CHANNEL	PRICE	CATEGORY	UNITS	NET	
3		10/1/2002	UT	Wholesale	Mid	Fruits	570	1206.91	
4		10/1/2002	UT	Wholesale	Mid	Books	555	1176.79	
5		10/1/2002	UT						
6		10/1/2002	UT						
7		10/1/2002	UT						

Immediate

```
myRange.Offset(1,5).Resize(1,2).Select
```

Tip

The combined functionality of the Offset and Resize properties is equivalent to that of the OFFSET function available on worksheets.

7 Press F5 to end the macro.

The Offset and Resize properties, along with the EntireRow, EntireColumn, and Current-Region properties, provide you with flexible tools for calculating new Range objects based on an original starting range. Often, the easiest way to work within a range is to first use the CurrentRegion property to establish the base range, and then use the Offset and Resize properties to manipulate the range.

Formatting a Range

Formatting contributes much to the usability of a worksheet. For example, borders can emphasize parts of a report and subtle horizontal bars can make a list easier to read.

Add Borders to a Range

Run Macro

1 In the Visual Basic Editor, click the Run Macro button, select TestRange, click Step Into, and then press F8 to initialize the *myRange* variable. In the Immediate window, type **Set myRange = Range("B2").CurrentRegion** and press Enter to assign the range containing the sample list to the variable.

Tip

If you don't have a TestRange macro, see the first two steps of the "Refer to a Relative Range" section earlier in this chapter.

Object Browser

2 Click the Object Browser button, and select Range in the list of Classes. In the list of Members, select the Borders property. The description indicates that this property returns a Borders object.

3 Click the word *Borders* in the description box to select the Borders object in the Classes list. In the list of Members, select the LineStyle property. The LineStyle property determines the type of line that will appear as the border.

The description indicates that the property returns a variant, which means there will not be an Auto List showing you the values you can use. You can, however, use the Object Browser to search for the appropriate values for the LineStyle property.

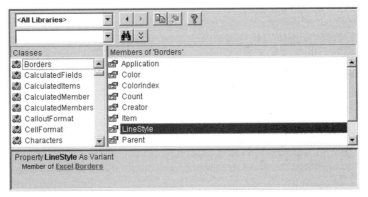

4 In the Search Text box above the Classes list, type **LineStyle** and click the Search button. In the Search Result pane that appears, select XlLineStyle in the Class list. The Members list shows all the possible constants you can use for the LineStyle property.

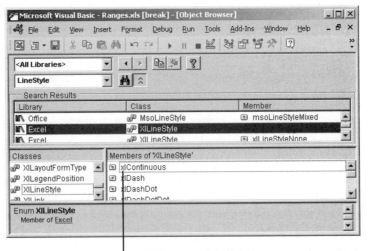

An enumerated list gives named constant values.

5 In the Immediate window, type **myRange.Borders.LineStyle = xlContinuous** and press Enter.

This adds a continuous border around each cell in the list range. When you assign a value to the LineStyle property of the Borders object, the property changes for the border of each cell in the entire range. The Borders object is actually a collection, and you can select specific borders within that collection.

Hide Search
Results

Go Back

6 In the Object Browser, click the Hide Search Results button. Then click the Go Back button (just above the Search button) repeatedly until Borders is again selected in the Classes list. Select the Item property in the Members list. The description shows that to select an item from the Borders collection, you use a value from the XlBordersIndex list.

7 In the description box, click XlBordersIndex to see the types of borders you can select.

The items beginning with *xlDiagonal* are diagonal lines through each cell in the range. The items beginning with *xlEdge* are borders around the edge of the entire range. The items beginning with *xlInside* apply to the borders between cells in the grid. If you want to change all the horizontal borders within the range, you would use the *xlInsideHorizonal* value.

The XlBordersIndex class is not really a class. There is no such thing as an XlBordersIndex object. It is, rather, an *enumerated list*. An enumerated list is used when a property or argument can accept only certain values. An enumerated list allows the object model designer to give each of those values a special name—for example, *xlInsideHorizontal*. The list of named values can then appear in an Auto List as you type a statement. Enumerated lists are included in the list of Classes, but with a special icon.

8 In the Immediate window, type **myRange.Borders(xlInsideHorizontal).LineStyle = xlDouble** and press Enter. This doubles the horizontal lines within the range.

	A	B	C	D	E	F	G	H	I
1									
2		DATE	STATE	CHANNEL	PRICE	CATEGORY	UNITS	NET	
3		10/1/2002	UT	Wholesale	Mid	Fruits	570	1206.91	
4		10/1/2002	UT	Wholesale	Mid	Books	555	1176.79	
5		10/1/2002	UT	Wholesale	Mid	Flowers	285	623.23	
6	Immediate								
7	`myRange.Borders(xlInsideHorizontal).LineStyle = xlDouble`								

If you want to change the border around all edges of a range, you can use the Borders collection four times, once for each edge of the range. To simplify the process, a Range object has a method that changes all four edge borders at once.

9 In the Object Browser, select the Range object in the Classes list. In the Members list, select BorderAround.

The description shows that the method takes up to four arguments, each of which is optional. The edge borders already have a continuous line style, so to darken the border, all you need to do is change the weight.

10 In the Immediate window, type **myRange.BorderAround Weight:=xlThick** and press Enter. This changes the edges of the range to a thick border.

	A	B	C	D	E	F	G	H	I
1									
2		DATE	STATE	CHANNEL	PRICE	CATEGORY	UNITS	NET	
3		10/1/2002	UT	Wholesale	Mid	Fruits	570	1206.91	
4		10/1/2002	UT	Wholesale	Mid	Books	555	1176.79	
5		10/1/2002	UT	Wholesale	Mid	Flowers	285	623.23	
6		10/1/2002	UT	Immediate					
7		10/1/2002	UT	`myRange.BorderAround Weight:=xlThick`					
8		10/1/2002	UT						

Borders can emphasize parts of a report. The Borders collection allows you to change all the borders at one time or choose a particular type of border to modify. The Border-Around method is a convenient shortcut for assigning a border to all the edges of a multi-cell range.

Tip

To clear all the borders within a range assigned to the *myRange* variable, you can use the statement *myRange.Borders.LineStyle = xlNone*.

Format Portions of a Range

To enhance the readability of a list, you might want to apply different colors to various ranges within the list. For example, you might want the background of the list to be light gray, with a medium gray for every third row. You might want to give a different format to the heading row—perhaps a dark gray background with light gray text.

Tip

If you are not stepping through the TestRange macro, with the current region surrounding cell B2 assigned to *myRange*, see the first step of the preceding section.

1 In the Object Browser, select the Range class. Then, in the list of Members, select the Interior property.

In the same way that the Borders property returns an object that controls the formatting of the borders of a range, the Interior property returns an object that controls the formatting of the interior of a range.

2 In the description box, click the word *Interior* to jump to the Interior object.

The list of properties includes two properties that change the interior color of a range—Color and ColorIndex. You should always use the ColorIndex property when assigning a color to a range. The ColorIndex property specifies one of the 56 colors in the Fill Color drop-down box. The color that corresponds to each number is arbitrary and has no correlation to the location of the color in the drop-down box. For example, index number for Gray – 25% (the lightest gray in the palette) is 15.

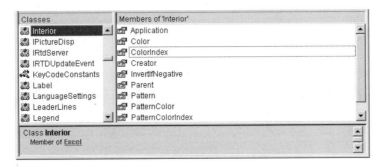

Important

In principle, the Color property allows you to assign any of over 16 million color values to the interior of the range. In practice, when you assign a value to the Color property, Excel finds the ColorIndex that is the closest approximation to the color you specified. In the following section, you will learn how to change the color of a range to any arbitrary color.

The ColorIndex and Color properties of the Interior object correspond roughly to the SchemeColor and RGB properties of the Fill object of a graphical shape. The RGB property, however, does allow you to assign any arbitrary color to the object. You can use the Fill object and RGB property only with shapes, not with ranges.

3 In the Immediate window, type **myRange.Interior.ColorIndex = 15** and press Enter to change the background of the entire sample list to light gray.

It will be easier to color every third row darker gray if you assign a simple counting number to a variable. You can first assign 3 to the variable, and then you can add 3 to it for each new row you want to format. The ColorIndex value for Gray – 40% (the second lightest available gray) is 48.

4 In the Immediate window, type **myRow = 3** and press Enter. Then type **myRange. Rows(myRow).Interior.ColorIndex = 48** and press Enter. This darkens the interior of the range in the third row of the list.

	A	B	C	D	E	F	G	H	I
1									
2		DATE	STATE	CHANNEL	PRICE	CATEGORY	UNITS	NET	
3		10/1/2002	UT	Wholesale	Mid	Fruits	570	1206.91	
4		10/1/2002	UT	Wholesale	Mid	Books	555	1176.79	
5		10/1/2002	UT	Wholesale	Mid	Flowers	285	623.23	
6		10/1/2002	UT						
7		10/1/2002	UT						
8		10/1/2002	UT						
9		10/1/2002	UT						

```
Immediate
  myRange.Interior.ColorIndex = 15
  myRow = 3
  myRange.Rows(myRow).Interior.ColorIndex = 48
```

5 Type **myRow = myRow + 3** and press Enter. Then click in the statement that assigns the dark gray and press Enter twice: once to darken the sixth row, and once to add three more to the counter. Execute those two statements two more times to darken the ninth and twelfth rows of the list.

	A	B	C	D	E	F	G	H	I
1									
2		DATE	STATE	CHANNEL	PRICE	CATEGORY	UNITS	NET	
3		10/1/2002	UT	Wholesale	Mid	Fruits	570	1206.91	
4		10/1/2002	UT	Wholesale	Mid	Books	555	1176.79	
5		10/1/2002	UT	Wholesale	Mid	Flowers	285	623.23	
6		10/1/2002	UT						
7		10/1/2002	UT						
8		10/1/2002	UT						

```
Immediate
  myRange.Rows(myRow).Interior.ColorIndex = 48
  myRow = myRow + 3
```

6 Type **Set myRange = myRange.Rows(1)** and press Enter. This changes the range variable to refer only to the first row of the list. You can now change the interior of this range to dark gray. The ColorIndex value for Gray – 80% is 56.

7 Type **myRange.Interior.ColorIndex = 56** and press Enter. This darkens the first row, making the text unreadable. You can change the font of the first row to light gray.

8 Type **myRange.Font.ColorIndex = 15** and press Enter.

	A	B	C	D	E	F	G	H	I
1									
2		DATE	STATE	CHANNEL	PRICE	CATEGORY	UNITS	NET	
3		10/1/2002	UT	Wholesale	Mid	Fruits	570	1206.91	
4		10/1/2002	UT	Wholesale	Mid	Books	555	1176.79	
5		10/1/2002	UT	Wholesale	Mid	Flowers	285	623.23	
6		10/1/2002	UT						
7		10/1/2002	UT						
8		10/1/2002	UT						
9		10/1/2002	UT						

```
Immediate
Set myRange = myRange.Rows(1)
myRange.Interior.ColorIndex = 56
myRange.Font.ColorIndex = 15
```

9 Press F5 to complete the macro.

Colors can enhance the readability of a report. To change the color of the cells in a range, you use the Interior property of the range. To change the color of the font, you use the Font property of the range. In either case, you change the color by assigning a number to the ColorIndex property.

Tip

To find the ColorIndex value for a color in the palette, record a macro while using the Fill Color box to change the color of a cell.

Change the Colors Available in a Workbook

Sometimes, the 56 standard colors in the workbook palette are not sufficient for your needs. For example, in the formatted list from the preceding section, the gray interiors in the body of the list are dark enough to make the text hard to read. Unfortunately, those are the lightest gray colors available in the standard palette. Fortunately, you can change the colors in the palette to any color you want. You simply assign a new value to the appropriate item from the Colors collection of the workbook object. The RGB function makes it easy to create a color value by designating the red, green, and blue components of a color. Each color component is a value from 0 to 255. Making the red, green, and blue components equal creates a shade of gray.

1 In the Immediate window, type **ActiveWorkbook.Colors(15) = RGB(220, 220, 220)** and press Enter. This lightens the color of the light gray from the 25% of the standard color to approximately 15%.

2 Type **ActiveWorkbook.Colors(48) = RGB(180, 180, 180)** and press Enter. This lightens the color of the medium gray from the 40% of the standard color to approximately 30%.

3 Type **ActiveWorkbook.Colors(56) = RGB(100, 100, 100)** and press Enter. This lightens the color of the dark gray from the 80% of the standard color to approximately 60%.

4 Type **ActiveWorkbook.ResetColors** and press Enter. This statement changes all the palette colors back to the original values.

5 If you want the lighter grays, re-execute the statements that change the workbook color palette.

The color palette applies to the entire workbook and is saved with the workbook. Changing the color palette gives you a great deal of control over the colors that can appear in your workbook. You can use subtle colors to enhance readability while avoiding the distractions of strong color changes.

Entering Values and Formulas into a Range

In addition to formatting ranges, you will also create macros that put values and formulas into cells and retrieve values from cells. First you should understand how references work in formulas in Excel, and then you can see how to create formulas in a macro.

Relative References

Most formulas perform arithmetic operations on values retrieved from other cells. Excel formulas use cell references to retrieve values from cells. Imagine, for example, a list of Retail prices and Wholesale costs.

	A	B	C
1		Retail	Wholesale
2	High	5.50	2.75
3	Mid	4.50	2.25
4	Low	3.50	1.75
5			

Suppose you want to add a column to the list that calculates the *gross margin*—the difference between the Retail price and the Wholesale cost—for each item. You would put the label **Margin** in cell D1 and then enter the first formula into cell D2. The formula subtracts the first Wholesale cost (cell C2) from the first Retail price (cell B2). So you would enter =B2-C2 into cell D2.

	A	B	C	D	E
1		Retail	Wholesale	Margin	
2	High	5.50	2.75	2.75	
3	Mid	4.50	2.25		
4	Low	3.50	1.75		
5					

=B2-C2

For each item in the High group, the gross margin is $2.75. Now you need to copy the formula to the other rows. The formula you typed into cell D2 refers explicitly to cells C2 and B2. When you copy the formula to cell D3, you want the formula to automatically adjust to refer to C3 and B3. Fortunately, when you copy the formulas, Excel adjusts the references because, by default, references are relative to the cell that contains the formula. (The Prices worksheet in the practice file contains these formulas.)

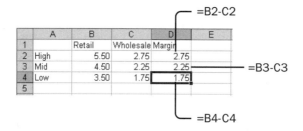

=B2-C2

	A	B	C	D	E
1		Retail	Wholesale	Margin	
2	High	5.50	2.75	2.75	
3	Mid	4.50	2.25	2.25	
4	Low	3.50	1.75	1.75	
5					

=B3-C3

=B4-C4

If the reference =C2 is found in cell D2, it really means "one cell to my left." When you copy the formula to cell D3, it still means "one cell to my left," but now that meaning is represented by the reference =C3.

Absolute References

Sometimes you don't want relative references. Imagine, for example, a worksheet that contains various quantities in column A and prices in row 2.

	A	B	C	D	E	F	G
1		Price				Discount	
2	Quantity	$5	$10	$15		10%	
3	10						
4	20						
5	30						
6	40						
7	50						
8							

Suppose you want to add formulas to calculate the revenue for each combination. To calculate the first revenue value (cell B3), you need to multiply the first price (cell B2) by the first quantity (cell A3). When you type =B2*A3 into cell B3, you get the correct answer, $50.

But if you copy that formula to cell B4, you get the ridiculous answer of $1000. That's because the cell references are relative. In this version of the formula, you're not really referring to cells B2 and A3; you're referring to "one cell above me" and "one cell to my left." When you put the formula into cell B4, "one cell above me" now refers to cell B3, not cell B2.

=B2*A3

	A	B	C	D	E	F	G
1		Price				Discount	
2	Quantity	$5	$10	$15		10%	
3	10	$50					
4	20	$1,000					
5	30						
6	40						
7	50						
8							

=B3*A4

You want the prices to adjust from column to column, and you want the quantities to adjust from row to row, but you always want the price to be from row 2 and the quantity to be from column A. The solution is to put a dollar sign ($) in front of the 2 in the first price reference (B$2) and in front of the A in the first quantity reference ($A3). The formula that should go into cell B3 is =B$2*$A3. The dollar sign "anchors" that part of the formula, making it absolute. When you copy the formula to the rest of B3:D7, you get correct answers.

=B$2*$A3

	A	B	C	D	E	F	G
1		Price				Discount	
2	Quantity	$5	$10	$15		10%	
3	10	$50	$100	$150			
4	20	$100	$200	$300			
5	30	$150	$300	$450			
6	40	$200	$400	$600			
7	50	$250	$500	$750			
8							

=D$2*$A7

The relative portion of the formula changes with the row or column of the cell that contains the formula. The absolute portion remains fixed.

If you want to modify the formula so that it also takes into account the discount value from cell F2, you must make both the row and the column of the discount reference absolute. The correct formula would be =B$2*$A3*(1-$F$2). (The Revenue worksheet in the practice file contains these formulas.)

R1C1 Reference Style

As a default, Excel displays letters for column headings and numbers for row headings, and the upper left cell in the worksheet is cell A1. Referring to cells by letter and number is called A1 reference style. In A1 reference style, however, cell references do not really say what they mean. For example, the reference =B3 says "cell B3," but it means "two cells to my left." You don't know what the reference really means until you know which cell contains the reference.

Excel has an alternate reference style that uses numbers for both column and row headings. In this alternate reference style, to refer to a cell you use the letter R plus the row number and C plus the column number. The upper left cell in the worksheet is therefore R1C1, and referring to cells by row and column numbers is called R1C1 reference style. In R1C1 reference style, cell references really do say what they mean.

To turn on R1C1 reference style, choose the Tools menu, click Options, and then click the General tab. Select the R1C1 Reference Style check box, and click OK. (To turn off R1C1 reference style, clear the check box.) The R1C1 Reference Style check box affects only formulas you enter directly into the worksheet. As you will see in the following section, a macro can enter formulas using either reference style, regardless of the setting in the Options dialog box.

Use this option to switch between
R1C1 and A1 notation.

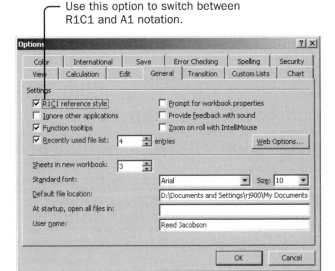

In R1C1 reference style, to specify a relative reference on the same row or column as the cell with the formula, you simply use an *R* or a *C*, without a number. For example, the reference =RC3 means "the cell in column 3 of the same row as me," and the reference =R2C means "the cell in row 2 of the same column as me."

To specify a relative reference in a different row or column, you indicate the amount of the difference, in square brackets, after the *R* or the *C*. For example, the reference =R5C[2] means "two columns to my right in row 5," and the reference =R[-1]C means "one cell above me."

The correct formula for calculating the gross margin on the Prices worksheet was =B$2-$C2, but only if the formula was entered into cell B2. In R1C1 reference style, the equivalent formula is =R2C-RC1, and it doesn't matter which cell gets the formula. The formula to calculate the discounted price on the Revenue worksheet was =B$2*$A3*(1-$F$2), at least for cell B2. In R1C1 reference style, the same formula is R2C*RC1*(1-R2C6), again, regardless of the target cell.

Important

When you use A1 reference style, the formula changes depending on which range you copy the formula into. When you use R1C1 reference style, the formula is the same, regardless of which cell it goes into.

Put Values and Formulas into a Range

You can explore the properties for putting values and formulas into a range by creating a simple list of incrementing numbers.

1 In the Visual Basic Editor, activate the Immediate window, type **Worksheets.Add** and press Enter to create a new, blank worksheet in the active workbook.

2   Type **Range("B2:B6").Select** and press Enter to select a sample starting range of cells.

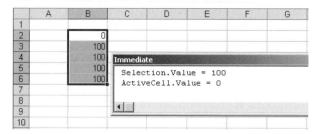

3   Type **Selection.Value = 100** and press Enter to fill all the cells of the selection with the number 100.

Value is a property of the range. When you set the Value property in conjunction with a multicell range, you change all the cells in the range.

Tip

You could just as well have used *Selection.Formula = 100* to assign the constant to the cell. The Formula property is equivalent to whatever you see in the formula bar when the cell is selected. The formula bar can contain constants as well as formulas, and so can the Formula property. When you assign a value to a cell, the Formula property and the Value property have the same effect.

4   Type **ActiveCell.Value = 0** and press Enter to change cell B2 to zero.

Only the active cell changes, not the selected cells. Entering a value in the active cell is equivalent to typing a value and pressing Enter. Entering a value in the selection is equivalent to typing a value and pressing Ctrl+Enter.

Suppose you want to enter a value in the cell above the active cell, whatever the active cell might be.

5   Type **ActiveCell.Offset(-1).Value = 1** and press Enter statement to change cell B1 to 1.

This statement starts with the active cell, uses the Offset property to calculate a new cell one up from that starting cell, and then sets the Value property for the resulting cell.

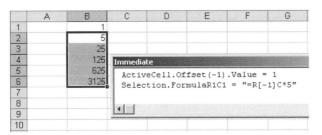

6 Type **Selection.FormulaR1C1 = "=R[-1]C*5"** and press Enter.

Now each of the selected cells contains a formula, not a constant. The FormulaR1C1 property expects a formula in R1C1 reference style. The reference *R[-1]C* always means "one cell above" regardless of which cell is active when you enter the formula.

7 Type **?ActiveCell.Value** and press Enter.

This statement displays the value 5 in the Immediate window. The Value property retrieves the result of any formula in a cell. When you retrieve the contents of the cell that contains a formula, the Value property gives you the result of the formula.

8 Type **?ActiveCell.Formula** and press Enter.

This statement displays the formula *=B1*5* in the Immediate window. When you retrieve the contents of a cell that contains a formula, the Formula property gives you the formula using A1 reference style. The setting in the Excel Options dialog box is ignored. If you want to retrieve the formula using R1C1 reference style, use the FormulaR1C1 property.

All cells have Formula, FormulaR1C1, and Value properties. The Value property and the Formula property are the same when you're writing to the cell. When you read the value of a cell, the Value property gives you the value, and the Formula property gives you the formula using A1 reference style. The FormulaR1C1 property is the same as the Formula property, except that it uses all references in R1C1 reference style, whether assigning a formula to the cell or reading the formula from a cell.

Tip

The Value property always gives you the unformatted value of the number in a cell. A cell also has a Text property, which returns the formatted value of the cell. The Text property is read-only because it's a combination of the Value property and the NumberFormat property.

Use the Address of a Range to Build Formulas

Sometimes you need a macro to create formulas that contain references. For example, suppose you have a range of cells such as the one on the Data worksheet and you want totals at the bottom of the two values columns. If the size of the range can change, you don't know until the macro runs which cells should be included in the SUM formula.

Sometimes the list, with headings, might extend from row 2 to row 4, in which case the formula for the values in the Units column should be =SUM(G3:G4) in cell G5. Another time, the range of cells might extend from row 2 to row 10, in which case the formula should be =SUM(G3:G10), this time in cell G11. Interactively, you would use the AutoSum button to create the formulas, but using the AutoSum button while recording a macro always generates formulas with specific addresses. You can't use the AutoSum button if you need to create a macro that can handle ranges of differing sizes. You need a macro that behaves like a simplified version of the AutoSum button.

1 In Excel, select the Data worksheet. Then activate the Visual Basic Editor, choose the Insert menu, click Module, and enter the following macro framework:

```
Sub MakeTotals()
    Dim myData As Range
    Dim myTotal As Range
    Set myData = Range("B2").CurrentRegion
    Set myData = _
        myData.Offset(1, 5).Resize(myData.Rows.Count - 1, 2)
    Set myTotal = myData.Rows(myData.Rows.Count + 1)

End Sub
```

2 Press F8 repeatedly until the End Sub statement is the next statement. In the Immediate window, type **myData.Select** and press Enter. Then type **myTotal.Select** and press Enter. The variables should contain references to the ranges G3:H14 and G15:H15, respectively. The expressions used to refer to the range all come from the "Referring to a Range" section earlier in this chapter. Your goal is to put a formula into each cell of the *myTotal* range that sums all the values from the corresponding column of the *myData* range.

	A	B	C	D	E	F	G	H	I
1									
2		DATE	STATE	CHANNEL	PRICE	CATEGORY	UNITS	NET	
3		10/1/2002	UT	Wholesale	Mid	Fruits	570	1206.91	
4		10/1/2002	UT	Wholesale	Mid	Books	555	1176.79	
5		10/1/2002	UT	Wholesale	Mid	Flowers	285	623.23	
6		10/1/2002	UT	Wholesale	Mid	Herbs	285	622.3	
7		10/1/2002	UT	Retail	Mid	Fruits	245	955.93	
8		10/1/2002	UT						
9		10/1/2002	UT						
10		10/1/2002	UT						
11		10/1/2002	UT						
12		10/1/2002	UT						
13		10/1/2002	UT	Wholesale	Mid	Books	30	67.5	
14		10/1/2002	UT	Retail	Mid	Books	28	126	
15									
16									

Immediate window:
```
myData.Select
myTotal.Select
```

3   Activate the Object Browser, and select the Range class. In the list of Members, select Address. The Address property returns a string and takes five arguments, each of which is optional.

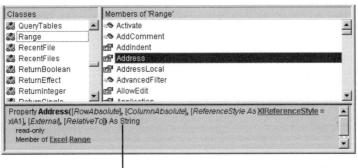

— The Address property returns a string.

4   In the Immediate window, type **?myData.Columns(1).Address** and press Enter.

This statement displays the reference *$G$3:$G$14*. This is the address of the first column of the data range. If you were to put this address inside a SUM function, the total would be correct for the first total, but the dollar signs mean that the reference is absolute. You need to make the column reference relative so that it will adjust as you put it into both columns of the totals row. The first two arguments of the Address property control whether the row and column references are absolute. The default value for each argument—*True*—produces an absolute reference.

5   Type **?myData.Columns(1).Address(True,False)** and press Enter.

This statement displays the reference *G$3:G$14*. This statement tells the Address property to make row references absolute but column references relative. You can now put this reference into the SUM function, creating a formula that is suitable for adding to the total range.

6   Type **?"=SUM(" & myData.Columns(1).Address(True,False) & ")"** and press Enter.

This statement displays the formula *=SUM(G$3:G$14)*. This is the final formula you will assign to the total range. The expression joins the first part of the SUM function with the reference returned by the Address property, and then adds the closing parenthesis. An ampersand character (&) joins pieces of text together.

7   Choose the View menu, and click the Last Position command.

This takes you to the macro where the End Sub statement is still the next statement.

8   Before the End Sub statement, insert the statement **myTotal.Formula = "=SUM(" & myData.Columns(1).Address(True, False) & ")"**. Then drag the Next Statement arrow back up to the new statement, and press F8 to execute it.

12	10/1/2002	UT	Retail	Mid	Flowers	35	157.5
13	10/1/2002	UT	Wholesale	Mid	Books	30	67.5
14	10/1/2002	UT	Retail	Mid	Books	28	126
15						2329	5865.31
16							

The totals appear in the row at the bottom, appropriately different for each column.

9 Press F8 to finish the macro, and then press F5 to run it again, adding a second row of totals.

This is a little silly, but it shows how the macro automatically adjusts as new rows are added to the data. The CurrentRegion property includes any new rows. The Address property calculates the appropriate reference for the SUM function.

Ranges are a powerful tool in Excel. You can select ranges, assign them to variables, add formulas to them, name them, and retrieve their addresses. By manipulating ranges, you can build powerful, dynamic worksheet models.

Tip

When you construct a formula by using the Address property of a range, the easiest approach is usually to use A1 reference style and assign the formula to the Formula property of the target range. When you enter a finished formula as a string into a macro statement, the safest approach is usually to use R1C1 reference style and assign the formula to the FormulaR1C1 property of the target range. (This is what the macro recorder does.) To convert a formula from A1 to R1C1 reference style, record a macro as you enter the A1 reference style formula into a cell.

Enhancing Recorded Selections

When you record a macro, the macro recorder dutifully follows all your actions, including selecting ranges before acting on them. You can make a macro do less work—and make it easier to read—by eliminating unnecessary selection changes. A powerful technique for eliminating unnecessary changes to the selection begins with watching for a statement ending in Select followed by one or more statements beginning with Selection or Active-Cell. What you do next depends on whether a single Selection (or ActiveCell) statement follows the Select statement or whether a group of them follow.

Simplify Select...Selection Pairs

When a single Selection statement follows a Select statement, you can collapse the two statements into one. Record and simplify a macro that puts the names of the months across the top of a worksheet.

1 In Excel, insert a blank worksheet and start recording a macro named **LabelMonths**. Type the labels **January**, **February**, and **March** in the cells B1, C1, and D1.

	A	B	C	D	E
1		January	February	March	
2					
3					

2 Turn off the recorder, and then edit the macro. The macro should look similar to the following code. (Your macro might be slightly different, depending on the key you press to enter the values into the cells.)

```
Sub LabelMonths()
    Range("B1").Select
    ActiveCell.FormulaR1C1 = "January"
    Range("C1").Select
    ActiveCell.FormulaR1C1 = "February"
```

```
    Range("D1").Select
    ActiveCell.FormulaR1C1 = "March"
    Range("D2").Select
End Sub
```

For each cell, you see the word *Select* at the end of one statement followed by either the word *Selection* or *ActiveCell* at the beginning of the next statement. You can delete both words, leaving only a single period. If a Select statement is the last one in a macro, you can delete it entirely.

3 Remove the unnecessary selections from the LabelMonths macro by deleting Select and ActiveCell each time they appear. The final macro should look like this:

```
Sub LabelMonths()
    Range("B1").FormulaR1C1 = "January"
    Range("C1").FormulaR1C1 = "February"
    Range("D1").FormulaR1C1 = "March"
End Sub
```

4 Insert a new blank worksheet, and test the macro. The labels appear in the cells, and the original selection doesn't change.

Why should you get rid of Select...Selection pairs? One reason is that doing so makes the macro run faster. Another reason is that running a macro can seem less disruptive if it doesn't end with different cells selected than when it started. But the most important reason is unquestionably that Select...Selection pairs in a macro are a dead giveaway that you're a beginner who uses the macro recorder to create macros. It's OK to use the macro recorder; you just have to cover your tracks.

Simplify Select Groups

When you eliminate a Select...Selection pair, be sure that only a single statement uses the selection. If you have a single Select statement followed by two or more statements that use the selection, you can still avoid changing the selection, but you must do it in a different way.

1 In Excel, select a sheet with labels in the first row and start recording a macro named **MakeBoldItalic**.

2 Click cell B1, click the Bold button, click the Italic button, and then click the Stop Recording button.

	A	B	C	D	E
1		*January*	February	March	
2					
3					

3 Edit the macro. It will look like this:

```
Sub MakeBoldItalic()
    Range("B1").Select
    Selection.Font.Bold = True
    Selection.Font.Italic = True
End Sub
```

Obviously, if you delete the first Select...Selection pair, you won't be able to predict which cells will become italicized.

4   Edit the macro to assign the range to a variable named *myRange*. Then replace the
     Selection object with the myRange object. The finished macro should look like this:

```
Sub MakeBoldItalic()
    Dim myRange As Range
    Set myRange = Range("B1")
    myRange.Font.Bold = True
    myRange.Font.Italic = True
End Sub
```

5   Change *"B1"* to *"C1"* in the macro, and then press F8 repeatedly to step through the
     macro. Watch how the format of the cell changes without changing which cell is originally
     selected.

6   Save the Chapter05 workbook.

Eliminating the selection when there's a group might not seem like much of a simplifica-
tion. With only two statements, it probably isn't. When you have several statements that
use the same selection, however, converting the selection to an object variable can make
the macro much easier to read.

Note

You could also replace the Select group with a With structure, like this:

```
With Range("B1")
    .Font.Bold = True
    .Font.Italic = True
End With
```

Here's what the With structure does secretly in the background: it creates a hidden variable,
takes the object from the With statement and assigns that object to the hidden variable, and
then puts the hidden variable in front of each "dangling" period. The End With statement dis-
cards the hidden variable.

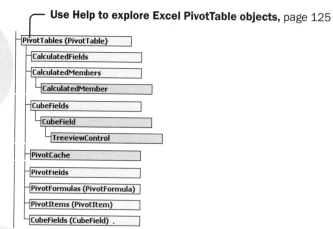

Use Help to explore Excel PivotTable objects, page 125

```
PivotTables (PivotTable)
  CalculatedFields
  CalculatedMembers
    CalculatedMember
  CubeFields
    CubeField
      TreeviewControl
  PivotCache
  PivotFields
  PivotFormulas (PivotFormula)
  PivotItems (PivotItem)
  CubeFields (CubeField) .
```

Customize labels and calculations, page 131

Expand and collapse items, page 132

Select ranges within a PivotTable report, page 134

	A	B	C	D	E	F	G
1	DATE	(All) ▼					
2							
3	Avg Units		PRICE ▼				
4	CHANNEL ▼	STATE ▼	High	Low	Mid	Grand Total	
5	Retail		111	92	111	104	
6	Wholesale	WA	287	354	167	259	
7		AZ	72	66	77	72	
8		CA	106	237	430	306	
9		NV	159	69	64	81	
10		OR	316	320	222	276	
11		UT	264	346	383	350	
12	Wholesale Total		226	254	217	232	
13	Grand Total		171	177	166	171	
14							

```
(General)                                          MakePivot

Sub MakePivot()
    Dim myCache As PivotCache
    Dim myTable As PivotTable
    Dim myField As PivotField
    Dim myItem As PivotItem
Workbooks.Open ("Orders.dbf")
Set myCache = ActiveWorkbook.PivotCaches.Add(xlDatabase, "Database")
Worksheets.Add
Set myTable = myCache.CreatePivotTable(Cells(1))
Set myField = myTable.PivotFields("Units")
myField.Orientation = xlDataField
myField.NumberFormat = "#,##0"
Set myField = myTable.PivotFields("State")
myField.Orientation = xlRowField
```

Use VBA statements to create and manipulate a PivotTable report, page 136

Chapter 6
Explore PivotTable Objects

After completing this chapter, you will be able to:

✔ **Build a PivotTable.**

✔ **Manipulate fields and items in a PivotTable.**

✔ **Use online Help topics to learn about Excel objects.**

Since the turn of the century, one of the mainstays of medical technology has been X-ray photography. One of the problems with an X-ray photograph, however, is that it shows you only the angle at which it was taken. If the bones or organs aren't properly aligned, the photograph might not reveal the problem. In 1974, the British company EMI Ltd. used the money it had made selling Beatles records to develop computerized axial tomography (CAT) scan technology. A CAT scan isn't limited by blind spots the way that conventional X-rays are.

A database report is like an X-ray photograph. It's an image, but it's a static image. If the rows and columns aren't properly defined, the person reviewing the report might miss important relationships. A PivotTable, in contrast, is like a CAT scan. It's a multidimensional view of the data that enables you to find the most meaningful perspective.

Orders.dbf

This chapter uses the practice file Orders.dbf that you installed from the book's CD-ROM. For details about installing the practice files, see "Using the Book's CD-ROM" at the beginning of this book.

Getting Started

1 In Microsoft Excel, open a new, empty workbook.

2 Save the workbook with the name **Chapter06** in the folder that contains the practice files for this book.

Building PivotTables

In Excel, each object class has its own list of methods and properties that you can use to manipulate objects belonging to that class. Many objects belong to collections or link to other objects.

Learn About PivotTable Objects in Help

The Microsoft Excel Visual Basic Reference portion of online Help contains an overview graphic that shows how Excel objects relate to each other.

1 On the Microsoft Visual Basic toolbar, click the Visual Basic Editor button to open Visual Basic. In the Ask A Question box, type **Excel Objects** and press Enter. In the list of suggested topics, click Microsoft Excel Objects.

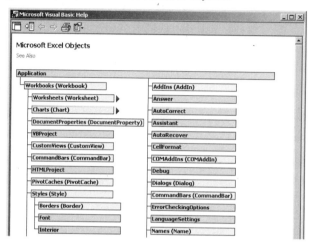

This figure shows the first part of the Excel object model. Each blue box represents an object class. Each yellow box represents two object classes: the collection class and the object class. The objects on the right belong directly to the Application object. The left side of the tree shows the Workbooks (Workbook) pair of objects, along with all the objects that belong to a Workbook. One pair of objects that belongs to a Workbook is the PivotCaches (PivotCache) pair of objects. A PivotCache object is an invisible location for storing the values that go into a PivotTable report.

2 Click the PivotCaches (PivotCache) box.

This takes you to the topic for the PivotCaches collection object. The topic shows the local context of the object, along with a brief description. At the top of the topic—and this is true of the topic for every object class—are links to pop-up windows containing the properties and methods for the object.

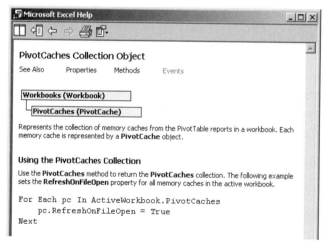

3 Click Methods, and click Add Method. Then expand the topic Add Method As It Applies To The PivotCaches Object. Each collection has a version of the Add method. The Add method for the PivotCaches collection requires two arguments that define the source for the data. The method then returns a reference to a PivotCache object.

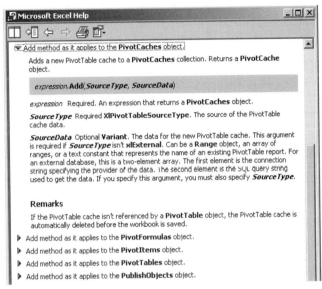

Back

4 Click the Back button twice to get back to the Microsoft Excel Objects topic.

A PivotTable does not belong to a Workbook, so it doesn't appear in the first part of the Excel object model. A PivotTable belongs to a Worksheet. Worksheet objects take a whole page of their own.

5 Click the red triangle to the right of the Worksheets (Worksheet) box.

The objects on the right belong directly to a Worksheet. The objects on the left belong to a Range object.

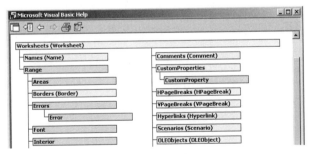

6 Scroll down to see the PivotTables (PivotTable) box and the objects that belong to it.

The most important PivotTable objects are PivotField objects (which are in the box with *PivotFields*), and PivotItem objects. You can see that a PivotTable object also points to the PivotCache object that contains data for that report.

```
PivotTables (PivotTable)
    CalculatedFields
    CalculatedMembers
        CalculatedMember
    CubeFields
        CubeField
            TreeviewControl
    PivotCache
    PivotFields
    PivotFormulas (PivotFormula)
    PivotItems (PivotItem)
    CubeFields (CubeField)
```

7 Close the Help window.

In this chapter, you will work with PivotCache, PivotTable, PivotField, and PivotItem objects.

Create a Basic PivotTable

The first step in creating a PivotTable is creating a cache. As you saw in the object model, a PivotCache object belongs to the workbook, not to a worksheet or PivotTable. You can have multiple reports linked to a single cache. You can put multiple reports on a single worksheet or in separate worksheets. Basing multiple reports on a single cache reduces the amount of memory Excel needs when working with large data sources.

1 In the Visual Basic Editor, click the Run Macro button, type **MakePivot** in the Macro Name box, and then click Create.

A module opens with a new, empty macro.

2 Insert the following variable declaration statements at the beginning of the macro:

```
Dim myCache as PivotCache
Dim myTable As PivotTable
Dim myField As PivotField
Dim myItem As PivotItem
```

Assigning objects to these variables enables Visual Basic to display Auto Lists that help you see methods and properties.

3 Press F8 twice to step to the End Sub statement. From the View menu, click the Immediate Window command. Move and size the Immediate window so that you can see the Excel window in the background.

4 In the Immediate window, type **Workbooks.Open "Orders.dbf"** and then press the Enter key to open the database workbook.

In a few seconds, the database appears. (The formatting of the first column is not important.) The active sheet in the database workbook is a worksheet that contains a range named Database. The Worksheet object's PivotTableWizard can create a PivotTable from a range named Database.

	A	B	C	D	E	F	G
1	DATE	STATE	CHANNEL	PRICE	CATEGORY	UNITS	NET
2	########	WA	Wholesale	High	Seattle	40	110.00
3	########	WA	Wholesale	High	Art	25	68.75
4	########	WA	Retail	High	Art	3	16.50
5	########	WA	Retail	Low	Environment	50	175.00
6	########	WA	Wholesale	Low	Dinosaurs	40	70.00
7	########	WA	Wholesale	Low	Seattle	35	61.25

Tip

If the Orders.dbf file doesn't open, click the Open toolbar button, change to the folder containing the practice files for this book, and then click Cancel before executing the statement.

5 In the Immediate window, type **Set myCache = ActiveWorkbook.PivotCaches. Add(xlDatabase, "Database")** and then press the Enter key.

Nothing seems to happen, but you have just created a PivotCache object. In this statement, the ActiveWorkbook property returns a reference to a Workbook object. The Pivot-Caches property returns a reference to the (initially empty) PivotCaches collection of that workbook. The Add method adds a new PivotCache object to the collection, using *xlDatabase* as the source type (the word *Database* refers to the list in an Excel worksheet, not to an external database), and *"Database"* as the name of the range that contains the list. The Add method returns a reference to the newly created PivotCache object, which the Set command assigns to the *myCache* variable. A PivotCache object has a method that can create a PivotTable report.

6 In the MakePivot macro, click anywhere in the word *PivotCache* and press F1. In the Context Help dialog box, leave the PivotCache object selected (the other option selects the PivotCache property topic), and click Help.

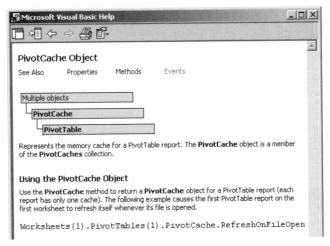

7 Click the Methods keyword, and click CreatePivotTable Method.

This method has one required argument—a Range object that can serve as the target location for the report. The method then returns a reference to a PivotTable object, which you can assign to a variable for later use.

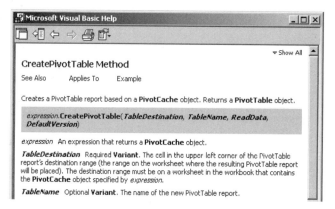

8   Close Help. In the Immediate window, type **Worksheets.Add** and press Enter.

This creates a new worksheet for the report.

9   Type **Set myTable = myCache.CreatePivotTable(Cells(1))** and press Enter.

This creates the simplest possible shell of a PivotTable report. (If the PivotTable Field List window appears, close it. You will be using Visual Basic to create and modify the PivotTable report.)

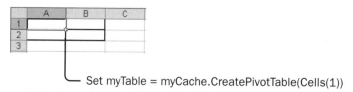

Set myTable = myCache.CreatePivotTable(Cells(1))

You've now used Microsoft Visual Basic for Applications commands to create a PivotCache and a PivotTable based on that cache.

Manipulate Pivot Fields

You did create a PivotTable, but it's not particularly informative. You still need to use the PivotTable to display summarized values from the source list. The source for a PivotTable report usually consists of a list with a lot of rows and a few columns. Each column is called a *field*, and the label at the top of the column is the name of the field. The list in Orders.dbf has seven fields. Date, State, Channel, Price, and Category are fields that contain words. Units and Net are fields that contain numbers. A PivotTable typically summarizes the number fields, sorting and grouping them by the fields that contain words.

1   In the Immediate window, type **Set myField = myTable.PivotFields("Units")** and then press the Enter key.

This action assigns the Units pivot field to a variable but does not put it onto the report.

2   Type **myField.Orientation = xlDataField** and then press the Enter key.

The label "Sum of UNITS" and a number appear in the body of the PivotTable. Because the Units field contains values, the PivotTable adds all the numbers in the Units column.

	A	B	C
1	Sum of UNITS	Total	
2	Total	564821	
3			

— myField.Orientation = xlDataField

The PivotFields collection contains one item for each of the seven fields in the database. You refer to a single item from the collection in the standard way—by name or by number. In this case, it's easier to remember the name of the Units field than it is to recall where it happens to fall in the database. Assigning *xlDataField* to the Orientation property summarizes the data in that field.

3 Now format the Units total. Type **myField.NumberFormat = "#,##0"** and then press the Enter key.

The number in the PivotTable looks much better with a comma. NumberFormat is a property of a PivotField object. It works in the same way as the NumberFormat property of a Range object.

	A	B	C
1	Sum of UNITS	Total	
2	Total	564,821	
3			

— myField.NumberFormat = "#,##0"

4 Type **Set myField = myTable.PivotFields("State")** and then press the Enter key.

This action assigns the State pivot field to the variable.

5 Type **myField.Orientation = xlRowField** and then press the Enter key.

Row headings appear, adding appropriate subtotals to the grand total that was already there. The gray box containing the word *State* is called a *field button*. It serves as a visible heading for the pivot field.

Tip

The CurrentPage property works only with page fields.

— Set myField = myTable.PivotFields("State")
myField.Orientation = xlRowField

	A	B	C
1	Sum of UNITS		
2	STATE ▼	Total	
3	AZ	25,341	
4	CA	112,385	
5	ID	1,860	
6	NV	51,634	
7	OR	179,516	
8	UT	40,068	
9	WA	154,017	
10	Grand Total	564,821	
11			

6 By now, you can probably guess how to turn the State field items into column headings. Type **myField.Orientation = xlColumnField** and then press the Enter key.

The state codes move from the side to the top of Sheet1. The field button moves above the state codes.

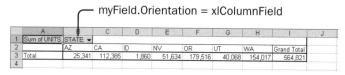

myField.Orientation = xlColumnField

7 Row and column fields group the data in the PivotTable. In the same way that you change pages in a magazine to select which part you want to see, you can filter the data in a PivotTable by using a *page field*. Type **myField.Orientation = xlPageField** and then press the Enter key. The State field button moves up to the upper left corner of the worksheet.

8 To filter the data (by state, for example), assign a state code to the CurrentPage property of the State page field. Type **myField.CurrentPage = "WA"** and press the Enter key. Then type **myField.CurrentPage = "CA"** and press the Enter key. The numbers change as you filter by different states.

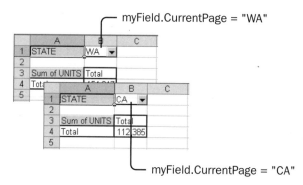

myField.CurrentPage = "WA"

myField.CurrentPage = "CA"

9 To remove a field from one of the visible areas of the PivotTable, assign it the *hidden* orientation. Type **myField.Orientation = xlHidden** and then press the Enter key.

The State field button disappears. The PivotTable still contains a pivot field named State, but the field button is no longer visible. The Orientation property of PivotFields is what makes the PivotTable "pivot."

myField.Orientation = xlHidden

	A	B	C
1			
2			
3	Sum of UNITS	Total	
4	Total	564,821	
5			

Make Multiple Changes to a PivotTable

The PivotTable object also has a shortcut method that can assign several fields to the different PivotTable areas all at once. You can find the method by looking at the PivotTable object in Help.

1 In the MakePivot macro, click in the word *PivotTable* and press F1. Leave the PivotTable object selected, and click Show. In the Methods list, click AddFields Method.

The topic shows that you can use this method to add row, column, and page fields all at once.

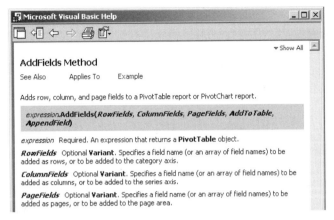

2 Close the Help window.

3 In the Immediate window, type **myTable.AddFields "Category", "State", "Channel"** and then press the Enter key.

The Category field becomes the row field, the State field becomes the column field, and the Channel field becomes the page field. The arguments of the AddFields method always appear in *Row, Column, Page* order.

myTable.AddFields "Category", "State", "Channel"

	A	B	C	D	E	F	G	H	I	J
1	CHANNEL	(All)								
2										
3	Sum of UNITS	STATE								
4	CATEGORY	AZ	CA	ID	NV	OR	UT	WA	Grand Total	
5	Art	5,292	28,787	295	14,275	53,185	6,080	26,263	134,177	
6	Dinosaurs	8,192	16,575	250	6,160	10,950	5,990	27,207	75,324	
7	Environment	3,356	14,685	170	5,070	35,965	5,345	22,500	87,091	
8	Humorous	1,577	6,970	290	1,784	7,466	8,140	1,423	27,650	
9	Kids	3,020	37,733	226	11,490	53,288	2,402	15,067	123,226	
10	Seattle					11,375		58,895	70,270	
11	Sports	3,904	7,635	629	12,855	7,287	12,111	2,662	47,083	
12	Grand Total	25,341	112,385	1,860	51,634	179,516	40,068	154,017	564,821	
13										

The Help topic indicates that each argument can consist of either a field name or an array of field names. You use an array when you want to add more than one field to an orientation.

4 To add more than one field to an orientation, you need to use multiple field names as a single argument. The Array function allows you to treat multiple field names as a single argument. Type **myTable.AddFields Array("State","Channel"), "Price", "Date"** and then press the Enter key.

Both State and Channel become row fields, Price becomes the column field, and Date becomes the page field.

myTable.AddFields Array("State","Channel"), "Price", "Date"

	A	B	C	D	E	F	G
1	DATE	(All)					
2							
3	Sum of UNITS		PRICE				
4	STATE	CHANNEL	High	Low	Mid	Grand Total	
5	AZ	Retail	783	2,869	3,789	7,441	
6		Wholesale	2,940	6,140	8,820	17,900	
7	AZ Total		3,723	9,009	12,609	25,341	
8	CA	Retail	6,152	5,229	10,414	21,795	
9		Wholesale	4,970	26,275	59,345	90,590	
10	CA Total		11,122	31,504	69,759	112,385	
11	ID	Retail	193	493	1,174	1,860	
12	ID Total		193	493	1,174	1,860	

5 When you have more than one field in a given area, you can swap the order of the fields using the Position property. The State field is still assigned to the *myField* variable. Type **myField.Position = 2** and then press the Enter key to swap the order of the State and Channel fields.

myField.Position = 2

	A	B	C	D	E	F	G
1	DATE	(All)					
2							
3	Sum of UNITS		PRICE				
4	CHANNEL	STATE	High	Low	Mid	Grand Total	
5	Retail	AZ	783	2,869	3,789	7,441	
6		CA	6,152	5,229	10,414	21,795	
7		ID	193	493	1,174	1,860	
8		NV	13,419	8,785	15,305	37,509	
9		OR	6,336	22,291	30,094	58,721	
10		UT	380	1,376	1,867	3,623	
11		WA	3,341	12,489	17,072	32,902	
12	Retail Total		30,604	53,532	79,715	163,851	

In summary, use the AddFields method of the PivotTable object to make major changes to a PivotTable; use the Orientation, Position, and CurrentPage properties of the PivotField objects to fine-tune the table.

Important

In addition to the PivotFields collection, the PivotTable object has subcollections that contain only PivotFields of a particular orientation. For example, the RowFields collection contains only the fields whose Orientation property is set to *xlRowField*. The subcollections are RowFields, ColumnFields, PageFields, DataFields, and HiddenFields. These collections don't have corresponding object classes. A member of the RowFields collection is still a PivotField object, not a RowField object. You never need to use any of these subcollections, but you might find them convenient. For example, if you know that there's only one row field, you can refer to it as RowFields(1), without worrying about its name or what its number is in the entire PivotFields collection.

Refining PivotTables

Once you've created a PivotTable with rows and columns in the proper orientation, you can make many refinements to the table. You can manipulate specific details within a field, change the appearance of the data, or even modify the worksheet ranges that contain portions of the PivotTable.

Manipulate Pivot Items

The unique values that appear in a PivotField are called *items*. You can manipulate individual items within a PivotField.

1 Type **Set myItem = myField.PivotItems("WA")** and then press the Enter key to assign the pivot item for Washington State to a variable.

2 Now that *myItem* refers to an individual pivot item, you can manipulate that item using its properties. Type **myItem.Position = 1** and then press the Enter key. A pivot item has a Position property, just as a PivotField does.

Set myItem = myField.PivotItems("WA")
myItem.Position = 1

	A	B	C	D	E	F	G
1	DATE	(All)					
2							
3	Sum of UNITS		PRICE				
4	CHANNEL	STATE	High	Low	Mid	Grand Total	
5	Retail	WA	3,341	12,489	17,072	32,902	
6		AZ	783	2,869	3,789	7,441	
7		CA	6,152	5,229	10,414	21,795	
8		ID	193	493	1,174	1,860	

3 Type **myItem.Name = "Washington"** and then press the Enter key.

myItem.Name = "Washington"

	A	B	C	D	E	F	G
1	DATE	(All)					
2							
3	Sum of UNITS		PRICE				
4	CHANNEL	STATE	High	Low	Mid	Grand Total	
5	Retail	Washington	3,341	12,489	17,072	32,902	
6		AZ	783	2,869	3,789	7,441	
7		CA	6,152	5,229	10,414	21,795	
8		ID	193	493	1,174	1,860	

The name of the pivot item displays in the PivotTable. If you don't like the way the database designer abbreviated state names, you can fix the problem in the PivotTable. Of course, sometimes it's better to leave conventions alone. Fortunately, the PivotItem object remembers for you what its original name was.

131

4 Type **myItem.Name = myItem.SourceName** and then press the Enter key.

The name changes back to the original. For obvious reasons, the SourceName property is read-only.

myItem.Name = myItem.SourceName

	A	B	C	D	E	F	G
1	DATE	(All)					
2							
3	Sum of UNITS		PRICE				
4	CHANNEL	STATE	High	Low	Mid	Grand Total	
5	Retail	WA	3,341	12,489	17,072	32,902	
6		AZ	783	2,869	3,789	7,441	
7		CA	6,152	5,229	10,414	21,795	
8		ID	193	493	1,174	1,860	

5 Perhaps changing the spelling of the state name isn't enough. Perhaps you don't like Washington state (in which case, I really do feel sorry for you) and want to eliminate it entirely. Type **myItem.Visible = False** and then press the Enter key.

myItem.Visible = False

	A	B	C	D	E	F	G
1	DATE	(All)					
2							
3	Sum of UNITS		PRICE				
4	CHANNEL	STATE	High	Low	Mid	Grand Total	
5	Retail	AZ	783	2,869	3,789	7,441	
6		CA	6,152	5,229	10,414	21,795	
7		ID	193	493	1,174	1,860	
8		NV	13,419	8,785	15,305	37,509	

6 Perhaps, however, you suddenly realize how foolish you are not to like Washington. Fortunately, you can put it back the same way you got rid of it. Type **myItem.Visible = True** and then press the Enter key.

7 Another useful thing you can do with a pivot item is to hide or show the detail to the right of a field. Try hiding the detail for the Retail channel. Type **Set myItem = myTable. PivotFields("Channel").PivotItems("Retail")** and then press the Enter key.

This action assigns the pivot item to the *myItem* variable.

8 Type **myItem.ShowDetail = False** and then press the Enter key.

All the states for the Retail channel collapse into a single row.

	A	B	C	D	E	F	G
1	DATE	(All)					
2							
3	Sum of UNITS		PRICE				
4	CHANNEL	STATE	High	Low	Mid	Grand Total	
5	Retail		30,604	53,532	79,715	163,851	
6	Wholesale	WA	26,430	60,255	34,430	121,115	
7		AZ	2,940	6,140	8,820	17,900	
8		CA	4,970	26,275	59,345	90,590	

Set myItem = myTable.PivotFields("Channel").PivotItems("Retail")
myItem.ShowDetail = False

Manipulating pivot items isn't generally as dramatic as manipulating PivotFields, but you can use the Position, Name, SourceName, Visible, and ShowDetail properties to refine the effect of the PivotTable.

Manipulate Data Fields

Data fields do the real dirty work of the PivotTable. This is where the numbers get worked over. Data fields are like other PivotFields in many ways, but they do have a few unique twists. You can see how data fields are different from other fields when you add a second data field.

1 Type **Set myField = myTable.PivotFields("Net")** and then press the Enter key to assign the Net field to the *myField* variable.

2 Type **myField.Orientation = xlDataField** and then press the Enter key to add a second data field.

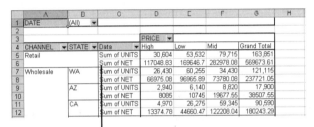

Set myField = myTable.PivotFields("Net")
myField.Orientation = xlDataField

As soon as you have two data fields in the PivotTable, you get a new field button, labeled *Data*. The Data field is not a field from the database. It's a temporary field that allows you to manipulate multiple data fields. The Data field begins as a row field, but you can change it into a column field.

3 Type **Set myField = myTable.PivotFields("Data")** and then press the Enter key.

This action assigns the temporary Data field to a variable. The statement works only if you have more than one data field.

4 Type **myField.Orientation = xlColumnField** and then press the Enter key.

Set myField = myTable.PivotFields("Data")
myField.Orientation = xlColumnField

	A	B	C	D	E	F
1	DATE	(All)				
2						
3			PRICE	Data		
4			High		Low	
5	CHANNEL	STATE	Sum of UNITS	Sum of NET	Sum of UNITS	Sum of NET
6	Retail		30,604	117048.83	53,532	169646.7
7	Wholesale	WA	26,430	66975.08	60,255	96965.89
8		AZ	2,940	8085	6,140	10745
9		CA	4,970	13374.78	26,275	44660.47
10		NV	4,440	11759.64	4,540	7945

When you made the State field into a row field, a button labeled *State* appeared on the PivotTable. The same was true for the other row, column, and page fields. But when you made Units and Net into data fields, you didn't see buttons labeled *Units* and *Net*. Rather, you saw the labels *Sum of UNITS* and *Sum of NET*. These summary fields are new, derived fields that have been added to the PivotTable. To refer to one of these fields, you must use the new name.

5 Type **Set myField = myTable.PivotFields("Sum of NET")** and then press the Enter key.

6 Type **myField.Orientation = xlHidden** and then press the Enter key.

The Sum of NET column disappears—along with the Data button—because there's now only one data field. To create a data field, you change the orientation of the database field. To remove a data field, you change the orientation of the derived field.

Set myField = myTable.PivotFields("Sum of NET")
myField.Orientation = xlHidden

	A	B	C	D	E	F	G
1	DATE	(All)					
2							
3	Sum of UNITS		PRICE				
4	CHANNEL	STATE	High	Low	Mid	Grand Total	
5	Retail		30,604	53,532	79,715	163,851	
6	Wholesale	WA	26,430	60,255	34,430	121,115	
7		AZ	2,940	6,140	8,820	17,900	
8		CA	4,970	26,275	59,345	90,590	
9		NV	4,440	4,540	5,145	14,125	

7 Type **Set myField = myTable.PivotFields("Sum of UNITS")** and then press the Enter key to assign the remaining data field to a variable.

8 The default calculation for a number field is to sum the values. The Function property of a data field allows you to change the way the PivotTable aggregates the data. Type **myField.Function = xlAverage** and then press the Enter key.

The values change to averages, and the label changes to *Average of UNITS*.

Set myField = myTable.PivotFields("Sum of UNITS")
myField.Function = xlAverage

	A	B	C	D	E	F	G
1	DATE	(All)					
2							
3	Average of UNIT		PRICE				
4	CHANNEL	STATE	High	Low	Mid	Grand Total	
5	Retail		111	92	111	104	
6	Wholesale	WA	287	354	167	259	
7		AZ	72	66	77	72	
8		CA	106	237	430	306	
9		NV	159	69	64	81	

9 If you don't want the label switching around on you, you can use the Name property to control it yourself. Type **myField.Name = "Avg Units"** and then press the Enter key. The label changes to *Avg Units*.

myField.Name = "Avg Units"

	A	B	C	D	E	F	G
1	DATE	(All) ▼					
2							
3	Avg Units		PRICE ▼				
4	CHANNEL ▼	STATE ▼	High	Low	Mid	Grand Total	
5	Retail		111	92	111	104	
6	Wholesale	WA	287	354	167	259	
7		AZ	72	66	77	72	
8		CA	106	237	430	306	
9		NV	159	69	64	81	

Tip

Once you replace the default name for the derived data field, Excel won't automatically change the name, even if you change the Function property. To have Excel automatically adjust the name, change the Name property to what the automatic name would be for the current function. For example, if the data field currently displays averages for the Units field, change the name to *Average of Units*.

> When you assign *xlDataField* to a field's Orientation property, you don't actually change the Orientation property for that field; rather, you create a new, derived field that has *xlDataField* as its Orientation property. These derived fields allow you to create multiple data fields from a single source field. Then you can set one derived data field to show sums, another derived field to show averages, and so forth.

The umbrella Data field, which exists only when the PivotTable has more than one data field, acts like an ordinary PivotField except that it can be assigned only to the row or column orientation.

Find PivotTable Ranges

A PivotTable resides on a worksheet. It doesn't use ordinary worksheet formulas to perform its calculations, but it does take up worksheet cells. If you want to apply a special format to a specific part of a PivotTable, or if you want to add formulas to cells outside the PivotTable that align with cells in the PivotTable, you need to know which cells contain which parts of the PivotTable. Fortunately, all the objects relating to PivotTables have properties to help you find the cells that contain the various parts of the PivotTable.

1 In the Immediate window, type **myTable.DataBodyRange.Select** and then press the Enter key.

> Excel selects the range containing the body of the data—that is, the DataBodyRange. When you type the period after the word *myTable*, Visual Basic displays the list of methods and properties. Several of the properties have names with the suffix *-Range*—for example, ColumnRange, DataBodyRange, DataLabelRange, and PageRange. All these properties that end in *-Range* return a range object of some kind.

	A	B	C	D	E	F	G
1	DATE	(All) ▼					
2							
3	Avg Units		PRICE ▼				
4	CHANNEL ▼	STATE ▼	High	Low	Mid	Grand Total	
5	Retail		111	92	111	104	
6	Wholesale	WA	287	354	167	259	
7		AZ	72	66	77	72	
8		CA	106	237	430	306	
9		NV	159	69	64	81	
10		OR	316	320	222	276	
11		UT	264	346	383	350	
12	Wholesale Total		226	254	217	232	
13	Grand Total		171	177	166	171	
14							

myTable.DataBodyRange.Select

2. You can also go the other way; you can find a PivotTable element that resides in a particular cell in Excel. Type **Range("D4").Select** and then press the Enter key to select cell D4.

Range("D4").Select

	A	B	C	D	E	F	G
1	DATE	(All) ▼					
2							
3	Avg Units		PRICE ▼				
4	CHANNEL ▼	STATE ▼	High	Low	Mid	Grand Total	
5	Retail		111	92	111	104	
6	Wholesale	WA	287	354	167	259	
7		AZ	72	66	77	72	

3. Type **Set myItem = ActiveCell.PivotItem** and press the Enter key.

The Low item from the Price field is assigned to the variable. Several of the properties in the Auto List begin with *Pivot-*. Each of these properties returns the appropriate object from the PivotTable that happens to fall on the range.

4. Type **myItem.DataRange.Select** and then press the Enter key to select the data cells "owned" by the Low Price item.

5. Type **ActiveWorkbook.Close False** and press Enter to close the Orders.dbf file.

Set myItem = ActiveCell.PivotItem
myItem.DataRange.Select

	A	B	C	D	E	F	G
1	DATE	(All) ▼					
2							
3	Avg Units		PRICE ▼				
4	CHANNEL ▼	STATE ▼	High	Low	Mid	Grand Total	
5	Retail		111	92	111	104	
6	Wholesale	WA	287	354	167	259	
7		AZ	72	66	77	72	
8		CA	106	237	430	306	
9		NV	159	69	64	81	
10		OR	316	320	222	276	
11		UT	264	346	383	350	
12	Wholesale Total		226	254	217	232	
13	Grand Total		171	177	166	171	
14							

When you see a property for a PivotTable object with the suffix *-Range*, you know that it returns a Range object of some kind. When you see a property for a Range object with the prefix *Pivot-*, you know that it returns an object that's in that cell.

Save Your Work

You've done a lot of exploring in the Immediate window. When you quit Excel, everything you've done will evaporate. You can save your explorations from the Immediate window by copying them into the MakePivot macro.

1 Press F8 to finish the macro.

2 Press Ctrl+A to select the entire contents of the Immediate window.

3 Press Ctrl+C to copy the contents of the Immediate window.

4 Click in the MakePivot macro, at the beginning of the End Sub statement. Press Ctrl+V to paste the contents of the Immediate window.

The new lines are not indented the way proper statements in a macro should be.

```
(General)                              ▼   MakePivot

    Sub MakePivot()
        Dim myCache As PivotCache
        Dim myTable As PivotTable
        Dim myField As PivotField
        Dim myItem As PivotItem
    Workbooks.Open ("Orders.dbf")
    Set myCache = ActiveWorkbook.PivotCaches.Add(xlDatabase, "Database")
    Worksheets.Add
    Set myTable = myCache.CreatePivotTable(Cells(1))
    Set myField = myTable.PivotFields("Units")
    myField.Orientation = xlDataField
    myField.NumberFormat = "#,##0"
    Set myField = myTable.PivotFields("State")
    myField.Orientation = xlRowField
```

5 Click in the middle of the first line that needs indenting, scroll to the bottom, and press and hold the Shift key as you click in the middle of the last line that needs indenting. Then press the Tab key to indent all the lines at once.

Save button

6 Save the Chapter06 workbook by clicking the Save button in the Visual Basic Editor. Close the Orders.dbf workbook without saving changes.

7 With the insertion point anywhere in the MakePivot macro, press F8 repeatedly to repeat (and review!) everything you did in this chapter.

Tip

In this exploration, you assigned several different objects in turn to each of the object variables. You might find your macros easier to read if you create a unique variable with a descriptive name each time you need to assign an object to a variable.

Here, for your reference, is the entire macro that you created in this chapter:

```
Sub MakePivot()
    Dim myCache As PivotCache
    Dim myTable As PivotTable
    Dim myField As PivotField
    Dim myItem As PivotItem

    Workbooks.Open "Orders.dbf"
    Set myCache = ActiveWorkbook.PivotCaches.Add( _
        xlDatabase, "Database")
    Worksheets.Add
    Set myTable = myCache.CreatePivotTable(Cells(1))

    Set myField = myTable.PivotFields("Units")
    myField.Orientation = xlDataField
    myField.NumberFormat = "#,##0"
    Set myField = myTable.PivotFields("State")
    myField.Orientation = xlRowField
    myField.Orientation = xlColumnField
    myField.Orientation = xlPageField
    myField.CurrentPage = "WA"
    myField.CurrentPage = "CA"
    myField.Orientation = xlHidden
    myTable.AddFields "Category", "State", "Channel"
    myTable.AddFields Array("State","Channel"), "Price", "Date"
    myField.Position = 2

    Set myItem = myField.PivotItems("WA")
    myItem.Position = 1
    myItem.Name = "Washington"
    myItem.Name = myItem.SourceName
    myItem.Visible = False
    myItem.Visible = True
    Set myItem = _
        myTable.PivotFields("Channel").PivotItems("Retail")
    myItem.ShowDetail = False
    Set myField = myTable.PivotFields("Net")
    myField.Orientation = xlDataField
    Set myField = myTable.PivotFields("Data")
    myField.Orientation = xlColumnField
    Set myField = myTable.PivotFields("Sum of NET")
    myField.Orientation = xlHidden
```

```
      Set myField = myTable.PivotFields("Sum of UNITS")
      myField.Function = xlAverage
      myField.Name = "Avg Units"

      myTable.DataBodyRange.Select
      Range("D4").Select
      Set myItem = ActiveCell.PivotItem
      myItem.DataRange.Select
      ActiveWorkbook.Close False
End Sub
```

This macro might not do much useful work, but now you understand how PivotTables work and how you can manipulate them using Visual Basic.

Loop with a counter using a For loop,
page 150

	A	B	C	D	E	F	G	H
1								
2	Old				New			
3	143	116	110		149	131	104	
4	133	136	114		131	134	100	
5	123	113	120		137	115	143	
6	103	148	129		116	115	130	
7								

	A	B
1	Events.xls	
2	Flow.xls	
3	Graphics.xls	
4	Loan.xls	
5	Ranges.xls	
6	Function.xls	
7	Budget.xls	
8	Chapter07.xls	
9		

Loop indefinitely
using a Do loop,
page 153

```
myStop = Range("A1").CurrentRegion.Rows.Count
For myRow = 3 To myStop
    If Cells(myRow, 1) <> Cells(myRow + 1, 1) Then
        Cells(myRow, 1).Select
        ActiveCell.PageBreak = xlPageBreakManual
    End If
Next myRow
Cells(myRow, 1).Select
```

Set a breakpoint,
page 155

Chapter 7
Control Visual Basic

After completing this chapter, you will be able to:

✔ Use conditional statements.

✔ Create loops using three different structures.

✔ Retrieve the names of files in a folder.

✔ Create breakpoints to debug long loops.

✔ Show progress while a macro executes a loop.

Walk outside and stand in front of your car. Look down at the tread on the right front tire. See that little piece of gum stuck to the tread? Well, imagine you're that little piece of gum. Imagine what it feels like when the car first starts to move. From the pavement, you climb higher and higher, as if you were on a Ferris wheel. Then you experience a pure thrill as you come back down the other side. (Who needs Disneyland, anyway?) But don't you think that by the five millionth revolution, you might start to get a little bored? Thwack, thwack, thwack, thwack. It really could get old after a while.

Just about anything you do is interesting—the first few times you do it. Repetition, however, can bring boredom. When you start doing the same task over and over, you start wanting somebody—or something—else to take it off your hands. This chapter will teach you how to record a repetitive task as a macro and then turn it into a little machine that works tirelessly to improve your life.

Flow.xls
Orders.dbf

This chapter uses the practice files Flow.xls and Orders.dbf that you installed from the book's CD-ROM. For details about installing the practice files, see "Using the Book's CD-ROM" at the beginning of this book.

Getting Started

1 Start Microsoft Excel, and change to the folder containing the practice files for this book.

2 Open the Flow workbook, and save a copy as **Chapter07**.

Using Conditionals

Recorded macros are, to put it bluntly, stupid. They can repeat what you did when you recorded the macro, but they can't behave differently in different circumstances. They can't make decisions. The only way that you can make your macros "smart" is to add the decision-making ability yourself.

Make a Decision

The Chapter07 workbook contains a macro named MoveRight. The MoveRight macro looks like this:

```
Sub MoveRight()
    ActiveCell.Offset(0, 1).Select
End Sub
```

This macro selects the cell to the right of the active cell. It has the keyboard shortcut Ctrl+Shift+R assigned to it. This macro works fine—most of the time.

1 With cell A1 selected, press Ctrl+Shift+R. The macro selects cell B1.

2 Press Ctrl+Right Arrow to select cell IV1, the rightmost cell on the first row, and press Ctrl+Shift+R.

Microsoft Visual Basic displays an error.

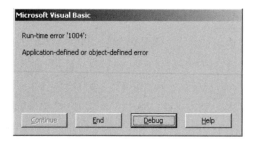

You can't select the cell to the right of the rightmost cell. An ugly error message appears. You'd rather have your macro simply do nothing if it can't move to the right.

Reset

3 Click the Debug button to jump to the code, and then click the Reset button to stop the macro.

4 Insert the statement **If ActiveCell.Column < 256 Then** after the Sub statement. Indent the main statement, and insert the statement **End If** before the End Sub statement. The revised macro should look like this:

```
Sub MoveRight()
    If ActiveCell.Column < 256 Then
        ActiveCell.Offset(0, 1).Select
    End If
End Sub
```

An If statement (a statement that begins with the word *If*) pairs with an End If statement. The group of statements from the If to the End If are called, collectively, an *If structure*.

Visual Basic looks at the expression immediately after the word *If* and determines whether it's *True* or *False*. This true-or-false expression is called a *conditional expression*. If the expression is *True*, then in a simple If structure such as this example, Visual Basic executes all the statements between the If statement and the End If statement. If the expression is *False*, Visual Basic jumps directly to the End If statement. You must always put the word *Then* at the end of the If statement.

5 Switch back to Excel, select cell IS1, and then press Ctrl+Shift+R four or five times.

The macro moves the active cell to the right until it gets to the last cell. After that it does nothing, precisely according to your instructions.

IR	IS	IT	IU	IV

You can make your macro smart enough to avoid an error.

The macro recorder will never create an If structure. This kind of decision is pure Visual Basic, and you must add it yourself. Fortunately, adding an If structure is easy.

6 Figure out a question with a "yes or no" answer. In this example, the question is, "Is the column number of the active cell less than 256?" You can then turn this question into the true-or-false conditional expression in an If statement.

7 Put the word If in front of the conditional expression, and put the word *Then* after it.

8 Figure out how many statements you want to execute if the conditional expression returns a *True* value.

9 Put an End If statement after the last statement that you want controlled by the If structure.

Using If structures makes your macro smart.

Make a Double Decision

Sometimes—such as when you're preventing an error—you want your macro to execute only if the conditional expression is *True*. Other times, you want the macro simply to behave differently depending on the answer to the question.

For example, suppose that you want a macro that moves the active cell to the right, but only within the first five columns of the worksheet. When the active cell gets to the fifth column, you want it to move back to the first cell of the next line, like a typewriter. In this case, you want the macro to carry out one action if the cell column is less than five (move to the right) and a different action if it isn't (move down and back). You can make the macro choose between two options by adding a second part to the If structure.

1 Switch to the Visual Basic Editor, and change the number 256 to **5** in the If statement.

2 Add the statement **Else** before the End If statement, and press the Enter key. Then press the Tab key and add the statement **Cells(ActiveCell.Row + 1, 1).Select** after the Else statement. The revised macro should look like this:

```
Sub MoveRight()
    If ActiveCell.Column < 5 Then
        ActiveCell.Offset(0, 1).Select
    Else
        Cells(ActiveCell.Row + 1, 1).Select
    End If
End Sub
```

The Else statement simply tells Visual Basic which statement or statements to execute if the conditional expression is *False*.

3 Press F5 repeatedly to execute the macro.

You see the selection move to the right and then scroll back to column A, much as a typewriter does.

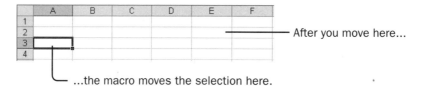

After you move here...

...the macro moves the selection here.

An If structure can contain a single part, executing statements only when the conditional expression is *True*, or it can have two or more parts, executing one set of statements when the conditional expression is *True* and a different set when it's *False*.

Tip

An If structure can also become much more complex than either of these two alternatives. To find out more about If structures, enter the words *if then* in the Ask A Question box of the Visual Basic Editor.

Ask Yourself a Question

In Chapter 2, you created a macro that asked you to enter a date. You used the Visual Basic InputBox function to do that. The InputBox function is excellent for asking a question, but you must be careful about what happens when you click the Cancel button.

The Chapter07 workbook contains a macro named TestInput that prompts for the date. The code in this macro should look familiar.

```
Sub TestInput()
    Dim myDate As String
    myDate = InputBox("Enter Month in MMM-YYYY format")
    MsgBox "Continue the macro"
End Sub
```

The macro prompts for a date. It then displays a simple message box indicating that it's running the rest of the macro.

1   Click in the TestInput macro. Press F5 to run the macro, type **Nov-2002** for the date, and then click OK.

The message box appears, simulating the rest of the macro.

Type a date, and then click OK.

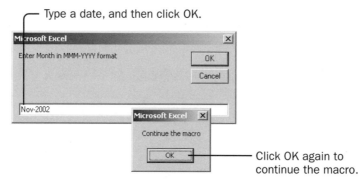

Click OK again to continue the macro.

2   Click OK to close the message box.

3 Press F5 to run the macro again, but this time click Cancel when prompted to enter the date.

The message box still appears, even though your normal expectation when you click Cancel is that you'll cancel what you started.

4 Click OK to close the message box.

You need a question to which the answer is "yes" if you want the macro to continue. An appropriate question is, "Did you enter anything in the box?" Clicking Cancel is the same as leaving the box empty. Whether you click Cancel or leave the box empty, the InputBox function returns an empty string (equivalent to two quotation marks with nothing between them). The operator <> (a less-than sign followed by a greater-than sign) means "not equal"; it's the opposite of an equal sign.

5 Before the MsgBox statement, enter the statement **If myDate <> "" Then**. Before the End Sub statement, enter **End If**. Indent the statement inside the If structure. The revised macro should look like this:

```
Sub TestInput()
    Dim myDate As String
    myDate = InputBox("Enter Month in MMM-YYYY format")
    If myDate <> "" Then
        MsgBox "Continue the macro"
    End If
End Sub
```

6 Press F5 to run the macro. Type a date, and click OK. The macro "continues."

7 Click OK to close the message box.

8 Now run the macro again, but this time click Cancel when prompted for a date. The macro stops quietly.

Whenever you allow user input in a macro, you must be sure to check whether the user took the opportunity to cancel the macro entirely.

Test for a Valid Entry

Testing for an empty string checks to see whether the user clicked the Cancel button, but it does not help you determine whether the value entered into the box is valid. You can add a second test to check the input value.

1 Run the TestInput macro again, but this time type **hippopotamus** in the input box and click OK.

The macro continues—the same as it would have if you had entered a date.

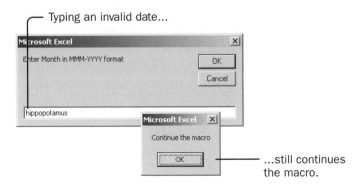

Typing an invalid date...

...still continues the macro.

2   Click OK to close the message box.

This behavior could be a problem. You need to check whether the box is empty, but you also need to check for a valid date. Visual Basic has an IsDate function that will tell you whether Visual Basic can interpret a value as a date. However, you want to check for a date only if the user didn't click Cancel. This calls for *nested* If structures.

3   Change the macro to look like this:

```
Sub TestInput()
    Dim myDate As String
    myDate = InputBox("Enter Month in MMM-YYYY format")
    If myDate <> "" Then
        If IsDate(myDate) Then
            MsgBox "Continue the macro"
        Else
            MsgBox "You didn't enter a date"
        End If
    End If
End Sub
```

Be sure to indent each statement in such a way as to make it clear which statement is governed by which If or Else statement. Visual Basic doesn't require proper indentation, but indentation is critical to help you (or someone following after you) interpret the macro the same way that Visual Basic does.

4   Run the macro at least three times. Test it with a valid date, with an invalid entry, and by clicking Cancel. The valid and invalid entries should display the appropriate messages. Clicking Cancel or leaving the box empty should display no message.

Tip

Visual Basic can interpret several different formats as dates. Try different date formats, such as 11/02, to see which ones Visual Basic interprets as dates.

Using the InputBox function can be a valuable way of making a macro useful across a wide range of circumstances. You must be careful, however, to check the result of the InputBox before you continue the macro. Typically, you need to check for three possibilities: valid input, invalid input, and Cancel. An If structure—and sometimes a nested If structure—can make your macro smart enough to respond to all the possible options.

Ask with a Message

The Visual Basic MsgBox function is handy for displaying simple messages. As its name implies, this function displays a message box. The MsgBox function can do much more than that, however. It can ask questions, too. Many times, when a macro asks a question, all it needs is a simple yes-or-no answer. The MsgBox function is perfect for yes-or-no questions.

Suppose that you have two macros. One is a long, slow macro named PrintMonth, and the other is a short, quick macro named ProcessMonth. You find that you often accidentally run the slow one when you mean to run the quick one. One solution might be to add a message box to the beginning of the slow macro that asks you to confirm that you intended to run the slow one.

The Chapter07 workbook includes a macro named CheckRun. You'll enhance this macro to see how to use a MsgBox function to ask a question. The macro looks like this before you start:

```
Sub CheckRun()
    MsgBox "This takes a long time. Continue?"
    MsgBox "Continue with slow macro..."
End Sub
```

1 Click in the CheckRun macro, and press F5 to run it. Click OK twice to close each message box.

The first message box appears to ask a question, but it has only a single button. To ask a question, you must add more buttons.

  The original macro displays two message boxes.

2 Move the cursor to the end of the first MsgBox statement. Immediately after the closing quotation mark, type a comma.

As soon as you type the comma, Visual Basic displays the Quick Info for the MsgBox function. The first argument is named *Prompt*. That's the one in which you enter the message you want to display. The second argument is named *Buttons*. This is an enumerated list of values. The default value for *Buttons* is *vbOKOnly,* which is why you saw only a single OK button when you ran the macro before.

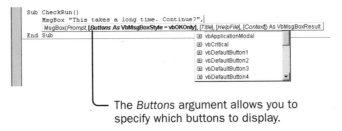

The *Buttons* argument allows you to specify which buttons to display.

Along with the Quick Info box, Visual Basic also displays the Auto List of possible values for the *Buttons* argument. You want the buttons to ask the question in terms of yes or no.

3 Scroll nearly to the bottom of the list, select *vbYesNo,* and then press the Tab key.

4 Press F5 to run the macro.

The first message box now has two buttons.

The message box asks a question, but it totally ignores your answer. You need to get the answer from the MsgBox function and then use that answer to control the way the macro runs.

5 Click Yes to close the first message box, and then click OK to close the second one. Then type the statement **Dim myCheck As VbMsgBoxResult** at the beginning of the macro. When you know a variable will contain only the value from an enumerated list, you can use the name of the list when you declare the variable. When you later write a statement to test the value of the variable, Visual Basic will display the list of possible values for you.

6 At the beginning of the first MsgBox statement, type **myCheck =** , and then put parentheses around the argument list of the MsgBox function. The revised statement should look like this:

```
myCheck = MsgBox("This takes a long time. Continue?", vbYesNo)
```

Important

When you use the return value of a function such as MsgBox, you must put parentheses around the argument list. When you don't use the return value, you must not use parentheses.

7 Insert these three statements before the second MsgBox statement:

```
If myCheck = vbNo Then
     Exit Sub
End If
```

When you create a conditional expression using the result of the MsgBox function, you must not check for *True* or *False*. MsgBox has many types of buttons it can display, so it has many types of answers. If you use *vbYesNo* as the *Buttons* argument, MsgBox will always return either *vbYes* or *vbNo*.

The Exit Sub statement causes Visual Basic to stop the current macro immediately. To avoid making your macros hard to understand, you should use Exit Sub sparingly. One good use for Exit Sub is when you cancel the macro at the beginning, as in this case.

8 Test the macro. Run it and click Yes, and then run it and click No. Make sure the rest of the macro runs only when you click Yes.

A message box is a powerful tool for asking simple questions. Be very careful to compare the answer to the correct constant rather than to *True* or *False*. Declaring a variable with the name of the enumerated list makes it easy to choose the correct constant. The MsgBox function is also a good example of when and when not to use parentheses around argument lists: use the parentheses if you use the return value of the function; otherwise, don't use them.

Creating Loops

In his classic book *The Wealth of Nations*, economist Adam Smith asked how much it would cost to make a single straight pin compared with how much it would cost to make 10,000 straight pins. The cost of one pin is almost as great as the cost of all 10,000 pins. Similarly, writing a macro that runs once is almost as much work as writing a macro that runs thousands of times in a loop.

Loop Through a Collection Using a For Each Loop

Excel allows you to protect a worksheet so that nobody can change anything in cells that aren't specifically unlocked. You must, however, protect each sheet individually. Suppose that you have a workbook containing budgets for ten different departments and that you want to protect all the worksheets.

The Chapter07 workbook includes a macro named ProtectSheets. Here's what it looks like:

```
Sub ProtectSheets()
    Dim mySheet As Worksheet
    Set mySheet = Worksheets(1)
    mySheet.Select
    mySheet.Protect "Password", True, True, True
End Sub
```

This macro assigns a reference to the first worksheet to the *mySheet* variable, selects that sheet, and then protects it. (Selecting the sheet really isn't necessary, but it makes it easier to see what the macro is doing.) Now see how you can convert this macro to protect all the worksheets in the workbook.

1 Click in the ProtectSheets macro, and press F8 repeatedly to step through the macro. Make sure you understand everything that the original macro does.

2 In the third line, replace *Set* with **For Each**, replace the equal sign with **In**, and remove the parentheses and the number between them.

3 Indent the next two statements, add a line break at the end of the second statement, and then type the statement **Next mySheet**. The revised macro should look like this:

```
Sub ProtectSheets()
    Dim mySheet As Worksheet
    For Each mySheet In Worksheets
        mySheet.Select
        mySheet.Protect "Password", True, True, True
    Next mySheet
End Sub
```

For Each acts just like Set. It assigns an object reference to a variable. But instead of assigning a single object to the variable, it assigns each object from a collection to the variable. Then, for each (get it?) object in the collection, Visual Basic executes all the statements down to the Next statement. Statements beginning with *For Each* and ending with *Next* are called For Each structures or For Each loops. (Technically, you don't need to put the variable name after Next. If you do use it, Visual Basic requires that it match the variable name after For Each. Always using a variable after Next can help you keep the right Next with the right For.)

4 Press F8 repeatedly to step through the macro, watching as it works on each worksheet in turn.

5 Switch to Excel, and try typing a value into a cell on any worksheet. (Then close the error message box that opens.)

6 Create a new macro named **UnprotectSheets** that unprotects all the worksheets. (Try to write the macro without looking at the finished code that follows. Hint: you'll need to use the *Unprotect* method of the worksheet object, with a single argument that gives the password.) Here's what your macro should look like:

```
Sub UnprotectSheets()
    Dim mySheet As Worksheet
    For Each mySheet In Worksheets
        mySheet.Select ' This statement is optional.
        mySheet.Unprotect "Password"
    Next mySheet
End Sub
```

7 Save the workbook, press F5 to test the UnprotectSheets macro, and try changing a value on a worksheet.

Looping through a collection is as easy as assigning a single value to an object. Just replace *Set* with *For Each*, specify the collection, and add a Next statement.

Tip

A For Each loop is a handy way of browsing collections in the Immediate window. However, in the Immediate window, everything you type must be on a single line. You can put multiple statements on a single line by separating the statements with colons. For example, here's what you'd type in the Immediate window to see the names of all the worksheets in the active workbook: **For Each x In Worksheets: ?x.Name: Next x.** (In the Immediate window, it's all right to use short, meaningless names for variables.)

Loop with a Counter Using a For Loop

Sometimes you want to perform actions repeatedly but can't use a For Each loop. For example, a For Each loop can work through only a single collection. If you want to compare two parallel collections—such as two ranges—you can't use a For Each loop. In that situation, Visual Basic has another, more generalized way to loop: a For loop.

The Compare worksheet in the Chapter07 workbook contains two named ranges. The one on the left is named Old, and the one on the right is named New. You can think of these as being an original forecast and a revised forecast. The cells in the Old range contain values. The cells in the New range contain a formula that will calculate a random number each time you press F9 to recalculate the workbook. (The formula in those cells is =ROUND(RAND()*50+100,0), which tells Excel to calculate a random number between 0 and 1, multiply it by 50, add 100, and round to the nearest whole number. Because the numbers are randomly generated, the ones you see will differ from the ones in the figure.)

	A	B	C	D	E	F	G	H
1								
2	Old				New			
3	143	116	110		103	142	106	
4	133	136	114		123	102	100	
5	123	113	120		135	108	143	
6	103	148	129		138	120	115	
7								

The New numbers are random sample numbers.

The Chapter07 module in the Visual Basic Editor contains a macro named CompareCells, which looks like this:

```
Sub CompareCells()
    Dim i As Integer
    Calculate
    i = Range("New").Cells.Count
    If Range("New").Cells(i) > Range("Old").Cells(i) Then
        Range("New").Cells(i).Interior.Color = vbYellow
    Else
        Range("New").Cells(i).Interior.Color = vbCyan
    End If
End Sub
```

The macro first executes the Calculate method, which is like pressing the F9 function key to calculate new values for all the cells in the New range. Then the macro compares only the last cell in the New range with the last cell in the Old range. If the New value is greater than the Old, the new value turns yellow; otherwise, it turns blue. The macro assigns the Count of cells in the range to the variable *i*. The macro uses that number several times, and *i* requires less typing than *Range("New").Cells.Count*.

Tip

If you're not comfortable with If structures, review the first half of this chapter.

Now see how you can convert this macro to compare all the cells at once.

1 Click in the CompareCells macro, and press F8 repeatedly to step through the macro. Make sure you understand everything the original macro does.

	A	B	C	D	E	F	G	H
1								
2	Old				New			
3	143	116	110		103	142	106	
4	133	136	114		123	102	100	
5	123	113	120		135	108	143	
6	103	148	129		138	120	115	
7								

The original macro compares the last cell of each range and flags the difference with a color change.

151

2 In the statement that assigns the Count to the variable, insert the word **For** in front of the variable, and then insert **1 To** after the equal sign.

3 Type **Next i** before the End Sub statement, and indent all the statements between For and Next. The revised macro should look like this:

```
Sub CompareCells()
    Dim i As Integer
    Calculate
    For i = 1 To Range("New").Cells.Count
        If Range("New").Cells(i) > Range("Old").Cells(i) Then
            Range("New").Cells(i).Interior.Color = vbYellow
        Else
            Range("New").Cells(i).Interior.Color = vbCyan
        End If
    Next i
End Sub
```

The keyword *For* works just like a simple assignment statement. It assigns a number to the variable. (The *For* keyword assigns a number to a variable, and *For Each* assigns an object reference to a variable.) The variable that gets assigned the number is called a *loop counter*. You specify the first value For should assign (in this case, 1) and the last value it should assign (in this case, the number of cells in the range).

Each time For assigns a number to the loop counter, Visual Basic executes all the statements down to the Next statement. Then For adds 1 to the loop counter and executes all the statements again, until the loop counter is greater than the value you specified as the last value.

4 Press F8 repeatedly to watch the macro work. Step through at least two or three loops, and then press F5 to finish the macro.

	A	B	C	D	E	F	G	H
1								
2	Old				New			
3	143	116	110		149	131	104	
4	133	136	114		131	134	100	
5	123	113	120		137	115	143	
6	103	148	129		116	115	130	
7								

A For loop allows you to loop through two collections at once.

In many cases, using a For Each loop is more convenient than using a For loop. However, a For loop is a more general tool in that you can always use a For loop to reproduce the behavior of a For Each loop. For example, here's how you could write the ProtectSheets macro without using For Each:

```
Sub ProtectSheets()
    Dim mySheet As Worksheet
    Dim i As Integer
    For i = 1 to Worksheets.Count
        Set mySheet = Worksheets(i)
        mySheet.Select
```

(continued)

continued

```
        mySheet.Protect "Password", True, True, True
    Next i
End Sub
```

If you were going to be marooned on a desert island and could take only one of these two looping structures with you, you'd probably be better off choosing For. Fortunately, however, you don't have to make the choice. In the many cases where For Each loops can work, use them and be happy. In cases where you need a numeric counter, use For loops.

Loop Indefinitely Using a Do Loop

A For Each loop works through a collection. A For loop cycles through numbers from a starting point to an ending point. In some situations, however, neither of these options works. For example, Visual Basic has a function that tells you the names of files in a folder (or directory). The function is named Dir, after the old MS-DOS operating system command of the same name. The first time you use Dir, you give it an argument that tells which kind of files you want to look at. To retrieve the name of the first Excel workbook in the current directory, you use the statement *myFile = Dir("*.xls")*. To get the next file that matches the same pattern, you use Dir again, but without an argument. You must run Dir repeatedly because it returns only one file name at a time. When Visual Basic can't find another matching file, the Dir function returns an empty string.

Suppose that you want to create a macro that retrieves the names of all the Excel files in the current folder. The list of files in the directory isn't a collection, so you can't use a For Each loop. You can't use a For loop either because you don't know how many files you'll get until you're finished. Fortunately, Visual Basic has one more way of controlling a loop: a Do loop.

The ListFiles macro in the Chapter07 workbook retrieves the first two Excel files from the current directory and puts their names into the first two cells in the first column of the active worksheet. Here's the original macro:

```
Sub ListFiles()
    Dim myRow As Integer
    Dim myFile As String

    myRow = 1
    myFile = Dir("*.xls")
    Cells(myRow, 1) = myFile

    myRow = myRow + 1
    myFile = Dir
    Cells(myRow, 1) = myFile
End Sub
```

Aside from the variable declaration statements, this macro consists of two groups of three statements. In each group, the macro assigns a row number to *myRow*, retrieves a file name using the Dir function, and then puts the file name into the appropriate cell. The first time the macro uses Dir, it specifies the pattern to match. The next time, the macro simply uses Dir without an argument to retrieve the next matching file.

Now see how you can convert this macro to loop until it has found all the files in the folder.

1   In the Chapter07 workbook, activate the Files worksheet. On the File menu, click Open, change to the folder containing the practice files for the book, and then click Cancel. Performing the actions in the preceding sentence ensures that the current folder contains Excel workbooks.

2   In the Visual Basic Editor, click in the ListFiles macro and press F8 repeatedly to step through the macro. (The names of the files your macro retrieves might differ from those in the figures.) Make sure you understand the original macro.

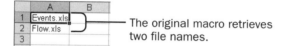 The original macro retrieves two file names.

Tip

As you step through the macro, move the mouse pointer over a variable name to see the current value stored in that variable.

3   Type **Do Until myFile = ""** on a new line after the first statement that contains a Dir function.

This statement begins the loop. You begin the loop after the first Dir function because you use Dir with an argument only once.

4   Type **Loop** on a new line after the second statement that contains a Dir function.

This statement ends the loop. After running this statement, Visual Basic goes back to the Do Until statement and checks to see whether it's time to quit.

5   Delete the second *Cells(myRow, 1) = myFile* statement. You don't need this statement because the loop repeats the assignment statement as many times as needed.

6   Indent the three statements between the Do and Loop statements. The revised macro should look like this:

```
Sub ListFiles()
    Dim myRow As Integer
    Dim myFile As String

    myRow = 1
    myFile = Dir("*.xls")
    Do Until myFile = ""
        Cells(myRow, 1) = myFile

        myRow = myRow + 1
        myFile = Dir
    Loop
End Sub
```

The phrase after Do Until is a conditional expression, precisely like one you'd use with an If structure. The conditional expression must be something that Visual Basic can interpret as either *True* or *False*. Visual Basic simply repeats the loop over and over until the conditional expression is *True*.

If you want to increment a number during the loop, you must enter a statement to do so. You must always be careful to cause something to happen during the loop that will allow the loop to end. In this case, you retrieve a new file name from the Dir function.

7 Press F8 repeatedly to watch the macro work. Step through at least two or three loops, and then press F5 to finish the macro.

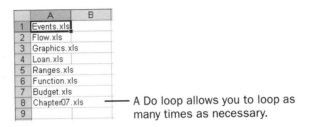

A Do loop allows you to loop as many times as necessary.

Important

If you run a macro that contains an infinite loop, stop the macro by pressing Ctrl+Break. (The Break key often functions the same as the Pause key.)

A Do loop is very flexible, but it's also a little bit dangerous because you have to be sure you provide a way for the loop to end. For example, if you forgot to add the statement to retrieve a new file name, or if you had included the argument to the Dir function inside the loop (so that Dir would keep returning the first file name over and over), you'd have what is called an *infinite loop*.

Tip

Do loop structures have several useful variations. You can loop *until* the conditional expression is *True* or *while* the expression is *True*. You can put the conditional expression at the top of the loop (in the Do statement) or at the bottom of the loop (in the Loop statement). To find out more about Do loop structures, enter the words *do loop* in the Ask A Question box of the Visual Basic Editor.

Managing Large Loops

A loop that executes only two or three times isn't much different from a program without a loop. It runs fast, and it's easy to step through to watch how each statement works. Once you start repeating a loop hundreds or thousands of times, however, you need some additional techniques to make sure the macro works the way you want it to.

Set a Breakpoint

The Chapter07 workbook includes a macro named PrintOrders. You can think of this macro as one that your predecessor wrote just before leaving the company. Or you can think of it as one that you almost finished three months ago. In either event, you have a macro that you don't completely understand and that doesn't work quite right.

The PrintOrders macro is supposed to print a copy of the entire Orders database, specifically one that is sorted by product Category. You give each Category manager the section of the report that shows orders only for that one category, so you need a new page every time the Category changes. Unfortunately, the macro doesn't do what it's supposed to. You need to find and fix the problem. Here's the macro as you first receive it:

```
Sub PrintOrders()
    Dim myRow As Long
    Dim myStop As Long
    Workbooks.Open FileName:="orders.dbf"
    Columns("E:E").Cut
    Columns("A:A").Insert Shift:=xlToRight
    Range("A1").CurrentRegion.Sort Key1:="Category", _
        Order1:=xlAscending, Header:=xlYes
    myStop = Range("A1").CurrentRegion.Rows.Count
    For myRow = 3 To myStop
        If Cells(myRow, 1) <> Cells(myRow + 1, 1) Then
            Cells(myRow, 1).Select
            ActiveCell.PageBreak = xlPageBreakManual
        End If
    Next myRow
    Cells(myRow, 1).Select
    ActiveSheet.PageSetup.PrintTitleRows = "$1:$1"
    ActiveSheet.PrintPreview
    ActiveWorkbook.Close SaveChanges:=False
End Sub
```

The best approach is probably to start stepping through the macro.

Open

1 Make sure the current folder is the one containing the practice files for this book. (On the File menu, click Open, change to the correct folder, and then click Cancel.)

2 In the Visual Basic Editor, click in the PrintOrders macro and then press F8 three times to jump over the variable declarations and open the database file. (The two variables are declared as Long, which means that they can hold whole numbers but aren't limited to the four-digit numbers of type Integer.)

In the original database, the Category field is in column E.

	A	B	C	D	E	F	G	H
1	DATE	STATE	CHANNEL	PRICE	CATEGORY	UNITS	NET	
2	11/1/1999	WA	Wholesale	High	Nuts	40	110.00	
3	11/1/1999	WA	Wholesale	High	Flowers	25	68.75	
4	11/1/1999	WA	Retail	High	Flowers	3	16.50	
5	11/1/1999	WA	Retail	Low	Fruits	50	175.00	

3 Press F8 three more times.

These statements move the Category field over to column A and then sort the list by Category.

The macro moves the Category field to column A and sorts the database by Category.

	A	B	C	D	E	F	G	H
1	CATEGORY	DATE	STATE	CHANNEL	PRICE	UNITS	NET	
2	Books	3/1/2001	CA	Wholesale	High	150	400.26	
3	Books	3/1/2001	CA	Retail	High	75	412.50	
4	Books	3/1/2001	OR	Wholesale	High	70	192.50	
5	Books	3/1/2001	WA	Wholesale	High	65	178.75	

4 Press F8 twice to assign a number to *myStop* and to start the loop. Hold the mouse pointer over *myStop* and then over *myRow* to see the values that were assigned. The value of *myStop* is 3300, and the value of *myRow* is 3. Those values appear to be correct. The loop will execute from row 3 to row 3300.

```
myStop = Range("A1").CurrentRegion.Rows.Count
For myRow = 3 To myStop
    myRow = 3 ls(myRow, 1) <> Cells(myRow + 1, 1) Then
            Cells(myRow, 1).Select
```

— The Data Tip box shows the value of the variable.

5 Press F8 several times.

Visual Basic keeps checking whether the cell in the current row matches the cell below it. How many rows are in the Books category? Pressing F8 repeatedly until the macro finds the last row in the category could take a very long time. But if you just press F5 to run the rest of the macro, you can't watch what happens when the condition in the If statement is *True*. If only there were a way to skip over all the statements until the macro moves into the If structure.

6 Click in the gray area to the left of the statement starting with ActiveCell. A dark red circle appears in the margin, and the background of the statement changes to dark red. This is a *breakpoint*. When you set a breakpoint, the macro starts stepping just before it would execute the breakpoint statement.

— Click in the left margin to create a breakpoint.

```
myStop = Range("A1").CurrentRegion.Rows.Count
For myRow = 3 To myStop
    If Cells(myRow, 1) <> Cells(myRow + 1, 1) Then
            Cells(myRow, 1).Select
            ActiveCell.PageBreak = xlPageBreakManual
    End If
Next myRow
Cells(myRow, 1).Select
```

7 Press F5 to continue the macro. The macro stops at the breakpoint. The active cell is the first one that the If statement determined is different from the cell below it.

— Visual Basic stops when it reaches the breakpoint.

```
myStop = Range("A1").CurrentRegion.Rows.Count
For myRow = 3 To myStop
    If Cells(myRow, 1) <> Cells(myRow + 1, 1) Then
            Cells(myRow, 1).Select
            ActiveCell.PageBreak = xlPageBreakManual
    End If
Next myRow
Cells(myRow, 1).Select
```

8 Press F8 to execute the statement that assigns a manual page break.

	A	B	C	D	E	F	G	H
801	Books	10/1/2002	UT	Wholesale	Mid	30	67.50	
802	Books	10/1/2002	UT	Retail	Mid	28	126.00	
803	Books	10/1/2002	NV	Wholesale	Mid	20	45.00	
804	Books	10/1/2002	AZ	Retail	Mid	19	85.50	
805	Books	10/1/2002	AZ	Retail	Mid	16	72.00	
806	Books	10/1/2002	WA	Retail	Mid	5	22.50	
807	Flowers	11/1/1999	WA	Wholesale	High	25	68.75	

— The page break appears in the wrong row.

The page break appears above the row, not below the row. This is a problem. The macro shouldn't set the page break on the *last* cell of a Category; rather, it should set the break on the *first* cell of a Category. The If statement should check to see whether the cell is different than the one *above* it.

9 Change the plus sign (+) in the If statement to a minus sign (–). The revised statement should look like this:

```
If Cells(myRow, 1) <> Cells(myRow - 1, 1) Then
```

Reset

10 Click the Reset button, press F5, and click Yes to reopen the Orders file. Then press F8 to watch the critical statement work—properly this time—as it assigns the page break after the Books category.

Setting a breakpoint is an invaluable tool for finding a problem in the middle of a long loop. In the following section, you'll learn an easy way to set a temporary breakpoint if you need to use it only once.

Set a Temporary Breakpoint

Suppose you're now stepping through the middle of the PrintOrders macro. The code to assign a page break seems to be working properly. There are still some statements at the end of the macro, however, that you'd like to step through.

1 Click the red circle in the margin to turn off the breakpoint.

2 Click anywhere in the *Cells(myRow, 1).Select* statement after the end of the loop. You want a breakpoint on this statement, but one that you need to use only once.

```
For myRow = 3 To myStop
    If Cells(myRow, 1) <> Cells(myRow - 1, 1) Then
        Cells(myRow, 1).Select
        ActiveCell.PageBreak = xlPageBreakManual
    End If
Next myRow
Cells(myRow, 1).Select
ActiveSheet.PageSetup.PrintTitleRows = "$1:$1"
```

Click in the statement where you
want a temporary breakpoint.

3 On the Debug menu, click the Run To Cursor command.

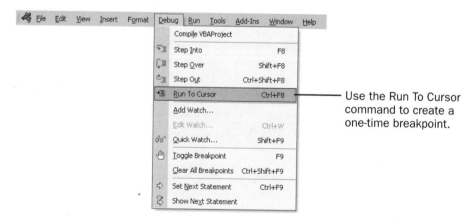

Use the Run To Cursor
command to create a
one-time breakpoint.

4 Press F8 three times to scroll to the bottom of the list, set the print titles, and preview the report.

5 Review the report. Click Next repeatedly to get to page 17 to see the end of the Books category.

Important

If you don't see the end of the Books category on page 17, simply click Next or Previous to locate the correct page. Your current printer driver might have placed the end of the Books category on a different page.

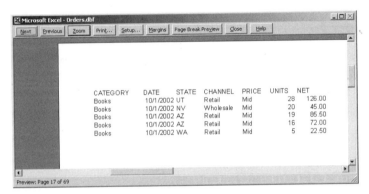

6 Close Print Preview, and press F8 twice more to finish the macro.

7 Save the Chapter07 workbook.

Turning off a breakpoint is just as easy as turning one on: just click in the left margin of the Visual Basic Editor window. But if turning a breakpoint on and off is still too much work, you can create a temporary one by running to the cursor.

Show Progress in a Loop

Even if the loop in a macro is working perfectly, you might get nervous about whether something has gone wrong if the macro takes a long time to execute. The best way to feel comfortable when a long loop is running (particularly if you're wondering whether you have time to go get a cup of coffee) is to show the progress of the loop.

You can show progress with any kind of loop. But a For loop lends itself particularly well to showing progress because at any point in the loop your macro can determine the current value of the loop counter and also what its final value will be.

1 In the PrintOrders macro, immediately following the For statement, insert this statement:

Application.StatusBar = "Processing row " & myRow & " of " & myStop

The status bar is the gray strip at the bottom of the Excel window that usually says "Ready." The StatusBar property of the Application object allows you to make the status bar say whatever you want. The best message is one that shows progress and also gives you an idea of how long the task will take.

The statement you added creates this message when it enters the loop the first time: "Processing row 3 of 3300." By using an ampersand (&) to join together message text with the numbers in the *myRow* and *myStop* variables, you can create a useful message. Just be careful to include an extra space before and after the numbers.

2 Press F5 to run the macro. Watch the status bar to see how the macro is progressing.

The status bar shows progress.

3 Close the Print Preview screen to let the macro finish. The status bar indicates that the macro is still running. The status bar doesn't automatically reset when your macro ends. To return control of the status bar to Excel, you must assign the value *False* to it.

4 After the Next statement, insert the statement:

```
Application.StatusBar = False
```

5 Run the macro again, close the Print Preview screen at the appropriate time, and then look at the status bar. It's back to normal.

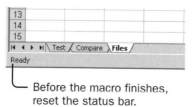

Before the macro finishes, reset the status bar.

6 Save the Chapter07 workbook.

Visual Basic provides extremely powerful tools for repeating statements in a loop. Coupled with the decisions that you can make using If structures, these tools let you create macros that are smart and very powerful.

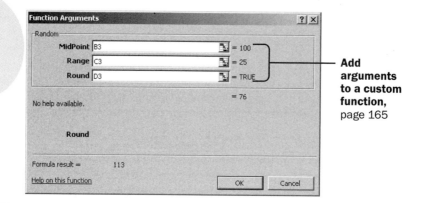

Add
arguments
to a custom
function,
page 165

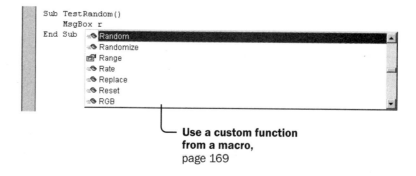

Use a custom function
from a macro,
page 169

Trap an error,
page 178

Chapter 8
Extend Excel and Visual Basic

After completing this chapter, you will be able to:

✔ Create and use custom functions.

✔ Handle errors that occur while a macro is running.

A bacteria cell doesn't have a nucleus. A cell without a nucleus is called a prokaryote. Prokaryotes are very important. The first known fossils, dating from three and a half billion years ago, are all prokaryotes. Prokaryotes are also very small. In 1999, Heide Schulz discovered the prokaryote species *Thiomargarita namibiensis* whose individual organisms grow to be as large as 3/4 millimeter—about the size of the head of a fruit-fly. This is astonishingly large for a bacteria but doesn't seem very large compared to, say, a puppy.

Probably the largest single-celled organism is *Caulerpa taxifolia*. It is a type of seaweed—algae, really—that has been an uncontrollable weed in the Mediterranean Sea since 1984 and was discovered off the coast near San Diego, California, in June 2000. A single Caulerpa plant—consisting of a single cell—can grow to just under a meter in length. In the grand scheme of things, a single-celled Caulerpa is not very big, but it is orders of magnitude larger than a single-celled Thiomargarita. The difference is due to structure. The Caulerpa has a nucleus. It has appendages and vacuoles and rhizomes. Structure enables functional size.

Recorded macros are like prokaryotes. The macro recorder puts everything you do into a single, unstructured procedure. And, like prokaryotes, single-procedure macros should be small. To get a large, sophisticated application to work properly, you must give it an internal structure—you must break it up into smaller procedures. And just as large, complex organisms need an immune system to deal with diseases, sophisticated applications need a mechanism for dealing with error conditions. In this chapter, you'll learn how to create custom functions, use arguments in procedures, and handle errors—tools you'll need to make more powerful applications.

Function.xls

This chapter uses the practice file Function.xls that you installed from the book's CD-ROM. For details about installing the practice files, see "Using the Book's CD-ROM" at the beginning of this book.

Getting Started

1 Start Microsoft Excel, and change to the folder containing the practice files for this book.

2 Open the Function workbook, and save a copy as **Chapter08.**

Creating Custom Functions

Once you assign a value to a variable, you can use that value in any expression. For example, after you assign the number 25 to the variable *myAge*, the value of the conditional expression *myAge > 20* would be *True* because 25 is greater than 20. You use the variable as if it were the value that it contains.

A function is like a variable, except that a function is smarter. A function is a variable that figures out its own value whenever you use it. For example, Microsoft Visual Basic has a function named *Time*. When you use the conditional expression *Time > #8:00 PM#*, the Time function checks the time on your computer's clock each time you use the expression.

Visual Basic has many built-in functions. Excel also has many built-in functions. Those functions are useful, but they aren't customizable. Even if you find a Visual Basic function that's "this close" to what you need, you can't worm your way into the innards of Visual Basic to change the way it works. You can, however, create a function of your own. Because your function can take advantage of any of the Excel or Visual Basic built-in functions, and because you can customize your function however you want, you get the same benefit you would get if you could tweak the built-in functions directly.

Use a Custom Function from a Worksheet

Both Excel and Visual Basic have functions that return a random number between 0 and 1. The Excel function is named RAND( ), and the Visual Basic function is named *Rnd*. You can use the Excel function in a worksheet cell, but you can use the Visual Basic function only in a macro.

You can't customize the Visual Basic Rnd function or the Excel RAND( ) function, but you *can* create a custom random-number function—let's call it *Random*—that you can use from Excel. Why would you want to create your own random-number function when you could use Excel's built-in one for free? Because you want your Random function to behave just a little differently than Excel's. Once you create your own function, you can make it do whatever you want.

1   Enter the formula **=Random()** into cell A3 on the TestFunction sheet.

Excel displays the #NAME? error value because the Random function doesn't exist yet.

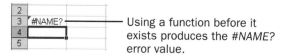

Using a function before it exists produces the #NAME? error value.

Run Macro

2   Click the Run Macro button, type **Random** in the Macro Name box, and then click Create.

3   Double-click the word *Sub* at the beginning of the macro, and replace it with **Function.**

The End Sub statement changes to End Function. You've now created a function. Next you need to tell Excel what to use as the value of the function.

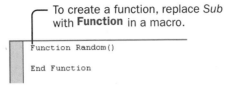

To create a function, replace *Sub* with **Function** in a macro.

```
Function Random()

End Function
```

4 Type the statement **Random = Rnd** as the body of the function. The revised function should look like this:

```
Function Random()
    Random = Rnd
End Function
```

The way you tell a function what value to return is by assigning a value to the name of the function, as if the function name were a variable. This function simply takes the value of the Visual Basic Rnd function and assigns it to the Random function.

Insert Function **5** Switch back to Excel, select cell A3, and then click the Insert Function button next to
f_x the formula bar. Excel displays the Function Arguments window, which explains that the Random function doesn't take any arguments. Click OK to enter the random number into cell A3.

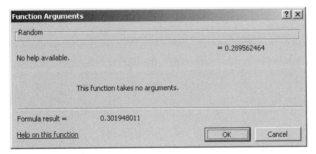

That's all there is to creating a simple worksheet function. In the Visual Basic Editor, you replace the word *Sub* with *Function*, and then somewhere in the function, you assign a value to the function name. In Excel, you put the function name into a formula, followed by parentheses.

Add Arguments to a Custom Function

Suppose that you want random whole numbers equal to 100 plus or minus 25. Or that you want random whole numbers equal to 1000 plus or minus 100. The Excel RAND( ) function can't give you that kind of random number. Neither, for that matter, can yours, but because yours is a custom function, you can add capabilities to it by adding arguments.

To specify random-number ranges such as those just mentioned, you need three arguments: one to specify the midpoint, one to specify the plus or minus range, and one to specify whether or not to round the final number. You can add those arguments to your function.

1 In the Visual Basic Editor, type **Midpoint, Range, Round** between the parentheses after the name of the function. The statement that contains the function name and its arguments is called the *function declaration* statement. In this statement, you declare the name of the function and also the names of all the arguments. The revised function declaration statement should look like this:

```
Function Random(Midpoint, Range, Round)
```

These three words are arguments to the function. You can use them inside the function as variables that have been prefilled with values.

2 Change the statement that assigns a value to the function name to this:

```
Random = Rnd * (Range * 2) + (Midpoint - Range)
```

The Rnd function returns a random number between 0 and 1. If Range is equal to 25, that means you want numbers from 25 below the midpoint to 25 above the midpoint, for a total range of 50. Multiplying Rnd by Range * 2 would then give you a random number between 0 and 50. If the target midpoint is 100, you need to add 75 (that is, 100 − 25), to the random number. That's what this statement does.

3 Insert these three statements to round the number if requested:

```
If Round Then
    Random = CLng(Random)
End If
```

In Visual Basic, a *Long* is a whole number that can include large numbers. The Visual Basic function CLng converts a number to a Long, rounding it along the way. You round the random number only if the value of the *Round* argument is *True*. (Because the value of the *Round* argument already equals *True* or *False*, you don't need to compare it to anything to get a conditional expression.) The complete function should look like this:

```
Function Random(Midpoint, Range, Round)
    Random = Rnd * (Range * 2) + (Midpoint - Range)
    If Round Then
        Random = CLng(Random)
    End If
End Function
```

Tip

To see other functions that convert between data types, click CLng and press F1.

4 In Excel, enter **100** into cell B3, **25** into cell C3, and **TRUE** into cell D3. You'll use these values for the *Midpoint*, *Range*, and *Round* arguments of your function.

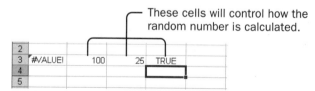

These cells will control how the random number is calculated.

Insert Function **5** Select cell A3, and click the Insert Function button next to the formula bar.

The Function Arguments window appears, showing you the three new arguments of your function.

The Function Arguments window displays
the custom arguments you created.

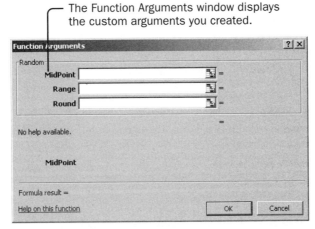

6 Click in the Midpoint box, and then click in cell B3. Click in the Range box, and then click
in cell C3. Click in the Round box, and then click in cell D3. Then click OK.

Link the arguments to worksheet cells.

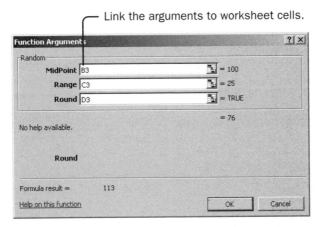

After adjusting the formula, cell A3 contains a random number between 75 and 125. You
use arguments to pass values to a function.

7 Change cell B3 to **1000** and cell C3 to **100**. The value of cell A3 changes to a random
number between 900 and 1100. Whenever you change the value of a cell that the function refers to, the function calculates a new answer. Adding arguments is a way to make
functions more flexible.

The function uses these values...

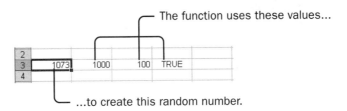

...to create this random number.

Make a Function Volatile

Most functions recalculate only when the value of a cell that feeds into the function changes. Other functions (such as Excel's RAND( ) function), called *volatile functions*, recalculate whenever any cell on the worksheet changes or whenever you press F9. You can make your function volatile; it will then calculate a new random number whenever you press F9.

1 In Excel, press F9 repeatedly to see that the random number in cell A3 doesn't change.

2 In the Visual Basic Editor, insert this statement after the statement containing the name of the function:

```
Application.Volatile True
```

3 Switch back to Excel, and press F9.

The random number in cell A3 changes. Press F9 several times to verify that the function generates random numbers in the appropriate range.

Most of the time, you don't want custom functions to be volatile. You want the function to recalculate only when a value that feeds into it changes. For those few cases in which you do want the formula to recalculate, just use the Application object's Volatile method with *True* as an argument.

Make Arguments Optional

The only problem with your new enhanced Random function is that it's now more complicated to use in those simple cases in which you don't need the new arguments. If you put *=Random()* into a cell, omitting the arguments, Excel displays the *#VALUE!* error value. To avoid this error, you can tell Visual Basic that you want the arguments to be optional. Then you specify default values to use if the argument isn't supplied.

1 In the Visual Basic Editor, type the word **Optional** in front of each of the three argument names. The revised statement should look like this:

```
Function Random(Optional Midpoint, _
    Optional Range, Optional Round)
```

You don't have to make all the arguments optional, but once you make one argument optional, all the arguments that follow it must be optional as well. In other words, you place optional arguments at the end of the argument list.

2 Type **= 0.5** after the word *Midpoint*, **= 0.5** after the word *Range*, and **= False** after the word *Round*. Break the statement into two lines after the first comma. The resulting statement should look like this:

```
Function Random(Optional Midpoint = 0.5, _
    Optional Range = 0.5, Optional Round = False)
```

You can specify a default value for any optional argument. You assign the default value to the argument name in the same way you would assign a value to a variable—by using a simple equal sign.

3 In Excel, enter **=Random()** into cell A4. A random number between 0 and 1 appears.

4 Delete the formulas in cells A3 and A4 so that you can step through other macros later in the chapter without stepping through the custom function.

Optional arguments allow you to add powerful features to a function while keeping it easy to use in cases in which you don't need the extra features. To make an argument optional, add *Optional* before the argument name. To add a default value for an optional argument, assign the value to the argument name the same way you would if it were a variable.

Use a Custom Function from a Macro

You can use a custom function from a macro just as easily as you can use it from a worksheet cell.

1   In the Visual Basic Editor, type **Sub TestRandom** at the bottom of the module, and then press the Enter key to start creating a macro.

2   Type **MsgBox** and a space.

Visual Basic shows the Quick Info box with the arguments for MsgBox.

3   Press Ctrl+Spacebar to show the list of global methods and properties, and then press R to scroll down to the words that begin with an R.

Your custom function appears as a method in the list of global methods and properties.

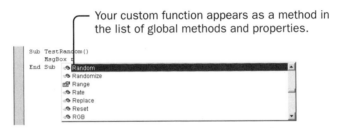

Your Random function is automatically included in the list. Your function has the icon for a method next to it. Excel methods are simply functions built into Excel. You create new global methods simply by writing new functions.

4   Press the Tab key to insert the function name into the statement, and then type an opening parenthesis to begin the argument list. Visual Basic displays the Quick Info box with the arguments for your custom function. The Quick Info box even shows the default values for the optional arguments.

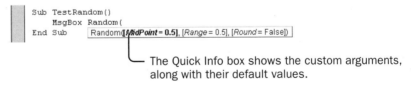

The Quick Info box shows the custom arguments, along with their default values.

5   Type **200, 5, True** as the list of arguments, and then type a closing parenthesis.

6   Press F5 to run the macro. Click OK when your random number appears.

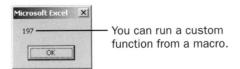

You can run a custom function from a macro.

A function is a procedure like a Sub procedure, except that it returns a value that you can use either in a cell in Excel or from a macro.

Important

A function used in a worksheet cell can include only those actions that can be executed while Excel is recalculating a worksheet. (Remember that some cells might even recalculate more than once.) Actions such as opening files or displaying message boxes can be included in functions that are called from macros, but if you include them in a function that's called from a worksheet, the function simply returns the #VALUE! error value.

Handling Errors

Believe it or not, computer programs don't always work perfectly. Every now and then, you might actually write a macro that doesn't quite do what you want. These errors come in several types.

- **Syntax errors**   These are mistakes such as using an opening quotation mark and leaving off the closing quotation mark. When you type a statement into a procedure, the Visual Basic Editor checks the statement for syntax errors as soon as you leave the statement.

- **Compiler errors**   Some mistakes can't be detected on a single-line basis. For example, you might start a For Each loop but forget to put a Next statement at the end. The first time you try to run a procedure, Visual Basic translates that procedure (along with all the other procedures in the module) into internal computer language. Translating to computer language is called *compiling*, and errors that Visual Basic detects while translating are called *compiler errors*. Syntax errors and compiler errors are usually easy to find and fix.

Tip

Visual Basic can check for spelling errors when you use variables. From the Visual Basic Tools menu, select the Options command and then select the Require Variable Declaration check box. After you do this, Visual Basic adds the statement Option Explicit to any new module that you create. When Option Explicit appears at the top of a module, Visual Basic displays a compiler error any time you use a variable that you didn't explicitly declare.

- **Logic errors**   The computer can never detect some mistakes. For example, if you mean to change a workbook caption to *My Workbook*, but you accidentally spell the caption *My Werkbook*, the computer will never complain. Or if you compare the new values with the wrong copy of the old values, the computer won't find the error for you. You can toggle breakpoints, step through the procedures, and watch values, but you still have to find the problem on your own.

- **Run-time errors**   Sometimes a statement in a procedure works under some conditions but fails under others. For example, you might have a statement that deletes a file on your hard disk. As long as the file exists and can be deleted, the statement works. If, however, the file doesn't exist, Visual Basic doesn't know what else to do but quit with an error message. These errors can't be detected until you run the procedure, so they're called *run-time errors*. Some run-time errors indicate problems. Other run-time errors are situations that you can anticipate and program Visual Basic to deal with automatically. Visual Basic has tools that can help you deal with any kind of run-time error.

Ignore an Error

Suppose you want to create a macro that creates a temporary report worksheet. The macro gives the name Report to the report worksheet and replaces any existing Report worksheet in the active workbook. The Chapter08 workbook contains a macro named MakeReport that creates and names the Report worksheet. Here's the original macro:

```
Sub MakeReport()
    Dim mySheet As Worksheet
    Set mySheet = Worksheets.Add
    mySheet.Name = "Report"
End Sub
```

The macro adds a worksheet, assigning a reference to the new worksheet to the *mySheet* variable. It then changes the Name property of the sheet.

1   In the Visual Basic Editor, click in the white space at the bottom of the module, and press F5 to display the Macros dialog box. Select the MakeReport macro, and click Edit. Then press F5 to run it.

You should see a new worksheet named Report in the active workbook. The macro works fine. Or at least it seems to work fine. But what happens if you run the macro again?

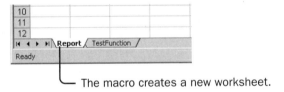

— The macro creates a new worksheet.

2   Press F5 again to run the macro a second time.

Visual Basic displays an error message informing you that you can't rename a sheet to the name of an existing sheet. The solution is simple: all you have to do is delete the old Report sheet before you rename the new one.

— As a default, a run-time error displays a dialog box like this one.

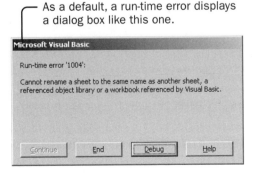

3 Click the End button to remove the error message, and then insert these two statements before the one that renames the worksheet:

```
Application.DisplayAlerts = False
Worksheets("Report").Delete
```

Turning off alert messages keeps Excel from asking whether you really want to delete the sheet.

Press F8 repeatedly to step through the macro. (If the macro steps through the Random function, stop the macro and clear the formulas from cell A3 and A4 of the Test worksheet. Then step through the macro again.) The macro creates a new worksheet, deletes the old Report worksheet, and then renames the new worksheet. Once again, the macro works fine. Or at least it seems to work fine. What happens if there's no Report worksheet in the workbook?

4 Switch to Excel, delete the Report worksheet, switch back to the Visual Basic Editor, and press F5 to run the macro.

Once again, you get an error message, this time informing you that the subscript is out of range. In other words, there's no item named Report in the Worksheets collection.

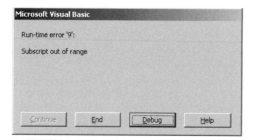

The interesting thing about this error is that you really don't care. You were just going to delete the worksheet anyway. If it already doesn't exist, so much the better.

5 Click the End button to clear the error message, and insert this statement above the one that deletes the worksheet:

```
On Error Resume Next
```

This statement tells Visual Basic to ignore any run-time errors and simply continue with the next statement.

6 Press F5 to test the macro. Test it again now that the Report worksheet exists.

Finally the macro seems to work properly. Some errors deserve to be ignored.

Ignore an Error Safely

When you use an On Error Resume Next statement, Visual Basic ignores all run-time errors until you turn error checking back on or until Visual Basic gets to an End Sub or End Function statement. When you tell Visual Basic to ignore errors, you should be careful that you don't ignore errors you didn't mean to ignore.

1 In the MakeReport macro you created in the previous section, remove the quotation marks from around the word *"Report"* in the statement that gives the worksheet a new name.

Extend Excel and Visual Basic 8

Removing these quotation marks creates a run-time error. The revised, erroneous statement should now look like this:

```
mySheet.Name = Report
```

Important

If the statement *Option Explicit* appears at the top of the module, delete it.

2 Press F5 to test the macro.

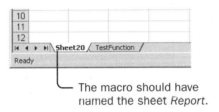

The macro should have named the sheet *Report*.

The macro appeared to run just fine, but you don't have a Report worksheet when you're done. Visual Basic interpreted the word *Report*, without the quotation marks, as a new (empty) variable and was unable to assign that empty name to the worksheet. Unfortunately, because you told Visual Basic to ignore errors, it didn't even warn you of a problem. (Of course, if you had inserted Option Explicit at the top of the module, Visual Basic would have complained about using an undefined variable.)

The best way to ignore errors for just one or two statements is to put the statements into a Sub procedure of their own. When Visual Basic gets to an End Sub or End Function statement, it cancels the effect of the On Error Resume Next statement.

3 Create a new Sub procedure named DeleteSheet. When you're finished, this procedure will quietly delete the Report worksheet if it exists.

4 Move the three statements that delete the worksheet into the DeleteSheet macro. The new macro should look like this:

```
Sub DeleteSheet()
    Application.DisplayAlerts = False
    On Error Resume Next
    Worksheets("Report").Delete
End Sub
```

The On Error Resume Next statement loses its effect at the End Sub statement, so you just ignore a possible error in the single Delete statement. This is a much safer way to ignore a run-time error.

5 In the MakeReport macro, type **DeleteSheet** where the three statements had been. The revised MakeReport macro (still containing the error) should look like this:

```
Sub MakeReport()
    Dim mySheet As Worksheet
    Set mySheet = Worksheets.Add
    DeleteSheet
    mySheet.Name = Report
End Sub
```

The MakeReport macro no longer contains an On Error Resume Next statement, so Visual Basic should be able to alert you to the error.

173

6 Press F5 to run the macro, and click the End button to close the error box.

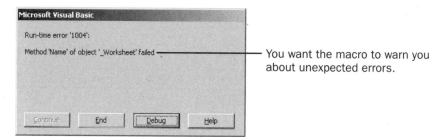

You want the macro to warn you about unexpected errors.

7 Replace the quotation marks around the sheet name in the last line of the MakeReport macro, and test the macro when the report file exists as well as when it doesn't.

This time, the macro really does work properly. It ignores the error you want to ignore and warns you of other, inadvertent errors.

Generalize the DeleteSheet Routine

The DeleteSheet macro you created in the previous section quietly deletes the Report worksheet if it happens to exist. Unfortunately, it deletes only the Report worksheet. What if you sometimes need to delete a sheet named Report and other times need to delete a sheet named Analysis? This DeleteSheet macro has too much potential to limit it to deleting only one specific sheet. You can add an argument to generalize the DeleteSheet routine, in much the same way that you added an argument to the Random function earlier in this chapter.

1 Type **SheetName** as an argument name between the parentheses after the DeleteSheet macro name.

2 Replace *"Report"* with **SheetName** in the body of the DeleteSheet macro. *SheetName* shouldn't have quotation marks around it.

3 Type **"Report"** after *DeleteSheet* in the MakeReport macro. Here's what the two revised macros should look like:

```
Sub MakeReport()
    Dim mySheet As Worksheet
    Set mySheet = Worksheets.Add
    DeleteSheet "Report"
    mySheet.Name = "Report"
End Sub

Sub DeleteSheet(SheetName)
    Application.DisplayAlerts = False
    On Error Resume Next
    Worksheets(SheetName).Delete
End Sub
```

The DeleteSheet macro now knows absolutely nothing about the name of the sheet it will delete. It will simply delete whatever sheet it's given, without asking any questions and without complaining if it discovers its services aren't really needed.

4 Press F5 to test the MakeReport macro.

5 Create a new macro named MakeAnalysis. Make it an exact copy of the MakeReport macro, except have it create a sheet named Analysis. The macro should look like this:

```
Sub MakeAnalysis()
    Dim mySheet As Worksheet
    Set mySheet = Worksheets.Add
    DeleteSheet "Analysis"
    mySheet.Name = "Analysis"
End Sub
```

6 Test the MakeAnalysis macro.

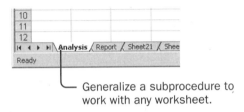

Generalize a subprocedure to work with any worksheet.

The DeleteSheet macro now not only avoids the inconveniences associated with deleting a worksheet but is also a generalized tool—an enhancement to the built-in capabilities of Excel—that you can use from any macro you want.

Check for an Error

When you use the On Error Resume Next statement in a macro, Visual Basic allows you to do more than merely ignore the error. Visual Basic contains a special debugging object named *Err*. The Err object has properties that you can check to see whether an error has occurred and, if so, what the error is.

Suppose that you want to create a Report worksheet but you don't want to delete any existing Report sheets. Instead, you want to add a suffix to the worksheet name, much as Excel does when you add a new worksheet. The Chapter08 workbook includes a macro named MakeNextReport. This macro creates a sheet named Report1. Here's the original MakeNextReport macro:

```
Sub MakeNextReport()
    Dim mySheet As Worksheet
    Dim myBase As String
    Dim mySuffix As Integer

    Set mySheet = Worksheets.Add
    myBase = "Report"
    mySuffix = 1

    On Error Resume Next
    mySheet.Name = myBase & mySuffix
End Sub
```

This macro creates a new worksheet and then tries to name it using *Report* as the base name and *1* as the suffix. The On Error Resume Next statement tells Visual Basic not to stop if Excel is unable to rename the sheet.

1 Go to the MakeNextReport macro, and then press F8 repeatedly to watch the macro work.

The new worksheet should rename properly.

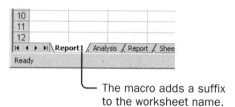

— The macro adds a suffix
to the worksheet name.

2 Step through the macro a second time.

The second time, the macro quietly fails, leaving the new sheet with the wrong name.

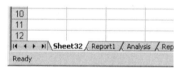

It would be nice if this macro were smart enough to increment the suffix if the initial rename fails. While a macro is ignoring errors, the Number property of the Err object is the key to knowing whether a statement failed.

3 Add the following statements immediately before the End Sub statement:

```
If Err.Number <> 0 Then
    mySuffix = mySuffix + 1
    mySheet.Name = myBase & mySuffix
End If
```

The If statement checks to see whether the error number is something other than 0. A nonzero error number indicates that a statement failed. If a statement failed—that is, if the statement that attempted to rename the sheet failed—the macro increments the suffix and tries again.

4 Step through the macro.

The code detects the failed rename and tries again, successfully renaming the sheet to Report2. If you run the macro again, however, it silently fails.

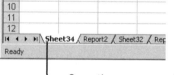

— Sometimes you need to check
for more than one error.

It would be nice if this macro were smart enough to keep incrementing the suffix until it finds one that works. That sounds like a job for a loop structure, and since you can't know when the loop begins or how many times you'll have to repeat the loop, you should use a Do loop.

5 Replace the word *If* with **Do Until**, remove the word *Then* at the end of the statement, and change the not-equal sign (<>) to an equal sign (=). Then change *End If* to **Loop**. The last few lines of the macro should look like this:

```
On Error Resume Next
mySheet.Name = myBase & mySuffix
Do Until Err.Number = 0
    mySuffix = mySuffix + 1
    mySheet.Name = myBase & mySuffix
Loop
```

The loop checks to see whether the rename occurred successfully. If not, the loop increments the suffix, tries the rename again, and checks again until there's no error—at least, that's what you want it to do.

6 Press F8 repeatedly to step through the macro. The first time the macro tries to name the report sheet, it fails because Report1 already exists. As a result, the macro proceeds into the loop. At the end of the loop, the macro tries again to rename the sheet but fails again because Report2 already exists, so the macro reenters the loop a second time. At the end of the loop, the macro tries a third time to rename the sheet. This time the sheet renames properly.

7 Keep stepping through the macro. Something's wrong. The macro goes into the loop again, renaming the sheet as Report4 and then as Report5. This renaming could go on forever.

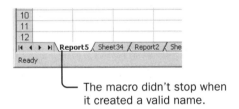

The macro didn't stop when it created a valid name.

The macro doesn't realize that the error is over. The value of Err.Number didn't automatically change back to 0 just because the macro successfully renamed the worksheet. You need to tell the macro that the error is no longer relevant.

Reset

8 Click the Reset button to stop the macro. Then, on the line immediately following the Do statement, type the statement **Err.Clear**. Clear is the name of a method for the Err object. Clear resets the error number to 0 and makes Visual Basic forget that an error ever occurred.

Important

Some macro statements change the Err.Number value back to 0 when they complete successfully. Others don't. To be safe, you should clear the Err object before a statement that you want to check and then inspect the value of Err.Number immediately after that statement executes.

9 Press F5 to test the macro. Test it again. And again. The macro is now able to create a new report sheet, incrementing as much as necessary—but no more!

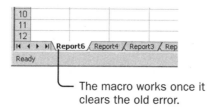

The macro works once it clears the old error.

Checking the value of Err.Number is meaningful only after you use an On Error Resume Next statement. Errors that occur above the On Error Resume Next statement cause Visual Basic to halt the macro with an error message box. Looking at the properties of the Err object is a good way to gain control over the way your macro handles errors.

Trap an Error

So far, you've seen three ways to handle a run-time error: you can let Visual Basic display a standard error dialog box, you can ignore the error altogether, or you can check for a nonzero error number after each statement.

Having Visual Basic display an error message might not be a bad alternative if you're writing macros for yourself, but if you want to give a macro to someone else, you'll probably want more control over what the error message says. You should ignore errors only in special circumstances. Checking for a nonzero error value after every statement, however, can make your macros hard to read. Fortunately, Visual Basic can monitor the error value for you in a process called *trapping* an error.

Suppose, for example, that you had a macro that opens, prints, and closes several workbooks. It's possible that one of the workbooks might be missing when the macro runs. The Chapter08 workbook contains a macro named CheckFiles that opens and closes several of the practice workbooks that came with this book. (In the interest of conserving trees, the macro doesn't actually print the workbooks.)

One of the workbook file names has been misspelled. Here's the original macro:

```
Sub CheckFiles()
    Workbooks.Open "Graphics"
    ActiveWorkbook.Close
    Workbooks.Open "Ranges"
    ActiveWorkbook.Close
    Workbooks.Open "Bad File Name"
    ActiveWorkbook.Close
    Workbooks.Open "Budget"
    ActiveWorkbook.Close
End Sub
```

Naturally, you can't tell which of the files won't be found until the macro actually runs. If you run this macro, you'll see the standard Visual Basic error message. If necessary, click the End button to close the dialog box.

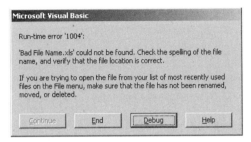

Here are the steps you follow to add special code that Visual Basic will run whenever an error occurs.

1 At the end of the macro, type the statement **ErrorHandler:** just before the End Sub statement. The statement ErrorHandler: is called a *label*. A label consists of a single word followed by a colon. (You can indent the label if you want, but you might prefer to keep it lined up with the Sub and End Sub statements because it behaves like an appendix to the macro.) A label must always end with a colon.

Tip

You can use any name you want for a label within the macro. You might want to always use the same name, such as ErrorHandler, as the error label in all your macros. That makes it easy to copy error-handling code from one macro to another.

2 After the error-handler label, type the statement **MsgBox Err.Number**. The statements below the label are the ones that the macro executes when it detects an error. These statements are called an *error handler*. The simplest error handler is a message box that displays the number of the error.

3 Immediately before the error-handler label, type the statement **Exit Sub**. You don't want the statements in the error handler to execute if the macro completes normally. If the macro gets to the Exit Sub statement, no error was detected.

4 At the top of the macro, just under the Sub statement, type the statement **On Error GoTo ErrorHandler**. This statement tells Visual Basic that if it sees a run-time error, it should drop whatever it's doing and jump immediately to the label you specify. You don't put a colon after the label name here. You use a colon only when you create the actual label.

5 Press F5 to test the macro.

Visual Basic should display a simple message box showing only the message number. Click OK to close the message box.

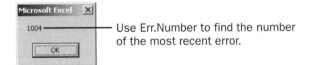

Use Err.Number to find the number of the most recent error.

You can make the message more elaborate. The Err object has a Description property that gives a longer text description of the error. That description is often a useful addition to an error message box. You can even add to the description with text of your own.

6 Delete the statement *MsgBox Err.Number,* and replace it with this statement:

```
MsgBox "Please notify Reed Jacobson of error " _
    & Err.Number & vbCrLf & vbCrLf _
    & Err.Description
```

You can string many pieces of text together to form an error message. Just put an ampersand between each piece. The word *vbCrLf* is a built-in Visual Basic constant that means "Carriage Return/Line Feed." Carriage Return/Line Feed is an archaic computer term for a new line and was often abbreviated as CRLF. You can put vbCrLf into a string anytime you want to force the message to go to a new line. (When you create your own macros, please substitute your name in the error message. Thanks.)

7 Press F5 to run the macro and see the more elaborate error message.

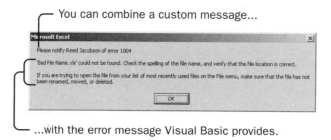

You can combine a custom message...

...with the error message Visual Basic provides.

The finished macro should look like this:

```
Sub CheckFiles()
    On Error GoTo ErrorHandler
    Workbooks.Open "Graphics"
    ActiveWorkbook.Close
    Workbooks.Open "Ranges"
    ActiveWorkbook.Close
    Workbooks.Open "Bad File Name"
    ActiveWorkbook.Close
    Workbooks.Open "Budget"
    ActiveWorkbook.Close
    Exit Sub
ErrorHandler:
    MsgBox "Please notify Reed Jacobson of error " _
        & Err.Number & vbCrLf & vbCrLf _
        & Err.Description
End Sub
```

If you're creating an application for someone else to use and you don't want that person ever to see the Visual Basic default error dialog box, you should always include an error handler in every macro that the user launches directly. If you have some statements for which the error should be handled differently—either ignored or checked on a statement-by-statement basis—put those statements into a separate procedure and use an On Error Resume Next statement within that procedure. Visual Basic automatically restores the error handler when the procedure ends.

Errors are a frustrating but inevitable part of life when working with computers—that's especially the case when the human error factor compounds the likelihood of other types of errors. Of course, not all errors are equal. Some are serious, some are trivial, and some are even useful. It's fortunate that Visual Basic provides flexible tools for dealing with all kinds of errors.

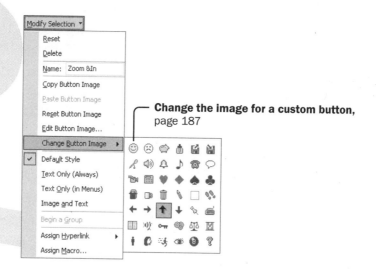

Change the image for a custom button,
page 187

Convert a toolbar button into a menu command,
page 188

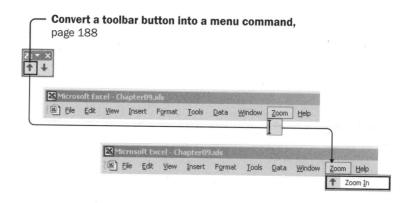

Run a macro when the user changes the selection,
page 202

Chapter 9
Launch Macros with Events

After completing this chapter, you will be able to:

✔ **Create custom toolbar buttons.**

✔ **Create custom menu commands.**

✔ **Create custom command buttons.**

✔ **Create worksheet and workbook event handlers.**

My grandmother used to embroider names on outfits for us with her sewing machine. She had a powerful old sewing machine, with lots of pulleys, levers, and loops. When she changed the thread, she had to poke the new thread up, over, and through countless turns, spools, and guides, before even getting to the needle. I still don't know how she managed embroidering the names. She'd move levers and twist the fabric, and the names somehow appeared. She was very good, and the results were beautiful. Few people could create embroidered names the way she did.

Now even I can embroider names onto clothes. I flip the thread around a couple of guides and the machine is threaded. I type in the name, select the lettering style, and push another button to embroider the name. The machine sews in all directions so I don't even have to turn the fabric. Anyone can use a sewing machine these days.

One purpose of macros is to make your own life simpler. An even more important purpose might be to enable others to accomplish tasks that they wouldn't be able to do without your help. In this chapter and the chapters that follow, you'll learn how to make macros easy for others to use.

Events.xls

This chapter uses the practice file Events.xls that you installed from the book's CD-ROM. For details about installing the practice files, see "Using the Book's CD-ROM" at the beginning of this book.

Getting Started

1 Start Microsoft Excel, and change to the folder that contains the practice files for this book.

2 Open the Events workbook, and save a copy as **Chapter09**.

Creating Custom Toolbars and Menus

You might feel perfectly comfortable running a macro by pressing a shortcut key combination or even pressing F5 in the Microsoft Visual Basic Editor. But if you're going to give a macro to somebody else, you want to make it as easy to run as possible. One way to make a macro easy to run is to integrate it into the Excel environment. You can initiate most built-in commands by choosing a menu command or clicking a toolbar button. By adding your macros to menus and toolbars, you can make your macros seem as if they're integral parts of Excel.

Try the ZoomIn and ZoomOut Macros

The Chapter09 workbook already contains two simple macros, ZoomIn and ZoomOut. They are macros that you'll assign to custom toolbar buttons and menu commands. Here are the macros:

```
Sub ZoomIn()
    Dim myZoom As Integer
    myZoom = ActiveWindow.Zoom + 10
    If myZoom <= 400 Then
        ActiveWindow.Zoom = myZoom
    End If
End Sub

Sub ZoomOut()
    Dim myZoom As Integer
    myZoom = ActiveWindow.Zoom - 10
    If myZoom >= 10 Then
        ActiveWindow.Zoom = myZoom
    End If
End Sub
```

Each macro considers a new value for the Zoom property of the active window. If the new value is within the acceptable limits (between 10% and 400%, the range of zoom factors in Excel), it changes the property; otherwise it does nothing.

1 In the Visual Basic toolbar, click the Run Macro button. Select ZoomIn and click Edit.

2 Press F5 a few times to see how the worksheet zooms in. Step through the macro if you want, to become comfortable with how it works.

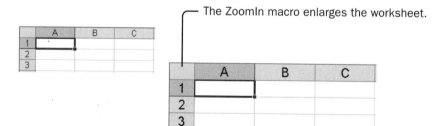

The ZoomIn macro enlarges the worksheet.

3 Go to the ZoomOut macro. Press F5 as necessary to return the window to the normal zoom level.

These are "typical" macros. In this chapter, you'll learn new ways to run them.

Create a Custom Toolbar

A toolbar button is a convenient way to launch a macro. A toolbar is small and easy to show or hide. An icon can make a toolbar button easy to find, and a ToolTip can make an icon easy to remember.

1 Activate the Excel window, right-click any toolbar, and click the Customize command.

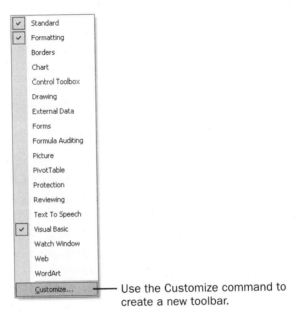

— Use the Customize command to create a new toolbar.

2 In the Customize dialog box, click the Toolbars tab.

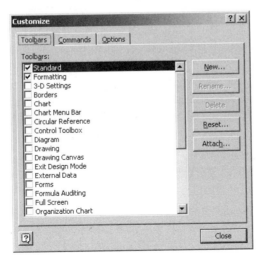

3 Click the New button, type **Zoom** as the name for the toolbar, and then click OK.

A new, empty toolbar appears. The Customize dialog box is still open and available to help you fill the toolbar.

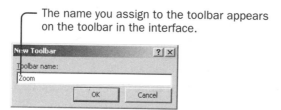

The name you assign to the toolbar appears on the toolbar in the interface.

4 Click the Commands tab in the Customize dialog box, and select Macros from the Categories list.

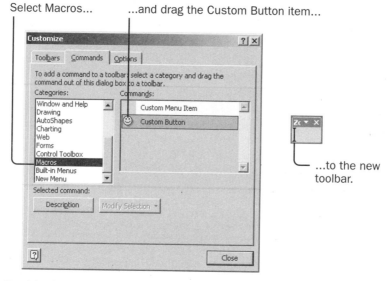

Select Macros...   ...and drag the Custom Button item...

...to the new toolbar.

5 Drag the Custom Button item (complete with its happy face) from the Commands list onto the Zoom toolbar.

When you drag the item onto the toolbar, the Modify Selection button becomes available in the Customize dialog box.

6 Click the Modify Selection button, press N to select the Name box, and type **Zoom &In** as the new name. Don't press the Enter key.

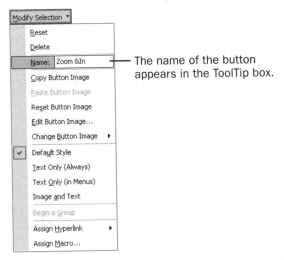

The name of the button appears in the ToolTip box.

The value in the Name box determines what the ToolTip for the toolbar button will display. The ampersand (&) precedes the letter that will be underlined if you use this command on a menu. The ampersand has no effect on the toolbar button, but put it there anyway.

7 Click the Change Button Image command, and click the Up Arrow icon.

The icon on the button changes, and the menu disappears.

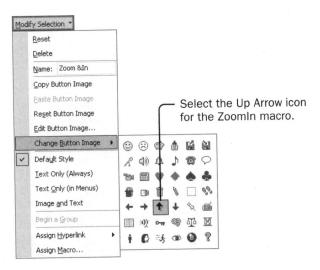

Select the Up Arrow icon for the ZoomIn macro.

Tip

If the menu disappeared before you could click the Change Button Image command, click the Modify Selection button again to redisplay the menu.

8 Click the Modify Selection button, and click the Assign Macro command. Select the ZoomIn macro, and then click OK.

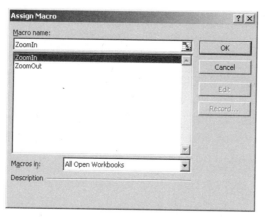

9 Repeat steps 4 through 8, but this time give the button the name **Zoom &Out**, select the Down Arrow icon, and assign the ZoomOut macro to the button.

10 Click the Close button in the Customize dialog box, and then try the toolbar buttons. Hold the mouse over the button to see the ToolTip appear. Hide and redisplay the toolbar.

Zoom In —— The custom button displays a ToolTip, just as a built-in button does.

Once you have a macro, it's easy to assign it to a toolbar button. Use the Customize dialog box to create and add buttons to the toolbar. Use the Modify Selection button to change the name, icon, and macro for a button.

Create a Custom Menu

A menu command is another convenient way to launch a macro. A menu command stays out of the way, reducing clutter on the desktop. The menu it belongs to, however, is always available, whereas a toolbar can be temporarily hidden.

In Microsoft Office XP, a menu is really just a specialized toolbar, which means that adding a command to a menu is just as easy as adding a command to a toolbar.

1 Right-click any toolbar, and click the Customize command to display the Customize dialog box.

2 If you don't see the Zoom toolbar, try moving the Customize dialog box out of the way. Click the Commands tab, and select New Menu from the Categories list.

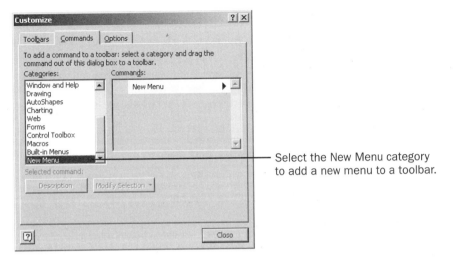

Select the New Menu category
to add a new menu to a toolbar.

The New Menu category has only a single item: New Menu. You can use this item to create a new menu on a menu bar or a new submenu on an existing menu. You can even add a menu to a toolbar.

3 Drag the New Menu item up to the Excel menu bar, dropping it between the Window and Help menus.

The new menu appears
in the Excel menu bar.

4 Click the Modify Selection button, change the value in the Name box to **&Zoom**, and press the Enter key.

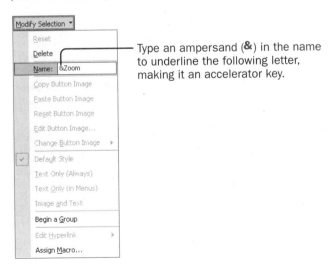

Type an ampersand (**&**) in the name
to underline the following letter,
making it an accelerator key.

If you look closely at the Zoom menu, you can see that the letter *Z* is underlined. That's because there's an ampersand (&) in front of the *Z* in the menu item name. The underlined letter, which lets you execute the command by pressing the Alt key followed by that letter, is called an *access key* or an *accelerator key*.

You could add brand new commands to the Zoom menu, but since you already have the toolbar buttons on the Zoom toolbar, you can copy them to the Zoom menu. (You should put commands on both a toolbar and a menu bar, giving a user the choice of which to use.)

5 Drag the Zoom In toolbar button (the one with the Up Arrow icon) up to the Zoom menu. A small, blank menu appears. Drag the button onto the menu, and then press and hold the Ctrl key as you release the mouse button.

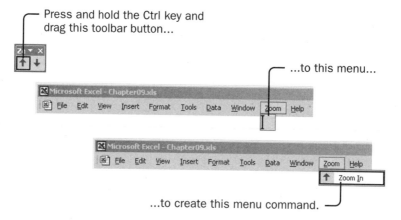

Press and hold the Ctrl key and drag this toolbar button...

...to this menu...

...to create this menu command.

Tip

When copying a toolbar button, be careful not to release the mouse button too soon. If you don't press and hold the Ctrl key when you release the mouse button, you'll move the toolbar button rather than make a copy. If you do accidentally move the button, simply press and hold the Ctrl key as you drag it back from the menu to the toolbar.

The command name for the new menu item is the same as the ToolTip for the toolbar button. The command name has the letter *I* underlined because you had the foresight to add the ampersand when you created the button in the "Create a Custom Toolbar" section earlier in this chapter. When you add a name to a toolbar button, insert an ampersand in front of the letter that you would want underlined if you were to move the button to a menu.

6 Drag the Zoom Out toolbar button up to the Zoom menu, and press and hold the Ctrl key as you release the mouse.

7 Close the Customize dialog box, and try the menu commands. Test them using the keyboard shortcuts. Press Alt, Z, I, and Alt, Z, O to make sure the accelerator keys work properly.

When you add a command to a toolbar, you can easily copy it to a menu. Or if you add a command to a menu, you can easily copy it to a toolbar. The general term that includes both toolbars and menus is *command bar.* The Customize dialog box for command bars makes moving between toolbars and menus delightfully simple.

Run Macros from a Closed Workbook

Normally, you can run a macro only when the workbook that contains the macro is open. Toolbar buttons and menu commands, however, have a unique capability: they remember where to find a macro, even when that macro's workbook is closed.

New

1   Save and close the Chapter09 workbook. Click the New button to create a new workbook.

2   Click the Zoom In toolbar button on the Zoom toolbar.

The Chapter09 workbook automatically opens and hides behind the active workbook, and the macro runs. Depending on your macro security setting and whether you have signed the workbook, you might be prompted for permission to enable macros.

3   Close the temporary workbook that you created.

This will reveal the Chapter09 workbook.

Remove Menus and Toolbars

Toolbar buttons and menu commands customize a user's workspace. Once you create a custom menu or toolbar, it remains a part of Excel on that computer until you remove it. Since you probably won't be using the Zoom toolbar or menu on an ongoing basis, you should remove them now. Here's how:

1   Right-click any toolbar, and click Customize to show the Customize dialog box.

2   Click the Toolbars tab, select the Zoom toolbar in the list, click the Delete button, and then click OK.

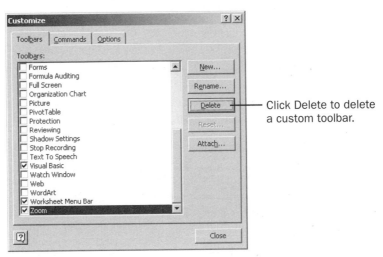

Click Delete to delete a custom toolbar.

3   Click the Zoom menu, press and hold the mouse button, and drag the menu off the menu bar and onto the Excel worksheet.

The menu permanently disappears.

While the Customize dialog box is visible, drag the menu off the menu bar to delete the menu.

4 Click the Close button in the Customize dialog box.

Toolbar buttons and menu commands are effective tools for customizing a user's copy of Excel. They remain available and active even when you close the workbook containing the macros they're attached to. Sometimes, however, you might want to give someone a button that's available only when a specific workbook is open. A command button works like that.

Creating Custom Command Buttons

Toolbar buttons and menu commands respond to a single event: a click. You tell the button or command which macro to run by using the Assign Macro command. Command buttons, on the other hand, not only can trigger an event when you click them, but also can respond to additional events, such as the simple movement of the mouse above the button. Because command buttons can respond to a complex set of events, they require a whole new way of linking a macro to the button. This new approach uses what are called *event handler procedures*. Event handler procedures are special macros that are linked to an object such as a command button. First create a command button, and then you can see how to add event handler procedures to make it work.

Create a Custom Command Button

A command button is useful for running macros that relate to a specific worksheet. Command buttons are usually large and easy to click, with a label describing what the button does.

Control Toolbox

1 With the Chapter09 workbook open, click the Control Toolbox button on the Visual Basic toolbar to display the Control Toolbox toolbar.

The Control Toolbox toolbar

The Control Toolbox is a toolbar that contains a number of controls that you can use on a worksheet or on a form. These controls are called *ActiveX controls*. An ActiveX control is a special kind of drawing object that carries out an action when you click it. The ActiveX control we'll work with in this chapter is the command button control.

Command Button

2 Click the Command Button button, and drag a rectangle on the worksheet from the upper left corner of cell A1 to the lower right corner of cell B2.

A command button appears on the worksheet. It has white handles on the edges, showing that it is currently selected.

	A	B	C
1	CommandButton1		
2			
3			

Tip

You can easily "snap" any drawing object to align with the corners of a cell by pressing the Alt key as you drag a rectangle for the object. You can also press and hold the Alt key to snap to cell gridlines as you move or resize an existing drawing object.

While the command button is selected, you can change its properties. As you're aware, you can use Visual Basic statements to change the properties of objects. ActiveX controls also have a special Properties window that allows you to change properties interactively.

Properties

3   On the Control Toolbox toolbar, click the Properties button.

The Properties window appears. The box at the top shows you which object's properties are being displayed. In this case, it's CommandButton1, which is a CommandButton object.

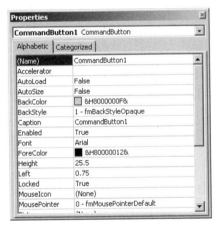

The Properties window shows various properties of the command button. One important property of the command button is its name. This property appears as *(Name)* in the Properties window. (The parentheses make the Name property sort to the top of the list.) The Name property affects how you use the button in your macros.

4   Replace the default value of the Name property with **btnZoomIn**.

You can't put spaces into the name. Many people use three-letter prefixes when naming controls. The three-letter prefix helps identify what kind of control it is; in this case, *btn* stands for *button*.

Type a new name for
the control here.

Changing the name of the button doesn't change the label displayed on it, however. That's
the function of the Caption property.

5   Replace the default value of the Caption property with **Zoom In**.

The caption on the button changes as soon as you change the Caption property. With
ActiveX controls, you don't use an ampersand to specify the accelerator key; instead,
there's a separate Accelerator property for that purpose.

Change the caption here...

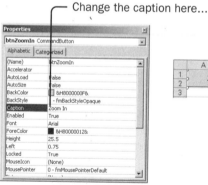
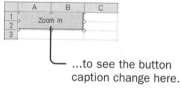

...to see the button
caption change here.

6   For this button, the letter *I* would make a good accelerator key. Type **I** as the value of the
Accelerator property.

As soon as you assign *I* to the Accelerator property, the letter *I* in the caption becomes
underlined.

The letter you type here will be underlined in the caption.

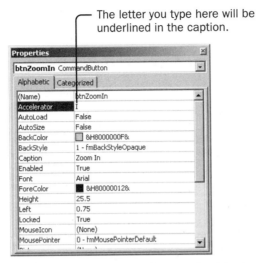

There's one more property that you should set when you create a custom command button. It controls how the command button interacts with the active cell in Excel. Suppose cell B4 is the active cell when you click the command button. You'd normally expect cell B4 to be the active cell even after clicking the button (unless the button runs a macro that changes the active cell). But the default behavior of a command button is to remove the dark border around the active cell, making it impossible to see which cell is active.

7 Scroll down to the TakeFocusOnClick property, and change it to *False* in the resulting drop-down list. (TakeFocusOnClick is a complicated name for a simple property. Setting it to *False* simply means, "Leave the active cell alone when you click this button.")

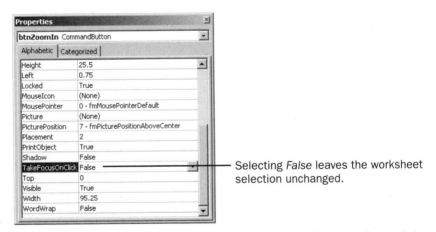

Selecting *False* leaves the worksheet selection unchanged.

You've now created and customized the command button. All that's left is to link it to a macro and make it run.

Link a Command Button to a Macro

You don't assign a macro to a command button. Instead, you create a macro with a special name, in a special place, and the macro automatically links to the button. Fortunately, the Control Toolbox has a button that will do all the work of naming the macro for you.

View Code

1 With the command button still selected, click the View Code button.

The first part of the name matches the object name.

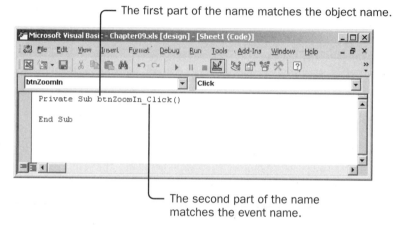

The second part of the name matches the event name.

The Visual Basic Editor window appears with a new macro. The word *Private* before the macro name means that this macro won't appear in the Run Macro dialog box. The macro name is btnZoomIn_Click. The name is important. The part of the name that precedes the underscore matches the name of the command button. The part of the name that follows the underscore matches the name of the event that this macro will handle. In this example, the macro runs whenever you click the button. A macro linked to an event like this is called an *event handler*.

Important

The word *procedure* is a more technical synonym for a macro. Excel uses the word *macro* because *macro recorder* is less intimidating than *procedure recorder*. In general, this book uses *macro* to refer to those procedures that you can run from the Macro dialog box and *procedure* to refer to functions and event handlers.

You could copy the code from the ZoomIn macro into the btnZoomIn_Click procedure, but it's easier simply to run that macro (since it already exists) from this one.

2 Type **ZoomIn** as the body of the procedure to make the procedure appear as follows:

```
Private Sub btnZoomIn_Click
    ZoomIn
End Sub
```

You're now ready to try clicking the button.

3 Switch back to Excel, click in any cell in the worksheet to deselect the button, and then click the button. The procedure doesn't run. You simply reselected the button.

You need some way of letting Excel know whether clicking an ActiveX control should run the event handler or simply select the control. You do that by controlling *design mode*.

When Excel is in design mode, clicking a control selects it. When Excel isn't in design mode (a condition called *run mode*), clicking a control runs the event handler procedure. Whenever you put an ActiveX control on a worksheet, Excel automatically switches to design mode.

Exit Design Mode

4 Click the Exit Design Mode button. The selection handles disappear from the command button.

5 Try the button: click it. Press Alt+I to try the accelerator key.

Design Mode

6 Click the Design Mode button to turn design mode back on, and click the command button. The command button becomes selected.

Attaching an event handler procedure to a control is different than attaching a macro to a toolbar button.

■ With a toolbar button, you can name the macro whatever you want and then use the Assign Macro dialog box to link the macro to the button. With an event handler, the combination of the name and the location of the procedure is what creates the link to the control.

■ With a toolbar button, you make Excel ignore events by opening the Customize dialog box. With a control, you do this by clicking the Design Mode button.

Create an Event Handler on Your Own

While you can create an event handler for a control by clicking the View Code button, you might find it enlightening to see how you can also create an event handler directly in the Visual Basic Editor.

1 Create a Zoom Out command button by roughly following steps 2 through 7 of the section "Create a Custom Command Button," as follows: Drag a rectangle on the worksheet from the upper left corner of cell A3 to the lower right corner of cell B4. In the Properties window, give it the name **btnZoomOut**, give it the caption **Zoom Out**, and assign the letter **o** as its accelerator. Also, set the TakeFocusOnClick property to *False*. Don't click the View Code button.

2 Switch to the Visual Basic Editor, and click anywhere in the btnZoomIn_Click procedure.

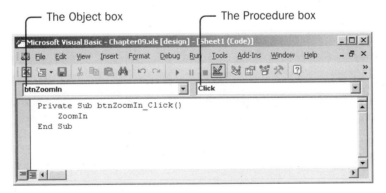

Above the code portion of the window are two boxes. The box on the left contains the first half of the procedure name (btnZoomIn), and the box on the right contains the second half of the procedure name (Click). These two boxes are named Object and Procedure, respectively.

3 Click the arrow next to the Object list.

The list shows all the objects related to the current worksheet that can have event handlers. In this case, they are btnZoomIn, btnZoomOut, and Worksheet.

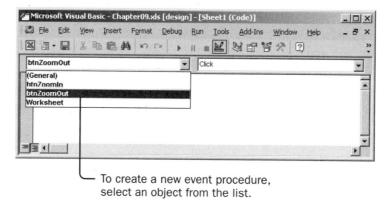

To create a new event procedure,
select an object from the list.

4 Select btnZoomOut from the list.

A new procedure appears. Click is the default event for a button, so the new procedure is named btnZoomOut_Click, which is precisely what you need.

5 Type **ZoomOut** as the body of the procedure.

6 Switch to Excel, turn off design mode, and try both buttons.

The lists at the top of the code window can help you build event handlers by combining an object name with an event name.

Make a Button Respond to Mouse Movements

The command button can recognize several different events. Three of the most useful events are a click (the Click event), a double-click (the DblClick event), and a mouse movement (the MouseMove event). The MouseMove event is especially fun to write an event handler for because it provides information to the procedure in the form of arguments.

1 In the Visual Basic Editor, select btnZoomOut from the Object list and then select Mouse-Move from the Procedure list.

Select the MouseMove event...

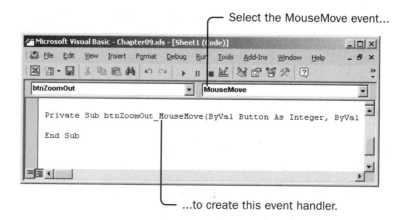

...to create this event handler.

The declaration for the new procedure is relatively long. This is what it looks like when divided into shorter lines:

```
Private Sub btnZoomOut_MouseMove( _
    ByVal Button As Integer, _
    ByVal Shift As Integer, _
    ByVal X As Single, _
    ByVal Y As Single)
```

This event handler procedure has four arguments: *Button, Shift, X,* and *Y.* (The word *byVal* means that Excel will ignore any changes the procedure makes to an argument.) The arguments communicate information to you that you can take advantage of as you write the macro. The *Button* argument indicates whether a mouse button is down as the mouse moves. The *Shift* argument indicates whether the Shift, Ctrl, or Alt key is pressed. The *X* and *Y* arguments indicate the horizontal and vertical position of the mouse.

2 Insert **ZoomOut** as the body of the new procedure, switch to Excel, and move the mouse over the Zoom Out button. (You don't even have to click. Just moving the mouse over the button causes the procedure to run. Events can happen quickly.)

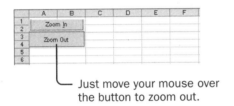

— Just move your mouse over
the button to zoom out.

You can use the arguments that the MouseMove event provides you to control the procedure. Specifically, if the value of the *Shift* argument is equal to 1, the Shift key is down. If the value of the *Shift* argument is equal to 2, the Ctrl key is down. If the value of the *Shift* argument is 3, both the Shift and Ctrl keys are down. You can change the procedure so that it zooms in when the Shift key is down and zooms out when the Ctrl key is down.

3 Replace the body of the btnZoomOut_MouseMove procedure with these statements:

```
If Shift = 1 Then
    ZoomIn
ElseIf Shift = 2 Then
    ZoomOut
End If
```

Tip

The ElseIf keyword allows you to combine Else and If statements into a single statement.

4 Switch to Excel, and try the event handler. Try moving the mouse by itself. Then try pressing and holding the Shift key as you move the mouse. Then try pressing and holding the Ctrl key as you move the mouse.

As you move the mouse over the button, you can practically see the procedure running over and over. Each time the button detects the mouse moving, it triggers another event and the event handler procedure runs again. Event handler procedures can be a powerful way to make things happen.

Explore the Visual Basic Project

You might wonder where all these event handlers are stored and how they relate to the macros that you create with the macro recorder. When you use the macro recorder to create a macro, the macro is stored in a module. You can have multiple macros in a single module, and you can have multiple modules in a workbook. (Each time you close and reopen a workbook, the macro recorder creates a new module for any new macros you record.) Event handler procedures for a command button are attached to the worksheet that contains that button. Visual Basic refers to all the code in a single workbook—whether the code is in a module or attached to a worksheet—as a *project*. The Visual Basic Editor has a special window that allows you to explore the project.

Project Explorer

1 In the Visual Basic Editor, click the Project Explorer button.

The Project window appears. The name of the project is VBAProject, and the name of the workbook (Chapter09.xls) appears in parentheses. Procedures can be stored either on module sheets (grouped under Modules in the Project window) or attached to workbooks and worksheets (grouped under Microsoft Excel Objects in the Project window).

Associated with each worksheet is a page that contains any code for that worksheet or for objects on that worksheet. When you create a new worksheet, a new code page appears in the Project window. When you delete a worksheet, the worksheet's code page disappears.

2 Double-click the entry labeled *Module1*.

The main Visual Basic Editor window displays the macros stored in Module1.

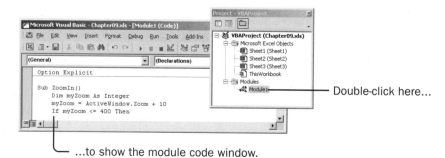

Double-click here...

...to show the module code window.

3   Double-click the entry labeled *Sheet1*.

The main Visual Basic Editor window displays the event handlers for the objects on Sheet1.

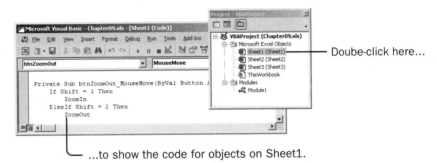

Doube-click here...

...to show the code for objects on Sheet1.

4   In Excel, drag the sheet tab for Sheet1 to the right, and then press and hold the Ctrl key as you release the mouse.

Excel creates a copy of the sheet. The copy's name is Sheet1 (2), and it has its own copy of the command buttons.

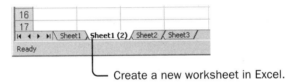

Create a new worksheet in Excel.

5   Switch to the Visual Basic Editor, and look at the Project window.

There's a new sheet in the list under Microsoft Excel Objects. The name in parentheses, Sheet1 (2), matches the name on the worksheet tab. The name in front of the parentheses, Sheet4, is a unique name that Visual Basic generates. Now that you have a sheet with Sheet4 as the internal name, if you use Insert Worksheet to create a new Sheet4, Visual Basic will give it Sheet5 as its internal name!

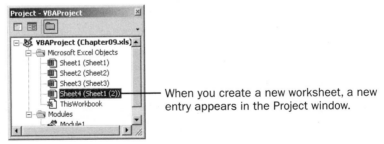

When you create a new worksheet, a new entry appears in the Project window.

6   Double-click the Sheet4 worksheet item in the Project window.

The main Visual Basic Editor window now shows the event handler procedures for the copies of the command buttons. These procedures look just like the procedures that are linked to the command buttons on Sheet1, but they're now separate entities. Even if you change the btnZoomIn_Click procedure on Sheet4, the btnZoomIn_Click procedure on Sheet1 remains unchanged.

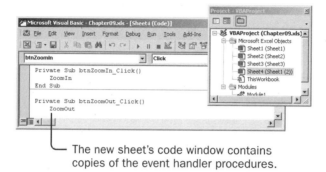

The new sheet's code window contains
copies of the event handler procedures.

7   In Excel, delete the Sheet1 (2) worksheet. Then switch back to the Visual Basic Editor
and look at the Project window.

As you probably anticipated, the entry for Sheet4 has disappeared, along with the procedures that were associated with it.

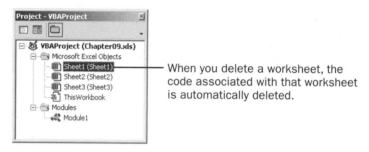

When you delete a worksheet, the
code associated with that worksheet
is automatically deleted.

Important

When you delete a worksheet that has event handler procedures associated with it, all the
procedures are destroyed with the worksheet. Save your work frequently when you write
event handlers for worksheets so that you can recover your work if you accidentally delete a
worksheet.

Handling Worksheet and Workbook Events

ActiveX controls aren't the only objects in Excel that can have events. Worksheets and
workbooks have events, too. Each of these objects has different events that it can
respond to.

Run a Procedure When the Selection Changes

1   In the Visual Basic Editor, activate the Sheet1 code window. (Activate the Project window,
and double-click Sheet1.)

2   From the Objects list, at the top left of the code window, select Worksheet.

A new procedure appears with the name Worksheet_SelectionChange. This event happens whenever you change the selection on the worksheet. It doesn't matter whether you
click in a cell or use the arrow keys to move around; the event happens either way.

A Worksheet object can respond to events.

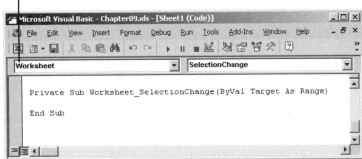

Just to see what events are available for a worksheet, click the arrow next to the Procedure list, at the upper right of the code window. The list shows the nine events that a worksheet can respond to. SelectionChange is the default event for a worksheet, just as Click is the default event for a command button.

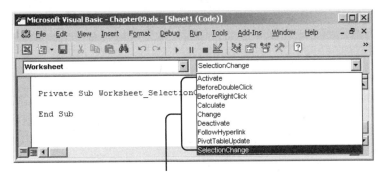

This list shows the available events
for the Worksheet object.

3 Press the Esc key to close the list of events, and enter these statements as the body of the Worksheet_SelectionChange procedure:

```
If ActiveCell.Interior.Color = vbCyan Then
    Selection.Interior.Color = vbYellow
Else
    Selection.Interior.Color = vbCyan
End If
```

Cyan is the Visual Basic name for the color labeled *Turquoise* in the Excel color palette. The procedure now changes all the selected cells to turquoise unless the active cell already happens to be turquoise.

4 Activate Sheet1 in Excel, and click in several different cells. Press arrow keys to move between cells. Drag a selection rectangle through several cells. The cell colors change each time you change which cells are selected.

	A	B	C	D	E	F	G	H
1	Zoom In							
2								
3	Zoom Out							
4								
5								
6								
7								
8								
9								
10								
11								

The event handler runs each time you change the selection.

5 Now activate Sheet2 and select a cell.

Nothing happens. The Worksheet_SelectionChange event handler is active only for the associated worksheet.

Handle an Event on Any Worksheet

When you create an event handler for the Sheet1 SelectionChange event, that handler applies only to that worksheet. If you activate Sheet2 and change the selection, nothing happens. Worksheet event handlers respond to events only on their own worksheet. To handle an event on any worksheet, you must use a workbook-level event handler.

1 In the Visual Basic Editor, activate the Project window and double-click the ThisWorkbook item.

2 From the Object list, select Workbook.

A new procedure appears with the name Workbook_Open. Open is the default event for a workbook. This is the event you'd use if you wanted to run a procedure every time you open the workbook.

A workbook can respond to events.

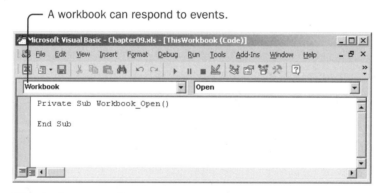

3 Click the Procedures list to see the events available for a workbook.

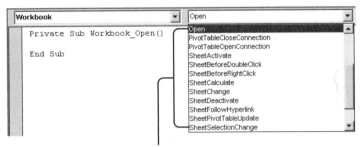

This list shows the events available for a Worksheet object.

A workbook can respond to any of 23 different events. It just so happens that 9 of the events begin with *Sheet*. These 9 workbook Sheet events correspond to the 9 events for a worksheet, except that they apply to any worksheet in the workbook, even worksheets that don't exist yet.

4 Select the SheetSelectionChange event.

This creates a new Workbook_SheetSelectionChange procedure.

5 Delete the Workbook_Open procedure. You won't need this one.

6 Type **Selection.Interior.Color = vbRed** as the body of the new procedure.

7 Switch to Excel, activate Sheet2, and click in various cells.

The cells change to red.

8 Activate Sheet1, and click in various cells.

The cells change to red. What happened to the SelectionChange event handler procedure for this sheet? It might seem that the event handler for the workbook replaces the one for an individual sheet, but that's not quite true. In fact, they both ran. The workbook one just ran last. The property for the interior color of the cell changed to blue (or yellow) and then quickly changed to red. You didn't see the intermediate color because Windows doesn't refresh the screen until the macro finishes. So all you ever see is the final color.

You can create event handler procedures for events that take place on a worksheet. You can put those event handler procedures either at the worksheet level or at the workbook level. If the procedure is at the workbook level, it handles events for all worksheets, regardless of whether a worksheet has an event handler of its own.

Suppress a Workbook Event

It might seem strange that a worksheet event handler wouldn't override a workbook event handler for the same event. In fact, having the worksheet event occur first gives you a great deal of control over how to take advantage of events.

If you want both event handlers to run, you don't have to do anything. If you want the worksheet event handler to suppress the workbook event handler, you can make the worksheet event handler tell the workbook event handler to do nothing. The way you do that is by creating a custom property at the workbook level.

1 Double-click ThisWorkbook in the Project window. At the top of the code window, enter this statement above the event handler procedure:

```
Public ProcessingEvent As Boolean
```

This declares *ProcessingEvent* as a *public* variable in ThisWorkbook. When you declare a variable above all the procedures in a module, the variable becomes visible to all the procedures in that one module and is called a *module-level* variable. If you use the word *Public* to declare a module-level variable, that variable is then visible to any procedure in the entire workbook. A public variable is essentially a simple property. Declaring the variable as Boolean means that it can be only *True* or *False*. If you don't assign something to it, it will be *False*.

2 Change the body of the Workbook_SheetSelectionChange event handler to this:

```
If ProcessingEvent = True Then
    ProcessingEvent = False
Else
    Selection.Interior.Color = vbRed
End If
```

The event handler will now change the color of the selection only if the *ProcessingEvent* variable is not *True*. If *ProcessingEvent* is *True*, the event handler changes the variable back to *False*. (If you didn't change *ProcessingEvent* back to *False*, suppressing the event handler once would disable this event handler until you close the workbook.)

3 Double-click Sheet1 in the Project window. In the Worksheet_SelectionChange event handler, type **ThisWorkbook.ProcessingEvent = True** just before the End Sub statement.

⎯ The public variable appears as a property in the list of methods and properties for the workbook.

The new ProcessingEvent property is in the list of members. It even has a standard Property icon next to it. With this statement, the worksheet event handler tells the workbook event handler not to do anything.

4 Activate Sheet1 in Excel, and change the selection.

The selection should change to yellow or blue. The worksheet event handler is suppressing the workbook event handler.

5 Activate Sheet3, and change the selection. The selection should change to red. The workbook event handler still functions properly as long as it's not suppressed by the worksheet.

Creating a simple custom property inside ThisWorkbook in the form of a public variable allows you to suppress the workbook event handler. You now have total control over which event handlers function at which time. You can have an event handler run only at the worksheet level, only at the workbook level, at both levels, or as a mixture.

Cancel an Event

Some events are made to be canceled. For example, Excel displays a shortcut menu when you right-click on a worksheet. What if you want to prevent the shortcut menu from appearing? You can create an event handler procedure that cancels that event.

Events that can be canceled all have the word *Before* in front of the event name. A worksheet has a BeforeDoubleClick event and a BeforeRightClick event. A workbook has corresponding SheetBeforeDoubleClick and SheetBeforeRightClick events, and also BeforeClose, BeforeSave, and BeforePrint events. Each event procedure that can be canceled has a *Cancel* argument. To cancel the corresponding event, assign *True* to the *Cancel* argument.

1 In the Sheet1 code window, select Worksheet from the Object list and BeforeRightClick from the Procedures list.

2 In the event handler procedure that appears, type **Cancel = True** as the body.

```
Worksheet                          ▼   BeforeRightClick                    ▼

    Private Sub Worksheet_BeforeRightClick(ByVal Target As Range, Ca
        Cancel = True
    End Sub
```

3 Activate Excel, and select Sheet1. Try right-clicking in a cell.

The color changes, but the shortcut menu doesn't appear. Your custom event handler executed before the built-in handler and prevented that built-in handler from executing.

4 Select Sheet2, and try right-clicking in a cell.

The color changes, and the shortcut menu also appears. Press Esc to remove the menu.

5 Save and close the Chapter09 workbook.

Toolbars and menus can be linked to macros. Command buttons, worksheets, and workbooks can be linked to event handlers. All these tools allow you to create applications that are easy for anyone to use.

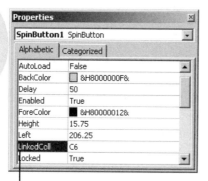

Set properties of custom controls, page 213

Add custom controls
linked to worksheet
cells, page 214

	A	B	C	D	E	F
1						
2		Price	$ 12,000			
3		Down	25%			
4		Loan	$ 9,000			
5		Interest	4.50%			
6		Years	6			
7		Payment	($142.87)			

D	E	F
	87 BMW 325	
	91 Mercury Sable $7,500	
	88 Nissan Pulsar I $3,350	
	90 Toyota Camry $5,950	
	88 Dodge Lancer $3,299	
	87 BMW 325 $4,959	
	91 Chev Camaro $3,796	
	88 Mazda MX6 $5,500	

Create a customized
drop-down list,
page 217

Chapter 10
Use Dialog Box Controls on a Worksheet

After completing this chapter, you will be able to:

✔ Add ActiveX controls to a worksheet.

✔ Link the value of a control to a worksheet cell.

✔ Link a list box to a worksheet range.

✔ Create a list box with multiple columns.

✔ Protect a worksheet that uses ActiveX controls.

Microsoft Excel is a great program. Many people purchase it to use at work. At least, people *say* they're going to use it at work. Of course, we all know the real reason most of us buy it: to calculate car payments. (The rest of us buy it for figuring out mortgage payments.) It's *after* buying it that we discover that it's also good for one or two other projects as well.

Anyway, suppose you have a friend who just bought Excel but doesn't know how to use it very well yet. You want to help out by building a model your friend can use for calculating car loan payments. You want your friend to be able to try several possible prices, interest rates, and repayment periods, but you want to minimize the chance for mistakes. Excel has some powerful tools to help you do just that.

Loan.xls

This chapter uses the practice file Loan.xls that you installed from the book's CD-ROM. For details about installing the practice files, see "Using the Book's CD-ROM" at the beginning of this book.

Getting Started

1 Start Excel, and change to the folder containing the practice files for this book.

2 Open the Loan workbook, and save a copy as **Chapter10**.

Using a Loan Payment Calculator

When you interact with Excel, you do so through Excel's graphical user interface. A graphical user interface includes menus, dialog boxes, list boxes, scroll bars, buttons, and other graphical images. A graphical user interface makes a program easier to learn and also helps reduce errors by restricting choices to valid options.

10 Use Dialog Box Controls on a Worksheet

Historically, creating a graphical user interface was the domain of professional computer scientists. More recently, users of advanced applications have been able to add graphical controls to custom dialog boxes. Now, with Excel, you can take advantage of dialog box–style controls directly on the worksheet, without doing any programming at all. These controls are called ActiveX controls.

In this chapter, you'll create a worksheet model to calculate a car loan payment. You'll add ActiveX controls to the worksheet to make it easy to use for a friend who's unfamiliar with worksheets. In the process, you'll become familiar with how ActiveX controls work, which will be useful when you create custom forms.

Create a Loan Payment Model

The Loan sheet of the practice workbook contains labels that will help you create a model that uses an Excel worksheet function to calculate the monthly payments for a car loan.

	A	B	C	D
1				
2		Price		
3		Down		
4		Loan		
5		Interest		
6		Years		
7		Payment		
8				

These are the labels for the loan payment calculator.

Cells B2 through B7 contain the labels Price, Down, Loan, Interest, Years, and Payment. Go through the following steps to create a fully functional loan payment calculator.

1 Type **$5000** in cell C2 (to the right of Price), type **20%** in cell C3 (to the right of Down), type **8%** in cell C5 (to the right of Interest), and type **3** in cell C6 (to the right of Years).

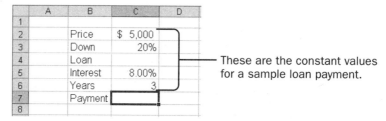

These are the constant values for a sample loan payment.

2 In cell C4 (to the right of Loan), type **=Price*(1-Down)** and press the Enter key.

The value $4,000 appears in the cell. Excel interprets which cells contain the price and down payment by looking at the labels next to the cells.

C4	▼	*fx* =Price*(1-Down)	
A	B	C	D
1			
2	Price	$ 5,000	
3	Down	20%	
4	Loan	$ 4,000	
5	Interest	8.00%	
6	Years	3	
7	Payment		
8			

The formula
=Price*(1-Down)
calculates the
loan amount.

Tip

If the word *#NAME?* appears in the cell, Excel is not set to accept labels in formulas. Point at the Tools menu, click Options, and select the Calculations tab. Select the Labels In Formulas check box, and click OK. Then re-enter the formula.

3 In cell C7 (to the right of Payment), type **=PMT(Interest/12,Years*12,Loan)** and press the Enter key. The payment amount, $125.35, appears in the cell. Once again, Excel uses the labels next to the cells to determine which cells you meant to use.

C7	▼	*fx* =PMT(Interest/12,Years*12,Loan)		
A	B	C	D	E
1				
2	Price	$ 5,000		
3	Down	20%		
4	Loan	$ 4,000		
5	Interest	8.00%		
6	Years	3		
7	Payment	($125.35)		

The formula
=PMT(Interest/12,Years*12,Loan)
calculates the loan payment.

The result is the monthly payment amount for the hypothetical car. The red text and the parentheses around the number in the worksheet indicate a negative number. Unfortunately, you don't receive this amount; you pay it. (If you want to change the monthly payment to a positive number, put a minus sign in front of *Loan* in the formula.)

Use the Loan Payment Model

1 Enter **$12000** in cell C2.

The loan amount should change to $9,600, and the payment should change to $300.83. This simple model calculates monthly loan payments for a given set of input variables. You change the input variables to anything you like, and the payment changes accordingly. You can even enter outlandish values.

	A	B	C	D
1				
2		Price	$12,000	
3		Down	20%	
4		Loan	$ 9,600	
5		Interest	8.00%	
6		Years	3	
7		Payment	($300.83)	
8				

— A new price...

...results in a new payment amount.

2 Enter **$1,500,000** as the price of the car.

This is a very expensive car. The payment formula bravely calculates the monthly payment, but you can't read it because it's too big.

	A	B	C	D
1				
2		Price	######	
3		Down	20%	
4		Loan	######	
5		Interest	8.00%	
6		Years	3	
7		Payment	######	
8				

— A price that's too big...

...produces an unusable result.

3 Press Ctrl+Z to change the price back to $12,000. (The monthly payment for the expensive car, in case you're interested, would be $37,603.64.)

One problem with this model is that it's *too* flexible. You can enter ridiculously large prices, even ridiculously high interest rates. (Try **500%**.) You can even enter something totally useless as the number of years, such as *Dog*. The wide spectrum of choices available, only a few of which are meaningful, might be confusing when your friend is using the model. You can add controls to the worksheet that will avoid possible confusion.

Creating an Error-Resistant Loan Payment Calculator

Excel has tools that enable you to make an error-resistant loan payment calculator. By restricting options to valid items, you can make your model less likely to produce erroneous results and also much easier to use. The Control Toolbox contains all kinds of useful ActiveX controls that you can put on a worksheet, such as list boxes, spin buttons, combo boxes, and so on.

Restrict the Years to a Valid Range

Start by making it difficult to enter an invalid number of years. Typically, for car loans you can borrow for up to five years in units of a year. Just to be safe, allow values from 1 to 6 for the number of years. A spin button is an effective way to specify such integer values.

Control Toolbox

1 Activate the Control Toolbox. (Click the Control Toolbox button on the Visual Basic toolbar.)

2 Click the Spin Button button on the Control Toolbox.

Spin Button

3 Press and hold the Alt key, and click near the upper left corner of cell E6. (Pressing the Alt key as you drag makes the control snap to the cell grid line.)

An ActiveX control has many properties. For most of the properties, you can simply accept the default values. Change only the properties for which you need a custom value.

4 Release the Alt key, and drag the lower right corner of the new spin button to the bottom center of cell E6.

This makes the spin button rotate sideways and fit on the row.

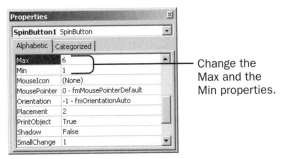

	A	B	C	D	E
1					
2		Price	$12,000		
3		Down	20%		
4		Loan	$ 9,600		
5		Interest	8.00%		
6		Years	3		◄ ►
7		Payment	($300.83)		
8					

Add a spin button control to
change the number of years.

Properties

5 Click the Properties button to display the Properties window.

6 Type **6** as the value of the Max property, and type **1** as the value of the Min property.

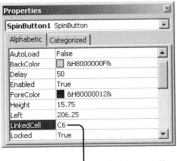

Change the
Max and the
Min properties.

You want the spin button to control the value in cell C6.

7 For the LinkedCell property, type **C6** and press the Enter key.

Enter a cell reference as the LinkedCell property
to cause the control to change the value of that cell.

Exit Design
Mode

8 Click the Exit Design Mode button, and try clicking the spin button.

The number in cell C6 changes as you click the spin button, and the payment amount changes accordingly. Now your friend will find it easy to select only valid loan duration values.

Restrict the Down Payment to Valid Values

Unfortunately, your friend can still enter an invalid value for the down payment percentage (*–50%*, for example, or *Dog*). You need to help out. A reasonable range of values for the down payment would be anywhere from 0% to 100%, counting in 5% increments. You specify the down payment as a percentage (which is a fraction, not an integer). The minimum change for a spin button is an integer, but you can still use a spin button as long as you utilize an extra cell to hold the intermediate value.

Copying the control makes both controls exactly the same size.

Design Mode

1 Click the Design Mode button to switch back to design mode.

2 Press and hold both the Alt key and the Ctrl key, and drag the spin button from cell E6 to cell E3. When you release the mouse button, a copy snaps to the upper left corner of cell E3.

Create a second spin button to control the down payment percentage.

	A	B	C	D	E
1					
2		Price	$12,000		
3		Down	20%		◄ ►
4		Loan	$ 9,600		
5		Interest	8.00%		
6		Years	6		◄ ►
7		Payment	($168.32)		
8					

3 In the Properties window, type **100** as the value of the Max property, **0** (zero) as the value of the Min property, and **H3** as the value of the LinkedCell property.

Cell H3 holds an intermediate—integer—value because the spin button can increment only in integers. Later, you will divide the value in cell H3 by 100 to convert the integer created by the spin button into a percentage suitable for use as a down payment.

4 As the value of the SmallChange property, type **5** and press the Enter key.

This property controls how much the number will change each time you click the control.

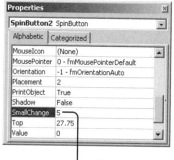

The SmallChange property controls how much the spin button changes when you click it.

Exit Design
Mode

5 Click the Exit Design Mode button, and then click the control.

The value in cell H3 changes to a multiple of 5 between 0 and 100. Now you need a value in cell C3 that changes between 0% and 100%.

6 Select cell C3, type **=H3/100**, and press the Enter key.

A percentage value appears in the cell.

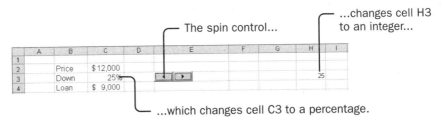

...changes cell H3 to an integer...

The spin control...

...which changes cell C3 to a percentage.

7 Click the spin button to see both the integer in cell H3 and the derived value in cell C3 change in tandem.

Restrict the Interest Rate to Valid Values

The interest rate is another input value your friend might enter incorrectly. The interest rate is similar to the down payment rate; both are percentages. You probably want to allow interest rates to vary by as little as 0.25%, and within a range from 0% through about 20%. Because you're allowing so many possible values, you'll have many more steps than with the down payment rate, so you'll use a scroll bar control instead of a spin button. Like a spin button, the scroll bar returns only integers, so you'll link the control to an intermediate cell.

Scroll Bar

1 Click the Scroll Bar button on the Control Toolbox, and then press and hold the Alt key as you click the upper left corner of cell E5.

2 Continue to press the Alt key as you drag the lower right corner of the new scroll bar to the lower right corner of cell E5.

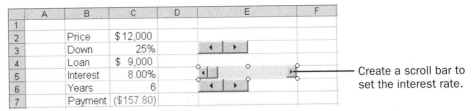

Create a scroll bar to set the interest rate.

3 In the Properties window, type **2000** as the value of the Max property, **25** as the value of the SmallChange property, **100** as the value of the LargeChange property, and **H5** as the value of the LinkedCell property. Press the Enter key.

4 Click the Exit Design Mode button, and try the scroll bar control by clicking the arrows as well as the area between them. If you click one of the arrows on either end, the number in cell H5 changes by 25 (the *SmallChange* value). If you click between the box and the end, the number changes by 100 (the *LargeChange* value).

5 Select cell C5, type **=H5/10000**, and press the Enter key. You divide by 100 to turn the number from H5 into a percentage and by another 100 (100 * 100 = 10000 total) to allow for hundredths of a percent.

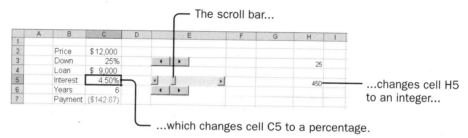

The scroll bar...

...changes cell H5 to an integer...

...which changes cell C5 to a percentage.

Now your friend can easily modify the number of years for the loan (using one spin button), the down payment percentage (using the other spin button), or the interest rate (using the scroll bar control).

Retrieving a Value from a List

You could specify the price of the car by creating another scroll bar, but the price of a car is actually determined by which car you want to buy. You know that your friend has been looking through the want ads and has come up with a list of used cars to consider. You can make the worksheet easy to use by allowing your friend to select the description of the car and have the price appear automatically in the Price cell.

Prepare a List of Cars

The Chapter10 practice file contains a list of cars that your friend is interested in and their prices. The list starts in cell K2. You can create a list box that displays this list of cars.

J	K	L	M
1			
2	91 Mercury Sable	$7,500	
3	88 Nissan Pulsar NX	$3,350	
4	90 Toyota Camry	$5,950	
5	88 Dodge Lancer ES	$3,299	
6	87 BMW 325	$4,959	
7	91 Chev Camaro	$3,796	
8	88 Mazda MX6	$5,500	
9			

1 Select cell K2, and press Ctrl+Shift+* to select the entire block of cells.

2 From the Insert menu's Name submenu, click Define. Type **CarList** as the name of the list, and click OK.

The defined name contains both the list of car names and the corresponding list of prices.

Type **CarList** here...

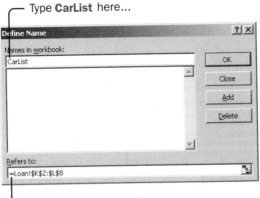

...to name the list of cars.

Combo Box

3 In the Control Toolbox, click Combo Box, press and hold the Alt key, and drag a rectangle from the upper left corner to the lower right corner of cell E2.

Create a Combo Box control to select the desired car.

	A	B	C	D	E	F
1						
2		Price	$12,000			
3		Down	25%			
4		Loan	$ 9,000			
5		Interest	4.50%			
6		Years	6			
7		Payment	($142.87)			

A combo box can have either of two styles. It can be a drop-down list box, allowing you to select only items from the list, or it can be a list box combined with an edit box, allowing you to enter new values as well as select from the list. Because you want to confine your friend to the existing list of cars, you want the combo box to be a drop-down list box.

4 In the Properties window, for the value of the Style property, select *2 – fmStyleDropDownList*.

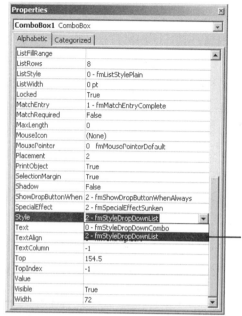

Select this style to select only items in the list.

5 Type **C2** as the value of the LinkedCell property, and press the Enter key.

The price from cell C2 appears as the value of the combo box. But because the combo box has a sunken appearance, the text in the box is too large to read. You can reduce the size of the font to make it visible.

6 Click the ellipsis button at the right of the Font property, change the font size to 8 points, and click OK. Now you can change the combo box to retrieve the list of cars.

Reduce the size of the font to make the text in the combo box readable.

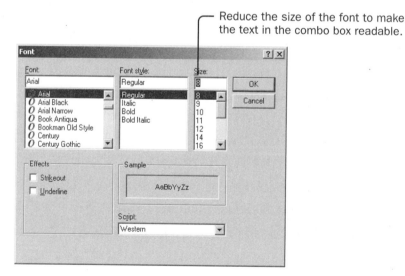

7 Type **CarList** as the value of the ListFillRange property, and press the Enter key.

Nothing seems to happen, but the combo box now knows to get its list of values from the CarList range. You can also watch the value of cell C2 change when you select a new car from the combo box.

Exit Design Mode

8 Click the Exit Design Mode button, click the arrow on the combo box, and select *90 Toyota Camry* from the list.

The name for the Toyota appears in the drop-down control, but also unfortunately in cell C2. The formula doesn't work well with a car name entered as the price.

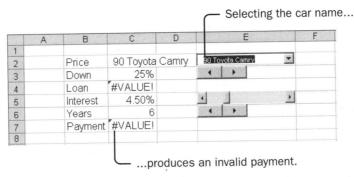

Selecting the car name...

...produces an invalid payment.

You can now select a car name from the combo box, but you want the combo box to put the price of the car—not the name of the car—into cell C2. Because the CarList range used to populate the list contains an extra column with the car prices, you can tell the combo box to get the value from that second column.

Retrieve the Price from the List

Design Mode

1 Click the Design Mode button, and click the combo box.

2 In the Properties window, type **2** as the value of the ColumnCount property.

The ColumnCount property informs the combo box that there are really two columns of values in the ListFillRange.

3 Type **2** as the value of the BoundColumn property, and press the Enter key.

The BoundColumn property tells the combo box which column's value to put into the linked cell. And sure enough, the price of the Toyota, $5,950, appears in the cell.

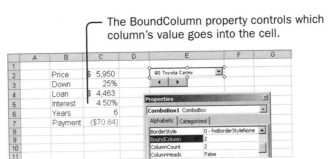

The BoundColumn property controls which column's value goes into the cell.

4 Turn off design mode, and click the arrow on the combo box.

Select the car from the list to
put the price into cell C2.

	A	B	C	D	E	F
1						
2		Price	$ 5,950		90 Toyota Camry ▼	
3		Down	25%		91 Mercury Sable $7,500	
4		Loan	$ 4,463		88 Nissan Pulsar I $3,350	
5		Interest	4.50%		90 Toyota Camry $5,950	
6		Years	6		88 Dodge Lancer $3,299	
7		Payment	($70.84)		87 BMW 325 $4,959	
8					91 Chev Camaro $3,796	
9					88 Mazda MX6 $5,500	

5 Select *87 BMW 325* from the drop-down list of cars. The price changes to $4,959.

	A	B	C	D	E	F
1						
2		Price	$ 4,959		87 BMW 325 ▼	
3		Down	25%		◄ ►	
4		Loan	$ 3,719			

Now your friend won't accidentally calculate the payment for a $1,500,000 car. Your friend can just select various cars from the list, and Excel will automatically insert the correct price in the Price cell.

Set the Column Widths

The combo box works fine, but while the list was dropped down, there was a horizontal scroll bar across the bottom. Even though there's plenty of room for the price, the combo box makes the price column just as wide as the car name column. As the default, a combo box uses the same width for each column. If, as in this example, you want the columns to have different widths, you can manually control the column widths.

1 Turn on design mode, and select the combo box.

2 In the Properties window, type **1 in; .5 in** as the value of the ColumnWidths property (to specify 1 inch for the first column and 0.5 inch for the second), and press the Enter key.

 The displayed value of the property changes to *72 pt; 36 pt*. This is the equivalent value in points. A point is equal to 1/72 inch. You can type the value of the property using inches (in), centimeters (cm), or points (pt), but the value is always displayed in points.

3 Turn off design mode, and click the combo box arrow.

 The combo box, complete with multiple columns, looks great!

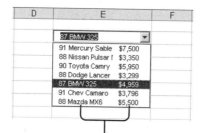

Columns can have custom widths.

Protecting the Worksheet

The model works fine now. It doesn't require any typing into cells. And you were able to create it without using any macros! The model still isn't bulletproof, however. There's nothing in the model to prevent your friend from accidentally typing, say, "Dog" in cell C2 as the price of the car, thereby destroying the formula.

You might protect the worksheet. That would keep your friend from typing invalid values into the model; but it would also unfortunately keep the ActiveX controls from changing the values of the linked cells. You can, however, set the worksheet protection in such a way that Visual Basic for Applications procedures can still change the cells. All you need are some simple event handler procedures to protect the model effectively.

Create an Event Handler for the Combo Box

Right now, each of the four ActiveX controls links directly to a cell. Before you can protect the worksheet, you must create four event handler procedures to put the new values into the cells.

1 Turn on design mode, and select the combo box.

View Code

2 In the Properties window, change the Name property to **cboPrice**. (The prefix *cbo* stands for "combo box.") Clear the LinkedCell property box, and then click the View Code button on the Control Toolbox.

A new event handler procedure named cboPrice_Change appears. *Change* is the default event for a combo box.

3 As the body of the macro, insert this statement:

```
Range("C2").Value = cboPrice.Value
```

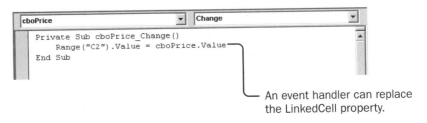

An event handler can replace the LinkedCell property.

Tip

For more information about locking cells, activate Excel and ask the Assistant for help using the keywords *locked cells*.

This event handler procedure changes cell C2 to match the new value of the combo box whenever that value changes.

4 Activate Excel, turn off design mode, and try out the combo box.

The value in cell C2 should change to the correct price each time you select a new car.

5 Repeat steps 1 through 4 for the spin button that sets the down payment percentage. Give it the name **spnDown**, clear the LinkedCell property box, and in its event procedure enter the following statement:

```
Range("C3").Value = spnDown.Value / 100
```

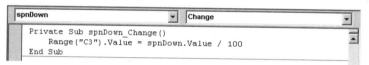

```
spnDown                          Change
    Private Sub spnDown_Change()
        Range("C3").Value = spnDown.Value / 100
    End Sub
```

6 Repeat steps 1 through 4 for the scroll bar. Give it the name **scrRate**, clear the LinkedCell property box, and in its event procedure enter the statement:

```
Range("C5").Value = scrRate.Value / 10000
```

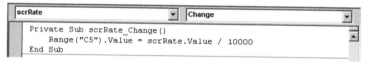

```
scrRate                          Change
    Private Sub scrRate_Change()
        Range("C5").Value = scrRate.Value / 10000
    End Sub
```

7 Repeat steps 1 through 4 for the spin button that sets the number of years. Give it the name **spnYears**, clear the LinkedCell property box, and in its event procedure enter the statement:

```
Range("C6").Value = spnYears.Value
```

```
(General)                        test
    Private Sub spnYears_Change()
        Range("C6").Value = spnYears.Value
    End Sub
```

8 Clear cells H3 and H5 since you no longer need the values in them.

You now have an event handler procedure for each control, and none of the controls is linked to a cell. You're finally ready to protect the worksheet.

Protect the Worksheet

You typically protect a worksheet by clicking the Protection command from the Tools menu and then clicking the Protect Sheet command. When you protect a worksheet this way, you can't subsequently change the value of any locked cells. Excel 2002 has many new options for items you can allow a user to change on a protected worksheet, but none of the standard options allow an ActiveX control to change the value in a cell while locking the cell from the user.

A macro, however, can protect a worksheet in such a way that a procedure—such as an event handler—can still change locked cells. This special kind of protection doesn't persist when you close and reopen the workbook, so you must protect the worksheet each time you open the workbook. Excel has an event that runs each time you open a workbook.

Project Explorer

1 Activate the Visual Basic Editor, click the Project Explorer button, and then double-click the ThisWorkbook object.

2 From the Object list (above the code window), select Workbook.

3   Insert this statement as the body of the Workbook_Open procedure:

```
Worksheets("Loan").Protect UserInterfaceOnly:=True
```

```
Private Sub Workbook_Open()
    Worksheets("Loan").Protect UserInterfaceOnly:=True
End Sub
```

4   The *UserInterfaceOnly* argument to the Protect method is what allows a macro to make changes even if a user or control can't.

5   Save and close the Chapter10 workbook. Then reopen it, allowing Excel to enable macros.

6   Try typing numbers into the model. Excel politely explains that the worksheet is protected.

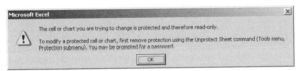

7   Try changing the model using the ActiveX controls. Everything works fine.

The loan payment calculator model is now robust and ready to give to your friend. Your friend can now experiment with various scenarios without having to worry about typing invalid inputs into the model. In fact, your friend can't type anything into the model—because the worksheet is protected. Besides, there's nothing to type. Your friend can control everything on the worksheet just by clicking controls with the mouse. One of the greatest benefits of a graphical user interface is the ability to restrict choices to valid values, thereby reducing or eliminating user error while also making a model easier to use.

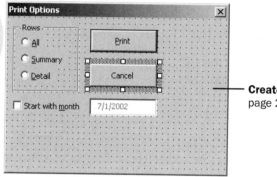

Create a custom form,
page 226

	A	B	M	N	O	P
1	Summary		Aug-2002	Sep-2002	Qtr3	Oct-2002
2	Projected Units		35000	36000	106000	37000
3	Projected Revenues		86000	87000	255000	88000
4	Projected Pretax Profit		40			
13	Total Variable					
21	Total Salaries					
23	Total Salaries and Bene		22			

Immediate

```
ShowView "Summary"
HideMonths "8/1/2002"
```

**Hide detail rows and
columns in a report,**
page 243

Use the Project Explorer to manage a project,
page 247

Chapter 11
Create a Custom Form

After completing this chapter, you will be able to:

✔ Create a custom form.

✔ Initialize a form.

✔ Check for invalid input values in a text box.

✔ Run macros from a form.

Get a 3-foot-by-4-foot piece of plywood and some cans of blue, yellow, and orange paint. Drip, dribble, splash, and spread the paint on the plywood. You now have—a mess. But put a $500 frame around the painted plywood, and you now have—a work of art! Even serious art doesn't look earnest without a good frame, and the best diamond brooch doesn't seem to be a precious gift if given in a paper bag.

Similarly, you can write macros that are practical, convenient, and useful, but until you put a frame around them—until you tighten up the edges, make them easy to use, and package them—you don't have a truly valuable application. Creating a custom form is an excellent way to make functionality easy to use and valuable. In this chapter, you'll learn how to create a custom form, create the functionality for the form, and link the two together into an integrated tool.

Budget.xls

This chapter uses the practice file Budget.xls that you installed from the book's CD-ROM. For details about installing the practice files, see "Using the Book's CD-ROM" at the beginning of the book.

Getting Started

1 Start Microsoft Excel, and change to the folder containing the practice files for this book.

2 Open the Budget workbook, and save a copy as **Chapter11**.

Creating a Form's User Interface

The Budget worksheet shows detailed budget information for the year 2002. It includes both detail and summary rows.

	A	B	C	D	E	F
1	Summary		Rates	Jan-2002	Feb-2002	Mar-2002
2	Projected Units			29000	30000	31000
3	Projected Revenues			71000	73000	75000
4	**Projected Pretax Profit**			28094.9	28332.9	31570.9
5						
6	Variable					
7		Potting Soil	0.095	2755	2850	2945
8		Pots	0.012	348	360	372
9		Seeds	0.002	58	60	62
10		Fertilizer	0.002	58	60	62

Suppose that you need to print different versions of the budget. The managers want a version that shows only the summary rows. The data entry person wants a version that shows only the detail rows, without the totals. The budget analyst wants both the detail and the summary rows but doesn't want to see months that are completed.

To make it easy to print the various versions of the report, you can create a custom dialog box, or *user form*. Here's the strategy for creating the form:

■ Design what the form will look like. The way the form looks and acts, called the *user interface,* is the first thing that the user sees, and it suggests how to use the form. The easiest way to design a form in Microsoft Visual Basic for Applications is to just jump in and create it.

■ Create the macros you need to make the form work. These are the procedures that interact with Excel objects. The tasks that the form executes are called its *functionality*. Adding functionality might involve making changes to the worksheet that enable the macros to work.

■ Make the form run the macros, and provide a way to show the form. Integrating the user interface with the functionality of the form is the final *implementation*. ˙

The process of designing the form's user interface can help you figure out what functionality you need to develop.

Create the Form

Visual Basic Editor

1 With the Chapter11 workbook open, click the Visual Basic Editor button.

The second button from the left on the Standard toolbar in the Visual Basic Editor allows you to insert a new object type. The object type inserted by the button changes to whatever you most recently used it for. The default is for the button to insert a UserForm.

Insert UserForm

2 Click the arrow next to the Insert UserForm button to display a list of objects that you can insert.

3 Click the UserForm option to create a new, empty user form.

The button might have a different picture depending on whether you've previously used it.

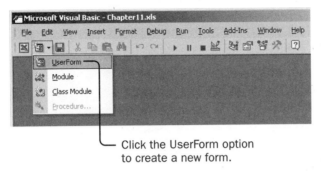

— Click the UserForm option
to create a new form.

The form is stored in your project just as a module is. You can "run" the form from Visual Basic for Applications in the same way that you run a macro.

Close

4 Click the Run Sub/UserForm button to display the form, and then click the Close button to close it.

By default, the caption of the form is UserForm1. The second form you create will be captioned UserForm2, and so on. The caption is a property; you can change the caption using the Properties window.

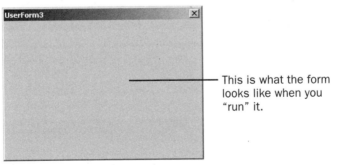

— This is what the form
looks like when you
"run" it.

Properties
Window

5 Click the Properties Window button, and change the value of the Caption property to **Print Options**.

The caption changes in the form as you change the value in the Properties window.

To change the form Caption...

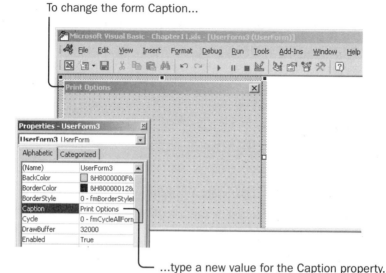

...type a new value for the Caption property.

6   Change the value of the (Name) property to **frmPrint**. (The Name property has parentheses around it, which cause it to appear at the top of the list.)

The prefix *frm-* is short for *form*. The *Print* part of the name tells you the intended purpose
of the form. If you ever need to refer to the form inside a procedure, you can use this
meaningful name.

That's all there is to creating a user form! Of course, you might want to put something a
little fancier inside it.

Add Option Buttons

In this exercise, you want the user to be able to choose one of three layouts when printing the report: all the rows, only the summary rows, or only the detail rows. Option buttons provide a way to select a single item from a short, predefined list. Generally, option
buttons go inside a frame.

When Visual Basic for Applications displayed the user form, it automatically displayed the
Toolbox for forms. This Toolbox is similar to the Control Toolbox you use to add ActiveX
controls to a worksheet.

Toolbox

1   Click the Form window. If you don't see the Toolbox, click the Toolbox button on the Standard toolbar to display it.

2   In the Toolbox, click the Frame button, and then click near the upper left corner of the form.

Frame

A large frame control appears on the form. You can move or resize the frame later.

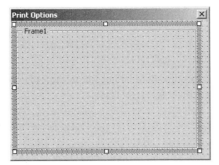

Your next task is to add the option buttons. You can avoid clicking the control button on the toolbox each time you add a button by double-clicking the control button. Double-clicking activates the button until you click it again.

OptionButton

3 Double-click the OptionButton button, click in three places on the form to create three buttons, and then click the OptionButton button again to turn it off.

You don't need to be exact in where you position the controls.

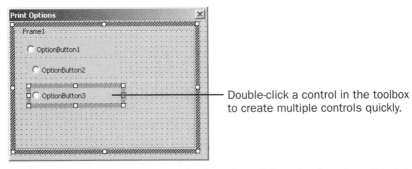

Double-click a control in the toolbox to create multiple controls quickly.

4 Activate the Properties window, and select Frame1 from the drop-down list at the top.

5 Type **Rows** as the value of the Caption property, and type **grpRows** as the value of the Name property. (The prefix *grp-* is short for *group*, which is an old name for a frame. The prefix *frm-* is commonly used as the prefix for a form.)

6 From the drop-down list, select OptionButton1. Type **All** as the value of the Caption property, **optAll** as the value of the Name property, and **A** as the value of the Accelerator property. (You've probably guessed what the prefix *opt-* is short for.) With the optAll control still selected, type **True** as the value of the Value property. Setting the Value property to *True* makes this the default option.

Tip
In the Toolbox, you can use the keyboard to jump to a new property by pressing Ctrl+Shift and the first letter of the property name. For example, to select the Accelerator property, press Ctrl+Shift+A.

7 Give the second option button the caption **Summary**, the name **optSummary**, and the accelerator key **S**.

8 Give the third option button the caption **Detail**, the name **optDetail**, and the accelerator key **D**.

9 Select all three option buttons by clicking between the bottom option button and the bottom of the frame and dragging a rectangle that touches each of the option button captions.

10 On the Format menu in the Visual Basic Editor, click Vertical Spacing, and then click Remove. From the Format menu, click Align and then click Lefts. Again, from the Format menu, click Size To Fit. Finally drag the group of controls up close to upper left corner of the frame, and resize the frame just to fit around the option buttons.

Use commands on the Format menu to clean up the form.

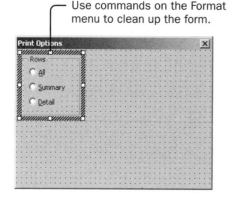

The Format menu provides powerful tools for getting the controls on a form to line up properly.

11 Save the workbook, press F5 to see how the option buttons will look (by clicking the option buttons), and then close the Print Options window.

You can select only one option button from the group.

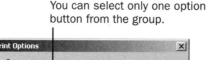

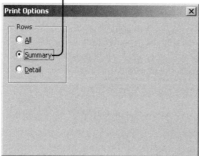

A frame with a set of option buttons is a good user interface for selecting a single option from a predefined list.

Add a Check Box with a Related Text Box

Your form needs some way for you to specify whether to print all the months or only the remaining months. This is basically a "yes or no" choice. The best control for a "yes or no" choice is a check box. When the check box is selected, the macro will print starting with the current month.

Also, even though the budget analyst says that the report should start with the current month, you know that exceptions inevitably will arise. You should therefore add a text box that lets you specify a different start month, just to be prepared.

CheckBox

1   With the form window visible, click the CheckBox button in the Toolbox, and then click below the frame on the form where you want the check box to appear.

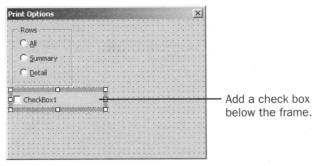

Add a check box below the frame.

2   In the Properties window, change the caption for the check box to **Start with month**, change the name to **chkMonth**, and change the Accelerator to **m**.

You must use a lowercase letter because the letter in the caption is lowercase. The accelerator character must match the character in the caption exactly.

3   Double-click the right size handle of the check box selection rectangle to shrink the rectangle to fit the caption.

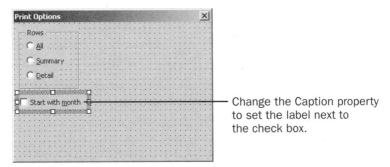

Change the Caption property to set the label next to the check box.

You'll now add the text box for the month immediately after the caption for the check box so that the contents appear to complete the *Start with month* caption.

TextBox

4   Click the TextBox button in the toolbox, and then click to the right of the check box caption.

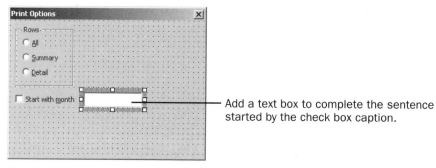

Add a text box to complete the sentence started by the check box caption.

5 Change the text box name to **txtMonth**, set the Value property to **7/1/2002**, and then change the Enabled property to **False**.

You won't need to change the value of the month if the check box is cleared. Setting the Enabled property to *False* makes the contents of the box appear gray. You want the text box to become enabled whenever the user selects the check box. This is a job for an event.

6 Double-click the chkMonth check box control.

A new window captioned as frmPrint (Code) appears. It contains a new event handler procedure, *chkMonth_Click*. The *Click* event is the default event for a check box.

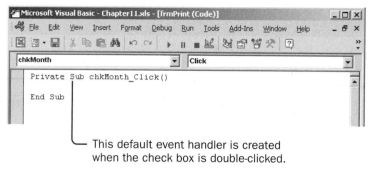

This default event handler is created when the check box is double-clicked.

7 Insert the following statement as the body of the new *chkMonth_Click* procedure:

```
txtMonth.Enabled = chkMonth.Value
```

This statement enables the text box whenever the check box is selected and disables the text box whenever the check box is cleared.

8 Save the workbook, press F5 to run the form, and click the check box a couple of times. Then close the form.

When the check box is selected...

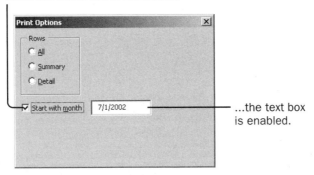

...the text box
is enabled.

9 When the check box is cleared, you can't change the date. When it's selected, you can.

Adding an event to the check box control makes the user interface work better, but it doesn't change anything in Excel. Even though the event is Visual Basic for Applications code, it is still part of the user interface of the form, not part of its functionality.

Initialize the Text Box

When you created the month text box, you assigned 7/1/2002 as a default date. Since most of the time you'll want the current month in that box, you can make the form easier to use by initializing the text box with the current month. To do so, you must calculate the appropriate date for the text box at the time you display the form.

1 Double-click the background of the form. A new procedure named *UserForm_Click* appears.

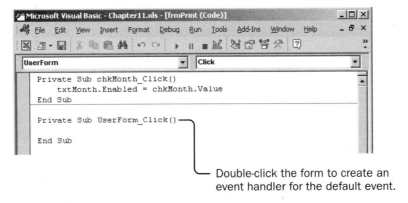

Double-click the form to create an
event handler for the default event.

The name of the object for a form is always *UserForm*. No matter what name you give the form, the event handler procedures always use the name *UserForm*. The default event for a form is *Click,* but you don't want to wait until the user clicks the form to initialize the month. You therefore need a different event.

2 From the Procedures list, select the Initialize event. After the *UserForm_Initialize* procedure appears, delete the *UserForm_Click* procedure.

3 Enter the following statement as the body of the procedure:

```
txtMonth.Value = Date
```

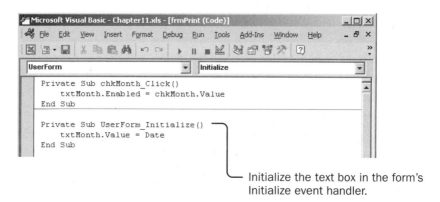

Initialize the text box in the form's Initialize event handler.

Date is a built-in Visual Basic function that returns the current date, based on your computer's internal clock.

4 Press F5 to run the form.

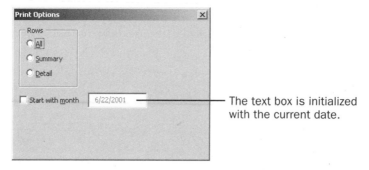

The text box is initialized with the current date.

The purpose of the date is to identify the month you want the report to start with. You'll create a macro that searches the top row of the worksheet to find a date that matches the one in the text box. The dates in the top row of the worksheet are all for the first day of the month. To find a match, therefore, the date in the text box must be for the first day of the month as well. The date that the macro puts into the text box, however, is the current date. Because it's highly unlikely that the current date is the first day of the month, you need a way to convert the current date to the first day of the current month.

5 Close the form, and then double-click the background to get back to the *UserForm_Initialize* procedure.

You're now going to create a custom function that will convert any date into the first day of the month.

6 Below the *UserForm_Initialize* procedure, add this custom function:

```
Function StartOfMonth(InputDate)
    If IsDate(InputDate) Then
        StartOfMonth = DateSerial _
```

```
        (Year(InputDate), Month(InputDate), 1)
    Else
        StartOfMonth = Empty
    End If
End Function
```

This function accepts an input date as an argument. It first checks to see whether the input date is a date or can be turned into one. If it can, the function extracts the year and the month from the input date and uses the DateSerial function to create a new date. You give the DateSerial function a year, a month, and a day, and it gives you back the appropriate date. The StartOfMonth function ignores the day portion of the input date and always uses 1 as the day instead. If for some reason the input date can't be interpreted as a date, the function returns the special value *Empty*. The *Empty* value is the same value used when a variable has never been initialized. The Visual Basic *Date* function in the *UserForm_Initialize* procedure always returns a valid date, so if you call only the StartOfMonth function from the *UserForm_Initialize* procedure, it doesn't have to handle an invalid date. But whenever you write a custom function, you should write it to work in a variety of possible situations. Returning an *Empty* value when the argument is an invalid date is one way to make your function more flexible.

Tip

If you want to test the function, you can do so from the Immediate window. Because this function is part of the code for a form object, however, you must include the form name before the function name. For example, you could test the function in the Immediate window by entering the following statement: **?frmPrint.StartOfMonth("May 23, 2002")**.

7   Change the statement in the *UserForm_Initialize* procedure to **txtmonth.Value = StartOfMonth(Date)**.

8   Press F5 to run the dialog box, check the date in the month box, and close the form.

The date should be the first day of the current month.

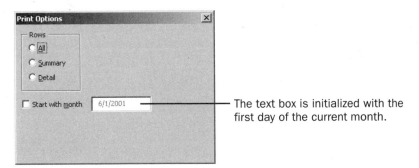

The text box is initialized with the first day of the current month.

Many controls need to be initialized. Some controls, such as the option buttons, can be initialized when you create the form. Other controls, such as the month text box, need to be initialized when you run the form, and the *Initialize* event handler is the place to accomplish that task.

Add Command Buttons

Your form allows you to specify what both the rows and columns of the report should look like. You still need a way to start printing. To do that, you add a command button. In theory, you don't need a cancel button because you can always just click the Close Window button to close the form. But a cancel button is easier to understand and use, and the whole purpose of a good user interface is to make the form easy to understand and use.

1 Activate the Form window.

CommandButton

2 Click the CommandButton button in the Toolbox, and then click on the form, to the right of the Rows frame.

3 Press and hold the Ctrl key, and drag the new button down to make a copy of it.

The top button will print the report, and the bottom one will not. Either button will close the form.

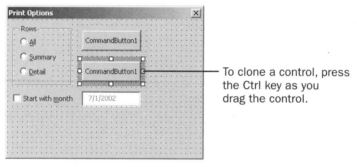

To clone a control, press the Ctrl key as you drag the control.

4 Change the caption on the top button to **Print**, assign **P** as the accelerator key, change the name to **btnPrint**, and change the Default property to **True**.

Only one command button on a form can be the default. A default button is the one that gets "clicked" when you press the Enter key.

5 Change the caption on the bottom button to **Cancel**, don't assign an accelerator key, change the name to **btnCancel**, and change the Cancel property to **True**.

Make one button into the default button...

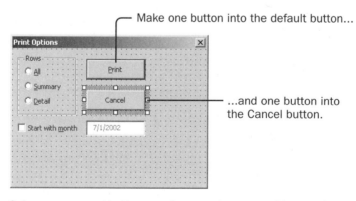

...and one button into the Cancel button.

Only one command button on a form can be a cancel button. A cancel button is the one that gets "clicked" when you press the Esc key. Normally, when you click a cancel button, you expect the form to close. A cancel button by itself, however, doesn't close the form. First you have to add an event handler to it.

6 Double-click the cancel button to create an event handler named *btnCancel_Click*, and enter the statement **Unload Me** as the body of the procedure.

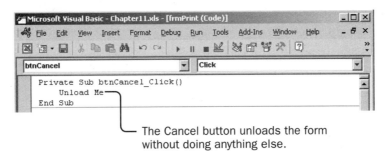

The Cancel button unloads the form without doing anything else.

The *Unload* command removes a form from memory. The *Me* keyword refers to the current form. The macro statement *Unload Me* therefore removes from memory the form that contains the control whose event handler is currently running.

7 Select btnPrint from the Objects list at the top of the code window to create a new procedure called *btnPrint_Click*, and enter these two statements as the body of the procedure:

```
Unload Me
MsgBox "Printing"
```

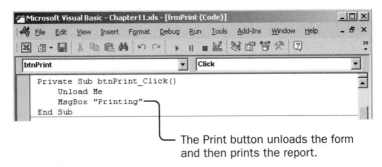

The Print button unloads the form and then prints the report.

The first statement removes the form, and the second statement is a placeholder until you add the functionality to print the report.

8 Save the workbook, and run the form several times. Try clicking the Cancel and Print buttons. Try pressing the Esc or Enter keys.

Press the Enter key to
"click" the default button.

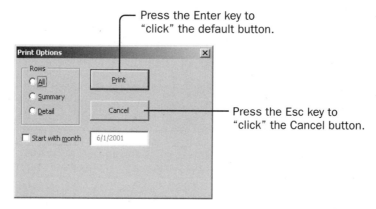

Press the Esc key to
"click" the Cancel button.

Pressing the Enter key or clicking the Print button should display the *Printing* message.
Pressing the Esc key or clicking the Cancel button should make the form disappear quietly.

Set the Tab Order for Controls

1   Run the form one more time. Select the Start With Month check box to enable the
month text box. Press the Tab key repeatedly. Watch the small gray box move from control to control.

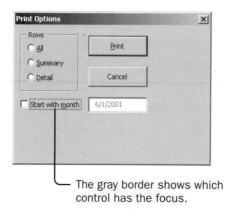

The gray border shows which
control has the focus.

The gray box identifies the control that has the *focus*. When you use the keyboard, you
can press the Tab key to move the focus from control to control.

2   Click Cancel to close the form.

Some people prefer to use the keyboard rather than a mouse. For them, you should make
sure that accelerator keys are properly defined and that the tab order is logical. For this
form, the tab order should be optAll, optSummary, optDetail, chkMonth, txtMonth,
btnPrint, and btnCancel. If that's not the tab order for your controls, the Visual Basic Editor provides a simple way to change the tab order.

3   Click the background of the form. From the View menu, click the Tab Order command.

The Tab Order dialog box shows five controls: grpRows, chkMonth, txtMonth, btnPrint, and
btnCancel. It treats the grpRows frame control (along with the controls it contains) as a

single item. If a control is out of place in the sequence, you simply select the control and click the Move Up or Move Down button to put it in the right place.

Tip

If you don't see a Tab Order command, move the mouse over the arrow at the bottom of the View menu.

Select the control that has the wrong tab order...

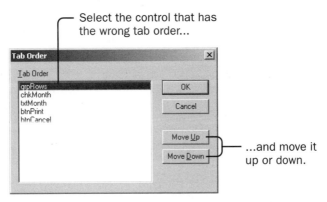

...and move it up or down.

4 After making any necessary adjustments, click OK to close the dialog box. Select the frame box (or any of the option buttons), and from the View menu, click the Tab Order command again.

This time, the Tab Order dialog box shows only the controls inside the frame.

Controls inside a frame have their own tab order.

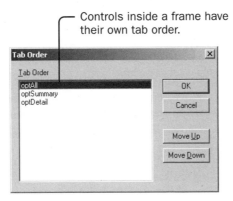

5 After making any necessary adjustments, click OK to close the dialog box. Save the workbook.

The tab order is easy to set, but remember that you need to set the order for the controls in each frame separately.

Preparing a Form's Functionality

The form now looks good. The next step is to build the functionality for printing the report. You need a way to change between the different row views, and you need a way to hide any unwanted columns. Excel can store different views of a worksheet that you specify, which you can then show later as needed. If you build some views into the worksheet, creating a macro to change between views will be easy.

Create Custom Views on a Worksheet

A custom view allows you to hide rows or columns on a worksheet and then give that view a name so that you can retrieve it easily. You need to create three views. The first view shows all the rows and columns. That one is easy to create. The second view shows only the total rows. The third view shows only the detail rows. Hiding the rows can be a tedious process. Fortunately, you need to hide them only once. You can also use Excel's Go To Special command to help select the rows faster.

1   Activate Excel. From the View menu, click the Custom Views command.

2   In the Custom Views dialog box, click the Add button, type **All** as the name for the new view, clear the Print Settings check box, leave the Hidden Rows, Columns And Filter Settings check box selected, and then click OK.

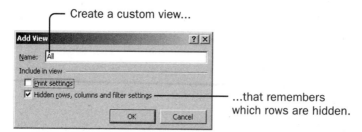

Create a custom view...

...that remembers which rows are hidden.

You just created the first view, the one with all rows and columns displayed. You now need to create the Summary view, showing only the total rows. That means that you need to hide the detail rows. You notice that only the detail rows have labels in column B.

3   Select column B. From the Edit menu, click Go To and then click Special. Select the Constants option, and click OK.

Only the cells in the detail rows are still selected.

The Constants option selects only cells that contain constants.

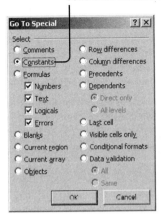

4 Hide the selected rows. (From the Format menu, click Row, and then click Hide.)

The rows with constants in Column B are hidden.

	A	B	C	D	E	F	G
1	Summary		Rates	Jan-2002	Feb-2002	Mar-2002	Qtr1
2	Projected Units			29000	30000	31000	90000
3	Projected Revenues			71000	73000	75000	219000
4	Projected Pretax Profit			28094.9	28332.9	31570.9	87998.7
5							
6	Variable						
13	Total Variable			7598	7860	8122	23580
14							
15	Salaries						
21	Total Salaries			16546	16546	16546	49638

The only remaining rows that you want to hide all have blank cells in column D. Does that give you any ideas?

5 Select column D. Click Edit, Go To, and Special. Select Blanks, and then click OK. Hide the selected rows as you did in step 4. This is the view for the managers.

The rows with constants in Column B or blanks in Column D are hidden.

	A	B	C	D	E	F
1	Summary		Rates	Jan-2002	Feb-2002	Mar-2002
2	Projected Units			29000	30000	31000
3	Projected Revenues			71000	73000	75000
4	Projected Pretax Profit			28094.9	28332.9	31570.9
13	Total Variable			7598	7860	8122
21	Total Salaries			16546	16546	16546
23	Total Salaries and Benefits			22337.1	22337.1	22337.1

6 With only these total rows visible, create another view named **Summary**. (From the View menu, click Custom Views, click Add, type **Summary**, clear Print Settings, and then click OK.) Now you need to create the detail view. For the detail view, you want to hide all the summary rows. The rows you want to hide have labels in the range A4:A54.

7 Show the All custom view to unhide all the rows. (From the View menu, click Custom Views, and with All selected, click OK.) Select the range A4:A54, use Go To Special to select the cells with constants, and then hide the rows. Select column D, and hide all the rows with blank cells.

The summary rows are hidden.

	A	B	C	D	E	F
1	Summary		Rates	Jan-2002	Feb-2002	Mar-2002
2	Projected Units			29000	30000	31000
3	Projected Revenues			71000	73000	75000
7		Potting Soil	0.095	2755	2850	2945
8		Pots	0.012	348	360	372
9		Seeds	0.002	58	60	62

8 With these detail rows visible, create a new view named **Detail**, again clearing the Print Settings option.

9 Save the workbook, and try showing each of the three views. Finish with the All view.

Creating the views is bothersome, but you have to do it only once. Once the views are created, making a macro to switch between views is easy.

Create a Macro to Switch Views

1 Start recording a macro named **ShowView**. Show the Summary view, turn off the recorder, and look at the macro. It should look like this:

```
Sub ShowView()
    ActiveWorkbook.CustomViews("Summary").Show
End Sub
```

A Workbook object has a collection named CustomViews. You use the name of the view to retrieve a CustomView item from the collection. A CustomView object has a Show method. To switch between views, all you need to do is substitute the name of the view in parentheses. And rather than create three separate macros, you can pass the name of the view as an argument.

2 Type **ViewName** between the parentheses after ShowView, and then replace *"Summary"* (quotation marks and all), with **ViewName**. The revised macro should look like this:

```
Sub ShowView(ViewName)
    ActiveWorkbook.CustomViews(ViewName).Show
End Sub
```

Next you'll test the macro and its argument using the Immediate window.

3 Press Ctrl+G to display the Immediate window.

4 Type **ShowView "Detail"** and press the Enter key.

The worksheet should change to show the detailed view.

	A	B	C	D	E	F
1	**Summary**		**Rates**	**Jan-2002**	**Feb-2002**	**Mar-2002**
2	Projected Units			29000	30000	31000
3	Projected Revenues			71000	73000	75000
7		Potting Soil	0.095			
8		Pots	0.012			
9		Seeds	0.002			
10		Fertilizer	0.002			

Immediate

ShowView "Detail"

— Test the procedure using
the Immediate window.

5 Type **ShowView "All"** and press the Enter key. Then type **ShowView "Summary"** and press the Enter key again. The macro works with all three arguments.

6 Close the Immediate window, and save the workbook.

You now have the functionality to show different views. Creating the views might not have been fun, but it certainly made writing the macro a lot easier. Also, if you decide to adjust a view (say, to include blank lines), you don't need to change the macro.

At this point, you need to create the functionality to hide columns containing dates earlier than the desired starting month.

Dynamically Hide Columns

You don't want to create custom views to change the columns because you'd need to create 36 different custom views—one for each month times the three different row settings. You need to change the columns dynamically, based on the choices in the dialog box. If you're going to hide columns, you'll start with column C and end with an arbitrary month specified. One good way to find the month is to use Excel's Find method.

1 In Excel, select all of row 1 and then start recording a macro named **HideMonths**.

2 From the Edit menu, click the Find command and then click the Options button to expand the dialog box. Type **5/1/2002** in the Find What box, select the Match Entire Cell Contents check box, and make sure the Look In drop-down list box says Formulas.

Important

If your system uses a date format other than mm/dd/yyyy (the default United States date format), you'll need to experiment to find the date format that works for you.

— Type the date here...

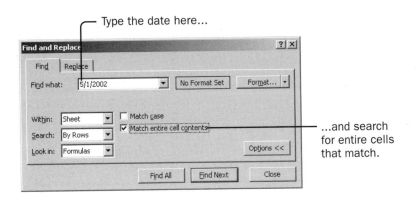

...and search
for entire cells
that match.

By searching for the formula, you look for the underlying date in the cell. The underlying date uses the system date format, regardless of how the cell happens to be formatted. By searching only entire cells, you make sure that 1/1/2002, for example, will find only January (1/1/2002), and not November (11/1/2002), which differs only by having an extra digit at the beginning.

3 Click Find Next, close the Find dialog box, stop the recorder, and then edit the HideMonths macro. Put a line continuation (a space, an underscore, and a new line) after every comma to make the statement readable. The macro should now look like this:

```
Sub HideMonths()
    Selection.Find(What:="5/1/2002", _
        After:=ActiveCell, _
        LookIn:=xlFormulas, _
        LookAt:=xlWhole, _
        SearchOrder:=xlByRows, _
        SearchDirection:=xlNext, _
        MatchCase:=False, _
        SearchFormat:=False).Activate
End Sub
```

The macro searches the selection (in this case, row 1), starting with the active cell (in this case, cell A1), searches for the specified date, and activates the matching cell. You don't want the macro to change the selection, and you don't want the macro to activate the cell it finds. Rather, you want the macro to assign the found range to a variable so that you can refer to it.

4 Make these changes to the macro: Declare the variable *myFind* as a Range. Change *Selection* to **Rows(1)** and *ActiveCell* to **Cells(1)**. Delete *.Activate* from the end of the Find statement, and add **Set myFind =** to the beginning. The revised macro looks like this:

```
Sub HideMonths()
    Dim myFind as Range
    Set myFind = Rows(1).Find(What:="5/1/2002", _
        After:=Cells(1), _
        LookIn:=xlFormulas, _
        LookAt:=xlWhole, _
        SearchOrder:=xlByRows, _
        SearchDirection:=xlNext, _
        MatchCase:=False, _
        SearchFormat:=False)
End Sub
```

If the Find method is successful, then *myFind* will contain a reference to the cell that contains the month. You want to hide all the columns from column C (the Rates column) to one column to the left of *myFind*.

5 Before the *End Sub* statement, insert this statement:

```
Range("C1",myFind.Offset(0,-1)).EntireColumn.Hidden = True
```

This selects a range starting with cell C1 and ending one cell to the left of the cell with the month name. It then hides the columns containing that range.

6 Save the workbook, and press F8 repeatedly to step through the macro. Watch as columns C through H disappear.

You'll be changing this subroutine to hide columns up to any date. You need some way of knowing whether or not the Find method finds a match. If the Find method does find a match, it assigns a reference to the variable. If it doesn't find a match, it assigns a special object reference, *Nothing*, to the variable. You can check to see whether the object is the same as *Nothing*. Because you're comparing object references and not values, you don't use an equal sign to do the comparison. Instead, you use a special object comparison word, *Is*.

Important

A variable that's declared as a variant contains the value *Empty* when nothing else is assigned to it. A variable that's declared as an object contains the reference *Nothing* when no other object reference is assigned to it. *Empty* means "no value," and *Nothing* means "no object reference." To see whether the variable *myValue* contains the *Empty* value, use the expression *IsEmpty(myValue)*. To see whether the variable *myObject* contains a reference to *Nothing*, use the expression *myObject Is Nothing*.

7 Add the If and End If statements around the statement that hides the columns, resulting in this If structure:

```
If Not myFind Is Nothing Then
    Range("C1", myFind.Offset(0, -1)) _
        .EntireColumn.Hidden = True
End If
```

If the Find method fails, it assigns *Nothing* to *myFind*, so the conditional expression is *False* and no columns are hidden.

8 Test the macro's ability to handle an error by changing the value for which the Find method searches, from *5/1/2002* to **Dog**. Then step through the macro and watch what happens when you get to the If structure. Hold the mouse pointer over the *myFind* variable and see that its value is *Nothing*.

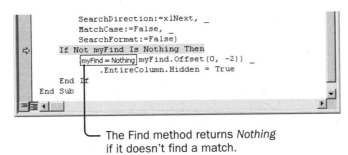

The Find method returns *Nothing* if it doesn't find a match.

If you search for a date that's in row 1, *myFind* will hold a reference to the cell containing that date, and the macro will hide the months that precede it. If you search for anything else, *myFind* will hold a reference to *Nothing*, and the macro won't hide any columns.

9 Press F5 to end the macro.

10 The final step is to convert the date to an argument. Type **StartMonth** between the parentheses after *HideMonths*, and replace "5/1/2002"or "Dog" (including the quotation marks) with **StartMonth**. The revised (and finished) procedure should look like this:

```
Sub HideMonths(StartMonth)
    Dim myFind As Range
    Set myFind = Rows(1).Find(What:=StartMonth, _
        After:=Cells(1), _
        LookIn:=xlFormulas, _
        LookAt:=xlWhole, _
        SearchOrder:-xlByRows, _
        SearchDirection:=xlNext, _
        MatchCase:=False, _
        SearchFormat:=False)
    If Not myFind Is Nothing Then
        Range("C1", myFind.Offset(0, -1)) _
            .EntireColumn.Hidden _
        = True
    End If
End Sub
```

11 Now test the macro. Press Ctrl+G to display the Immediate window. Enter **ShowView "All"** and then enter **HideMonths "8/1/2002"**.

The months before August are hidden.

	A	B	M	N	O	P
1	Summary		Aug-2002	Sep-2002	Qtr3	Oct-2002
2	Projected Units		35000	36000	106000	37000
3	Projected Revenues		85000	87000	255000	89000
4	Projected Pretax Profit		40			
13	Total Variable					
21	Total Salaries					
23	Total Salaries and Benet		22			

Immediate

```
ShowView "Summary"
HideMonths "8/1/2002"
```

12 Close the Immediate window, and save the workbook.

You now have macros that can handle the functionality of the form by hiding appropriate rows and columns. It's now time to put the form and the functionality together.

Implementing a Form

You've created a user interface that allows you to specify which rows and columns to print. You've also created the functionality for the form. The ShowView and HideMonths macros show the appropriate rows and columns. You now need to make the user interface drive the functionality. You need to implement the form.

For this form, the Print button is what formats and prints the report. You'll put all the code that links the form to the functionality into the *btnPrint_Click* procedure.

Implement Option Buttons

To implement the option buttons, you need a way to determine which option button value is *True*. The frame control has a Controls property that returns a collection of all the controls in the frame. You can loop through those controls and determine which option button value is *True*.

Project Explorer

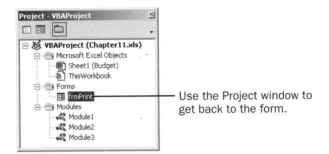

1 In the Visual Basic Editor, click the Project Explorer toolbar button, double-click the frm-Print form, and then close the Project window.

Use the Project window to get back to the form.

When you have a project with several components, the Project window is often the easiest way to get to the right place.

2 Double-click the Print button to show the *btnPrint_Click* event handler procedure.

3 Insert these statements at the beginning of the procedure, before the Unload Me statement:

```
Dim myControl As Control
Dim myView

For Each myControl In grpRows.Controls
    If myControl.Value = True Then
        myView = myControl.Caption
    End If

Next myControl
ShowView myView
```

This *For Each* loop inspects each control in the frame, looking for a value of *True*. You declare the loop variable as a Control (not as an OptionButton) because it's possible for a frame to contain other types of controls besides option buttons.

Tip

If you loop through the controls of a frame that contains controls other than option buttons, you should check to see whether the control is an option button. You can use the conditional expression *TypeName(myControl) = "OptionButton"* to determine whether the control is an option button.

The loop stores the caption of the selected option in a variable, and the macro later uses that variable as the argument when it runs the ShowView macro. What a fortuitous coincidence that you used the same names for the custom views as for the captions of the option buttons!

4 Save the workbook, and press F8 to run the form. (Press F8 repeatedly to step through the initialization procedures.) You can run the form by pressing F5 while either the form design window or the form code window is active, but the form code window must be active to use F8. If you press F8 to run the form, you can step through any event handler procedures triggered by controls on the form.

5 Click the Summary option, and then click Print. Press F8 repeatedly to step through the *btnPrint_Click* procedure. Close the message box as necessary.

An option button can be easy to implement if you plan ahead. In this example, giving the custom views in the worksheet the same names as the captions of the option buttons made the option buttons easy to implement. Also, if you were to add a fourth view option, all you'd have to do is define a new view on the worksheet and add an option button with the appropriate caption to the form. You wouldn't need to make any changes to any of the procedures.

Implement a Check Box

If the check box is selected, the Print button event handler should run the HideMonths macro. Actually, the HideMonths macro will do nothing if you give it a date that it doesn't find. You can take advantage of that by assigning to a variable either the date from the month box or an invalid value.

1 Double-click the Print button to show the *btnPrint_Click* procedure, and add the following statements after Dim myView:

```
Dim myMonth

If chkMonth.Value = True Then
    myMonth = txtMonth.Value
Else
    myMonth = "no date"
End If
```

These statements assign to the *myMonth* variable either the value from the month text box or an obviously invalid value.

2 Insert the statement **HideMonths myMonth** after the statement ShowView myView.

You place this statement after the ShowView statement because you want to change the view before hiding the months; showing the custom view redisplays all the hidden columns.

3 Save the workbook, and press F5 to run the form. Select the check box, type **9/1/2002** in the month box, and click Print. The worksheet now shows only the months starting from September.

The date in the text box of the form determines the first visible month.

	A	B	N	O
1	Summary		Sep-2002	Qtr3
2	Projected Units		36000	106000
3	Projected Revenues		87000	255000
4	**Projected Pretax Profit**		42260.9	121306.7

4 Click OK to close the message box.

Check for Errors in an Edit Box

What if you run the form and type *Dog* as the date? The macro shouldn't hide any columns, but it should point out the error. What if you type *4/15/2002* as the date? Ideally, the macro should convert *4/15/2002* to the appropriate *4/1/2002*. Look in the library of useful functions you've created during this project and see whether you can find one to convert a date to the start of the month.

1 Double-click the Print button. In the *btnPrint_Click* procedure, replace *myMonth = txtMonth.Value* with **myMonth = StartOfMonth(txtMonth.Value)**.

The StartOfMonth function converts a date to the first of the month. If the input date isn't a valid date, the function returns the *Empty* value. (That was remarkably prescient of you to write the StartOfMonth function to handle invalid dates.) If the *myMonth* variable contains the *Empty* value, you'll want to show a message and make the value easy to fix.

2 Insert these statements before the *Else* statement:

```
If myMonth = Empty Then
    MsgBox "Invalid Month"
    txtMonth.SetFocus
    txtMonth.SelStart = 0
    txtMonth.SelLength = 1000
    Exit Sub
End If
```

When you run the form, the macro appropriately displays a message box explaining the problem if you type an invalid date. After you close the message box, you should be able to just start typing a corrected value. For that to happen, however, the macro must move to the text box and preselect the current, invalid contents.

The SetFocus method moves the focus to the text box. Setting the SelStart property to 0 (zero) starts text selection from the very beginning of the text box. Setting the SelLength property to 1000 extends text selection to however much text there is in the box. Using an arbitrarily large value such as 1000 simply avoids having to calculate the actual length of the contents of the box.

3 Save the workbook, and then press F5 to run the form. Try enabling the month, typing **Dog**, and clicking Print. Try typing **Jun 23, 02** and clicking Print. (Close the message box.)

When you put an edit box onto a form, you must think about what the macro should do if the user enters an invalid value. In many cases, displaying an error message and preselecting the invalid entry is the best strategy. The SetFocus method and the SelStart and SelLength properties are the tools that allow you to implement that strategy.

Print the Report

The Print form now does everything it needs to do—everything, that is, except print. If you make the report display the report in print preview mode, you can then decide whether to print it or just admire it.

1 Double-click the Print button. In the *btnPrint_Click* procedure, replace MsgBox "Printing" with **ActiveSheet.PrintPreview**. After the report prints, you should restore the rows and columns in the worksheet.

2 After the statement ActiveSheet.PrintPreview, type the statement **ShowView "All"**.

3 Save the workbook, press F5 to run the form, select the Summary option, limit the months to August and later, click the Print button, and then click Zoom to see the beautiful report.

Use Print Preview to see what the report will look like.

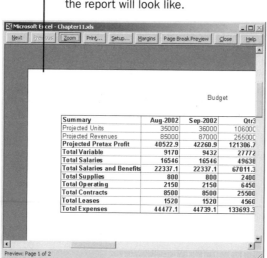

4 Close the Print Preview window.

The user interface of the form is now linked to its full functionality. All that's left is to provide a way for the user to run the form from Excel instead of from Visual Basic.

Launch the Form

To launch the form, you create a standard macro that displays the form. Once you've done that, you can make event procedures that automatically add a menu command when the workbook opens and remove the command when the workbook closes.

Project Explorer

1 Click the Project Explorer button to show the Project window, double-click the Module1 module (that is, the module that contains the ShowView and HideMonths macros), activate the code window, and scroll to the bottom of the module.

2 Insert this macro:

```
Sub ShowForm()
    frmPrint.Show
End Sub
```

The Show method of a form displays the form. To refer to the form, simply use the name that you gave it when you created it.

Tip

Ordinarily, you can't activate a worksheet while a form is displayed. When a form prevents you from selecting the worksheet, it's called a *modal* form. If you want the user to be able to use the worksheet while the form is displayed, add the argument **False** after the Show method. This creates what is called a *nonmodal* form.

3 In the Project window, double-click the ThisWorkbook object. Select Workbook from the Objects list, and insert these statements as the body of the *Workbook_Open* procedure:

```
Dim myButton As CommandBarButton
Set myButton = _
    Application.CommandBars("Worksheet Menu Bar").Controls.Add
myButton.Caption = "&Print Report"
myButton.Style = msoButtonCaption
myButton.BeginGroup = True
myButton.OnAction - "ShowForm"
```

The CommandBars collection works like any other collection; you specify an item using the name of the item. The Controls collection also works like other collections; you add an item—in this case, a command bar button—using the Add method. The Add method returns a reference to the new object, which you can assign to an object variable. Unless you specify otherwise, the Add method adds the control to the end of the collection.

Assigning a value to the Caption property sets the text for the command. Assigning *msoButtonCaption* to the Style property makes the control display the caption rather than an icon. The BeginGroup property adds a line before the command, separating it from the built-in commands. The OnAction property is the name of the macro you want to have run. This menu item will appear on the main Excel menu bar whenever you open the workbook.

4 From the Procedures list at the top of the code window, select BeforeClose. Insert these statements as the body of the *Workbook_BeforeClose* procedure:

```
ActiveWorkbook.Save
On Error Resume Next
Application.CommandBars("Worksheet Menu Bar") _
    .Controls("Print Report").Delete
```

The first statement saves the workbook. This prevents Excel from asking whether to save the workbook. The second statement keeps the macro from displaying an error if the Print Report command doesn't exist for some reason. The third statement deletes the new Print Report menu command. These statements will execute whenever the workbook closes, removing any trace of the Print Report command.

5 Switch to Excel, and then save and close the workbook.

6 Open the Chapter11 workbook and allow Excel to enable macros.

The new Print Report command appears on the main worksheet menu as soon as you open the workbook.

The new command appears on the main worksheet menu.

7 Click the new Print Report menu command, and then click Cancel.

8 Close the workbook.

The new command disappears. Your custom form is completely integrated with Excel.

Creating a fully usable form entails three major steps: creating the user interface, creating the functionality, and joining them together into a working tool. Now that you've created one form, go and create dozens more for your own projects.

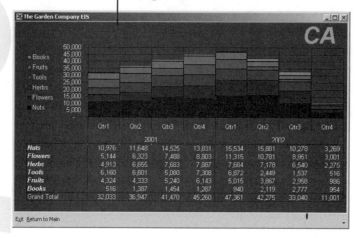

Create interactive management reports,
page 268

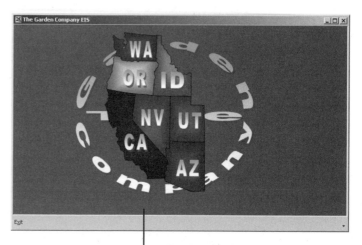

Create an animated splash screen,
page 281

QuickLook

Chapter 12
Create an Enterprise Information System

After completing this chapter, you will be able to:

✔ Retrieve data from an external database.
✔ Create a graphical front end to an application.
✔ Create an animated logo.
✔ Change and restore workbook settings.

While I was in college, I spent two years in Japan. Before leaving the United States, I spent two months in an intensive language training program. At the end of the two months, I was reasonably satisfied with my ability to speak Japanese. Then I arrived in Tokyo. For the first two weeks, I was unable to detect *any* similarity between the language I had studied and the language the local inhabitants were speaking. It was, shall we say, a humbling experience.

Within a few weeks, however, I was able to pick out words, and within a few months, I could communicate reasonably well. By the end of the two years, I once again felt reasonably satisfied with my ability to speak Japanese. And I learned along the way that classroom practice isn't the same as real-world experience.

Learning to write macros is in some ways similar to learning a new foreign language. Once again, classroom practice isn't the same as real-world experience. In this chapter, you'll build a simple but complete Enterprise Information System (EIS) that will allow people in all parts of a hypothetical enterprise to look at orders for the past two years. Creating a packaged application turns up numerous new real-world challenges that you don't encounter when building macros for yourself. This chapter will show you how to solve many such challenges.

Most of the concepts in this chapter have been introduced earlier in the book. This chapter shows how to put those concepts to work in packaging an application. This chapter also introduces a few new tricks that you might need.

Chapter12.xls

In addition to the main practice file Chapter12.xls, this chapter also uses the files Map.wmf, Orders.dbf, Orders.mdb, and Code12A.txt through Code12H.txt that you installed from the book's CD-ROM. For details about installing the practice files, see "Using the Book's CD-ROM" at the beginning of this book.

Getting Started

● Start Microsoft Excel. Make sure you have a blank workbook open.

Examining an Existing Enterprise Information System

In this chapter, you'll create an Enterprise Information System (EIS) that displays order information for each state in The Garden Company territory. It will be easier to understand what pieces you need to build if you have a vision of what you'll end up with. So let's take a look at the finished product before you start building it yourself.

Look at the Application

Open

1 Click the Open button, change to the folder containing the practice files for this book, select EIS.xls, and click Open.

2 Enable macros if asked.

When the workbook opens, it displays an introductory animation and shows you a colored, shaded map of the western United States.

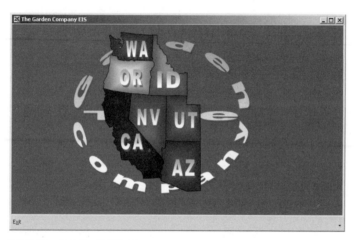

3 Click the map for California.

The screen switches to display quarterly orders for a two-year period, complete with a graph.

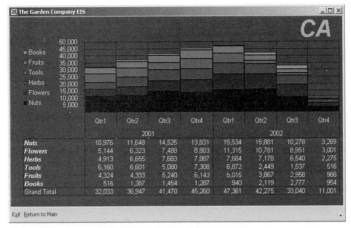

4 Click the Return To Main command at the lower left corner of the Workbook window to return to the map.

5 Click the Exit command at the bottom of the window to close the workbook.

This is a simple EIS. It displays information from one of the company's databases in an easy-to-use, visually powerful way.

Take a Closer Look at the Application

Many small details make the difference between an application that's intuitive and easy to use and one that's frustrating. Take another look at The Garden Company EIS, and notice some details worth including in your EIS.

1 Before reopening the EIS workbook, open and position several toolbars. Make the Excel window short and wide so that you can tell whether the application puts it back to the original size when it finishes.

Resize the window so that you can tell whether the application restores it properly.

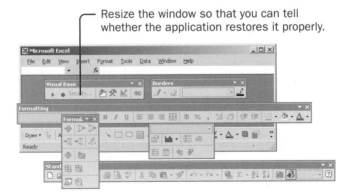

2 Open the finished Chapter12 workbook again. Wait for the animation to begin, but before it ends, press Ctrl+Break.

The animation stops, and the procedure that controls it jumps directly to its end and then displays the map. Animations are good for attracting attention, but they can be annoying to an impatient user. It's often a good idea to provide a mechanism for bypassing a lengthy animation.

3 Move the mouse over the notch where Nevada interlocks with Arizona. Click once when the mouse is over Nevada, return to the main sheet, and click again when the mouse is over Arizona. You can click anywhere within the exact border of the state to show the data for that state.

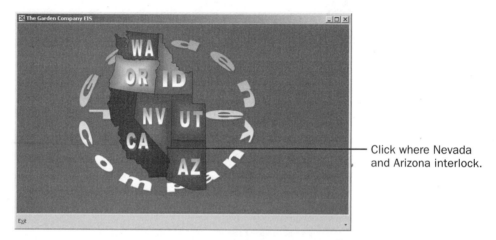

Click where Nevada and Arizona interlock.

This new screen with the table and the map is really a worksheet. Sometimes you want to use the features of an Excel worksheet but disguise that fact from the user.

4 Try selecting a cell on the worksheet.

This is a "look but don't touch" screen. The application makes use of a worksheet, but from the user's perspective, it could be a completely custom application. Although the data grid looks somewhat like a PivotTable, it also has some differences.

5 Look at the caption at the top of the application. The caption says *The Garden Company EIS* rather than *Excel*. The caption contributes to the custom appearance of the application.

6 Look at the button at the bottom of the screen. It appears to be a toolbar or a menu bar, but unlike most toolbars, it doesn't have a double bar at the left, so you can't move it. Many times in an EIS application, you want to limit the ways that the user can modify the environment.

7 Click the Exit button.

The Excel window returns to the way it was before—the same size and shape, with the same configuration of toolbars.

This EIS has many subtle features—features that you'll build into your EIS as you go through this chapter.

Charting Data from a Database

Your first task is to build the core functionality of the application—the data sheet. This sheet will use a PivotTable to retrieve the data from an external database. You'll link a chart to the PivotTable and then format the chart and the PivotTable to make a dramatic presentation.

Retrieve External Data into a PivotTable

The easiest way to retrieve data from an external database into a PivotTable is to use an Office Data Connection (odc) file. A data connection file contains all the information necessary to connect to any OLE DB data provider. OLE DB is a data connection technology that allows you to connect to a wide variety of data sources. Once you have created a data connection file, you can retrieve data into a list or a PivotTable report.

1 Save a new blank workbook as **Chapter12** in the folder containing the practice files for this book, replacing the copy of the finished workbook that you copied earlier. Then rename Sheet1 to **Data**.

2 From the Data menu, point at Import External Data and click Import Data. (Do not use the PivotTable And PivotChart Report command.) In the Select Data Source dialog box, select Connect To New Data Source and click the New Source button.

3 In the Data Connection Wizard dialog box, select Other/Advanced and click Next.

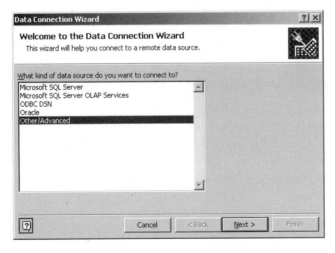

4 In the Data Link Properties dialog box, select Microsoft Jet 4.0 OLE DB Provider and click Next.

Clicking Next switches to the Connection tab.

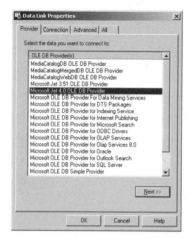

5 On the Connection tab, click the ellipsis button next to the box for entering a database name, navigate to the folder containing the practice files for this book, select Orders.mdb, and click Open. Then click OK.

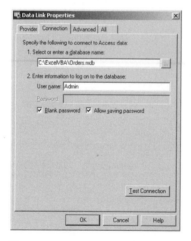

6 The next page of the wizard allows you to choose the table that contains the data. Leave the Orders table selected, and click Next.

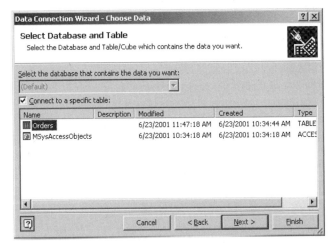

7 Type **The Garden Company** in the File Name box as the name for the new data connection file, and click Finish.

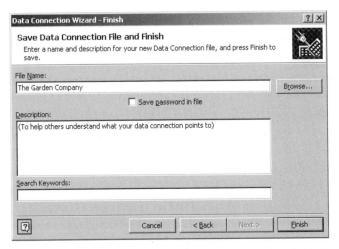

8 Back in the Import Data dialog box, click Create A PivotTable Report.

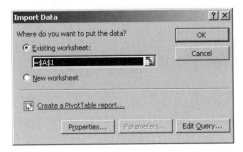

When you use the Import Data command, you can still create a PivotTable from the data connection you specify. The data connection is a simple file that you can transfer to another computer as needed.

Define the PivotTable

When you choose to create a PivotTable report from within the Import Data command, you are put directly into Step 3 of 3 of the PivotTable And PivotChart Wizard. You can now define the appearance of the PivotTable.

1 In the wizard, click Finish.

The shell of the PivotTable report appears, along with the PivotTable Field List. (If the PivotTable Field List does not appear, click the Show Field List button on the PivotTable toolbar. If the PivotTable toolbar is not visible, right-click any toolbar and click PivotTable.)

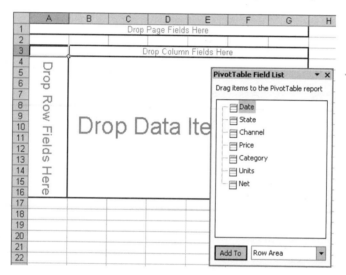

2 Drag the Category field to the Drop Row Fields Here area, drag State to the Drop Page Fields Here area, drag Date to the Drop Column Fields Here area, and drag Net to the Drop Data Items Here area. Then close the PivotTable Field List.

	A	B	C	D	E	F	G
1	State	(All) ▼					
2							
3	Sum of Net	Date ▼					
4	Category ▼	1/1/2000	2/1/2000	3/1/2000	4/1/2000	5/1/2000	6/1/2000
5	Books						
6	Flowers	4983.64	6472.32	4775.13	7805.35	7760.79	5578.9
7	Fruits	807.5	883.75	933.75	1022.5	3053.03	3280.36
8	Herbs	546.25	645.5	695.25	875.75	1916	2395.78
9	Nuts	668.25	841.6	979.75	1183.43	3279.41	3624.28
10	Tools			1117.25	1031.25	3976.54	4868.09
11	Grand Total	7005.64	8843.17	8501.13	11918.28	19985.77	19747.41

3 On the PivotTable toolbar, click the PivotTable menu, and then click Table Options. Turn off Grand Totals For Rows and AutoFormat Table, and then click OK. You'll apply custom formatting to the PivotTable, and you don't want Excel to automatically change the format each time you select a new state.

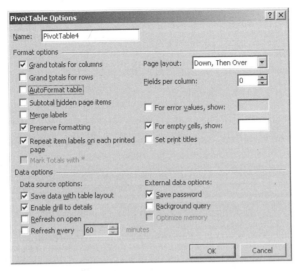

4 Click the PivotTable menu, point at Select, and click Entire Table. Then repeat, but click Data instead of Entire Table.

This selects all the data cells of the report.

5 On the Formatting toolbar, click the Comma Style button, and then click the Decrease Decimal button twice.

This formats the revenue values with commas, which makes the numbers easier to read.

	A	B	C	D	E	F	G	H
1	State	(All) ▼						
2								
3	Sum of Net	Date ▼						
4	Category ▼	1/1/2000	2/1/2000	3/1/2000	4/1/2000	5/1/2000	6/1/2000	7/1/2000
5	Books							
6	Flowers	4,984	6,472	4,775	7,805	7,761	5,579	6,689
7	Fruits	808	884	934	1,023	3,053	3,280	3,362
8	Herbs	546	646	695	876	1,916	2,396	2,207
9	Nuts	668	842	980	1,183	3,279	3,624	3,367
10	Tools			1,117	1,031	3,977	4,868	4,281
11	Grand Total	7,006	8,843	8,501	11,918	19,986	19,747	19,906

When you create the PivotTable, the data connection tells the PivotTable where the database is located. The data connection stores the entire location of the database. If you move the workbook or the database to a new location, the PivotTable won't be able to find the database. You can edit the connection string so that the report will find the database file in the current folder.

6 Point at the Data menu, click Import External Data, and then click Edit Query. Within the string in the Connection box, select and delete the path that precedes the Orders.mdb file name. Leave the rest of the connection string intact, and then click OK.

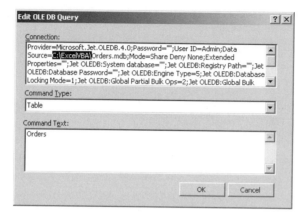

Tip

Even though you create a data connection file (The Garden Company) to create the report, the PivotTable internally stores the connection information and never uses the file again. If you don't need the data connection for a different purpose, you can remove it once the PivotTable is created.

To remove a data connection, simply act as if you were retrieving data for a new PivotTable report, but then right-click the data connection file and click Delete. If you need to modify the connection for an existing PivotTable report, select within the PivotTable, point at the Import External Data menu, and click Edit Query.

Enhance the Layout of the PivotTable Report

To improve the layout of the report, you want product categories to sort in descending order of revenue. You want to display quarters instead of months, and you want the same quarters always to appear, even if you select a state that did not sell any products during that quarter.

1 In the list next to the State button, select ID as the state and click OK.

The report shrinks, showing only categories and months in which sales actually occurred in Idaho. Notice also that the list of categories is sorted alphabetically, with Fruits appearing higher than Herbs or Tools, even though the revenue is lower.

	A	B	C
1	State	ID ▼	
2			
3	Sum of Net	Date ▼	
4	Category ▼	9/1/2002	10/1/2002
5	Books	1,665	1,733
6	Flowers	695	773
7	Fruits	398	318
8	Herbs	533	443
9	Tools	474	442
10	Grand Total	3,763	3,707

2 Double-click the Category tile (in the row area), again select the Show Items With No Data check box, and then click the Advanced button. Select Descending as the AutoSort option, and select Sum Of Net from the Using Field list box at the bottom of the AutoSort Options group. Then click OK twice.

All the categories now appear, sorted in descending order.

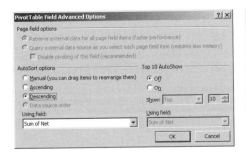
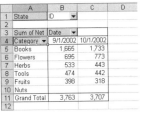

3 In the State list, select CA.

This switches the state to California. The Garden Company first started selling in California in August 2000. As a default, months before that month are hidden.

4 Double-click the Date tile (in the column area), select the Show Items With No Data check box, and then click OK.

This displays all the months, regardless of whether sales were made in that month in that state.

5 Right-click the Date tile, and on the Group And Show Detail submenu, click Group. In the By list box in the Grouping dialog box, deselect Months, select Quarters and Years, and then click OK.

This automatically groups the months into quarters and years, even though the quarter and year values are not in the original data source.

When you group dates, you end up with two rows of labels. A chart based on a PivotTable works just fine with one or more rows of labels. Because you specified Show Items With No Data for the Date field, the table shows extra "catch-all" dates at the beginning and end. You don't want those in the table. While you're at it, you can eliminate the year 2000 from the report, showing only the most recent two years.

6 Click the arrow next to the Years tile, deselect <1/1/2000, 2000, and >10/2/2002, and then click OK.

The unwanted periods disappear.

	A	B	C	D	E	F	G
1	State	CA					
2							
3	Sum of Net	Years	Date				
4		2001				2002	
5	Category	Qtr1	Qtr2	Qtr3	Qtr4	Qtr1	Qtr2
6	Flowers	11,954	9,916	10,623	11,253	8,011	6,061
7	Tools	9,559	10,397	10,883	9,405	9,035	7,429
8	Books	1,394	5,715	5,116	4,984	4,099	8,134
9	Herbs	4,656	4,899	5,268	6,169	4,599	3,444
10	Fruits	3,581	4,229	4,437	5,530	5,420	3,863
11	Nuts						
12	Grand Total	31,144	35,156	36,327	37,341	31,163	28,931
13							

The PivotTable report now shows the dates as quarters and years, sorts the product categories in descending order of sales, and retains the same row and column headings, regardless of which state is selected.

Format the PivotTable

The table looks good, except that you want a slightly more dramatic look for the EIS application. You also want the columns to keep the same width, instead of adjusting as the data changes. In addition, you will need a second copy of the PivotTable report that can serve as the data source for a PivotChart.

1 Insert a new column to the left of column A, and insert two new rows above row 1. Set the width of column A to 3.5, the width of column B (the category labels) to 18, the width of columns C through J (the data values) to 9, and the width of column K to 1.3.

Tip

If you want a chart based on a PivotTable to have a different orientation than the PivotTable, you need to make a second copy of the PivotTable to use as the basis for the chart. Because both PivotTables share the same data cache, creating a copy of the PivotTable doesn't require significant additional system resources.

2 Before continuing to format the PivotTable, make a copy of the Data sheet. Press and hold the Ctrl key as you drag the Data sheet tab to the right. Rename the new sheet **ChartData**, and reselect the Data sheet.

3 You want the background to be dark gray (leaving the black outlines in the PivotTable distinguishable) and the font for most of the cells to be light gray. Press Ctrl+A to select the entire Data worksheet. On the Formatting toolbar, click the Fill Color button and select Gray-80% (the top color in the rightmost column). Click the Font Color button, and select Gray-25% (the fourth color down in the rightmost column). Then select cell A1 to deselect the worksheet cells.

	A	B	C	D	E	F
1						
2						
3		State	CA ▾			
4						
5		Sum of Net	Years ▾ Date ▾			
6			2001			
7		Category ▾	Qtr1	Qtr2	Qtr3	Qtr4
8		Flowers	11,954	9,916	10,623	11,253
9		Tools	9,559	10,397	10,883	9,405
10		Books	1,394	5,715	5,116	4,984
11		Herbs	4,656	4,899	5,268	6,169
12		Fruits	3,581	4,229	4,437	5,530

4 Move the mouse pointer over the top of cell B7 until it turns into a black downward-pointing arrow, and then click.

This selects the Category labels.

Tip

If the mouse pointer never turns into a black arrow when you move it around over the labels of a PivotTable report, you do not have selections enabled for the report. To enable selections, click in the PivotTable, and on the PivotTable toolbar, click the PivotTable menu, the Select submenu, and the Enable Selection command.

5 Change the Category labels to bold and italic. Change the font color to White (the lower right color in the Font Color palette).

Click above the Category button
to select all the category labels.

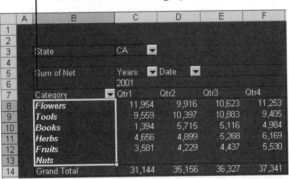

	A	B	C	D	E	F
1						
2						
3		State	CA ▾			
4						
5		Sum of Net	Years ▾ Date ▾			
6			2001			
7		Category ▾	Qtr1	Qtr2	Qtr3	Qtr4
8		*Flowers*	11,954	9,916	10,623	11,253
9		*Tools*	9,559	10,397	10,883	9,405
10		*Books*	1,394	5,715	5,116	4,984
11		*Herbs*	4,656	4,899	5,268	6,169
12		*Fruits*	3,581	4,229	4,437	5,530
13		*Nuts*				
14		Grand Total	31,144	35,156	36,327	37,341

You won't need the column headings from the PivotTable because the chart will have labels for the years and quarters. You can hide the top part of the PivotTable to get ready to add the chart, but first put a formula at the top of the sheet to show which state is currently displayed.

6 In cell J1, enter the formula **=C3**. Format the cell as right-aligned, bold, and italic, with 36 as the font size, and Turquoise (fourth row, fifth from the left) as the font color.

7 Hide rows 3 through 7. Then save the Chapter12 workbook.

Hide rows that contain unwanted
labels for the PivotTable.

The PivotTable is ready. Next you'll create a chart to display the PivotTable data.

Create a PivotChart

A chart can make the numbers in the table easier to interpret. To show both the total
orders for a state and what portion of those orders came from each category, a *stepped
area chart* is a good choice. A stepped area chart is a stacked column chart with no gaps
between the columns.

When you associate a chart with a PivotTable, the chart becomes a PivotChart. The row
headings in the PivotTable always correspond to the horizontal axis of the PivotChart.
You, however, want the dates as row headings in the PivotTable and as horizontal labels
in the PivotChart, so you need to base the chart on the copy of the PivotTable.

Chart Wizard

1 Activate the ChartData sheet, click in the PivotTable, and then click the Chart Wizard button to create a new PivotChart on a new sheet.

2 Drag the Category tile to the legend area, and drag the Year and Date tiles down to the
horizontal axis.

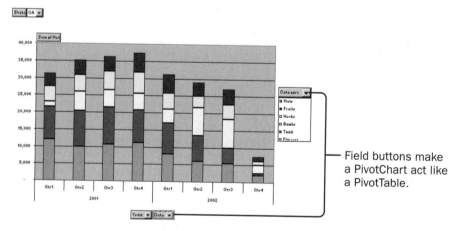

Field buttons make
a PivotChart act like
a PivotTable.

Rearranging the chart also rearranges the PivotTable it's based on. If you want to control
the orientation of a PivotTable report separately from a chart based on it, you must create
a separate copy of the report.

3 On the PivotTable toolbar, select the PivotChart menu and click Hide PivotChart Field
Buttons.

You won't be manipulating the chart anymore, so you won't need the field buttons on the chart.

4   Make a few more changes to the general chart layout. On the Chart menu, click Chart Options. On the Gridlines tab, select Category (X) Axis Major Gridlines. On the Legend tab, select Left as the placement option. Then click OK.

5   Double-click any of the columns, and select the Options tab. Change the Gap Width setting to 0, and click OK.

6   Before you move the chart to the sheet with the table, you need to ensure that the font won't change size. Double-click in the white space above the chart to format the Chart Area. On the Font tab, deselect the Auto Scale check box and then click OK.

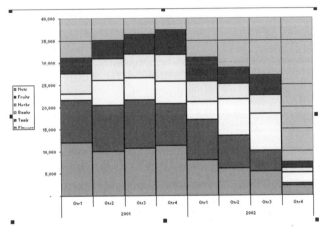

7   Now you can move the chart to the Data sheet. On the Chart menu, click Location, select As Object In Data, and then click OK.

The chart appears on the worksheet, overlapping the formatted tabular report.

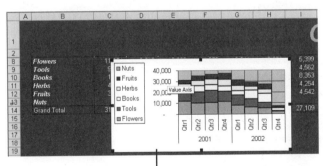

While the chart is opaque, make it overlap part of the PivotTable.

You want to position the chart above the grid, aligned so that the columns in the chart match up with the appropriate columns in the table. Changing the height of row 2 will give you enough room for the chart. If you change the chart so that it doesn't automatically resize with the underlying data cells, you can temporarily adjust row heights to precisely position the chart.

8 On the Format menu, click Selected Chart Area and select the Properties tab. Select the Don't Move Or Size With Cells option, and then click OK.

9 Change the height of row 1 to 20 and the height of row 2 to 183. Then press and hold the Alt key as you drag the upper left corner of the chart to the upper left corner of cell A2, and as you drag the lower right corner of the chart to the lower right corner of cell K2.

10 Change the height of row 1 to 40 and the height of row 2 to 150.

The chart overlaps the state identifier and part of the table, but that ensures that the pieces will all flow together when you make the chart transparent.

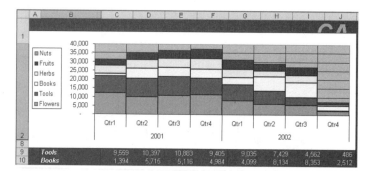

You can now turn off the row and column headings because you won't need them again.

11 If the chart is selected, press Esc to deselect it. On the Tools menu, select Options. Click the View tab, clear the Row And Column Headers check box, and then click OK.

When you move the mouse over items in a chart, a chart tip displays information about that item. You want the chart tips to display the value for any item, but you don't want the name of the item to show. You set a global charting option to make that change.

12 On the Tools menu, select Options. Select the Chart tab, clear the Show Names check box, and then click OK.

Format a PivotChart

You need to make the chart transparent so that it will integrate smoothly with the table. To make the chart completely transparent, you need to change the chart area, the plot area, and the legend. Rather than select and change each object interactively, you can make the changes using Microsoft Visual Basic for Applications from the Immediate window. While you're at it, you can change the color of the fonts in the chart to a light shade of gray.

1 Activate the Visual Basic Editor, and in the Immediate window type the following statements:

```
set x = Activesheet.ChartObjects(1).Chart
x.ChartArea.Font.ColorIndex = 54
x.ChartArea.Fill.ForeColor.SchemeColor = xlNone
x.ChartArea.Border.LineStyle = xlNone
x.Legend.Fill.ForeColor.SchemeColor = xlNone
x.Legend.Border.LineStyle = 0
x.PlotArea.Fill.ForeColor.SchemeColor=xlNone
x.PlotArea.Border.Color = vbBlack
```

Tip

To make Visual Basic show you lists of methods and properties, create a macro containing the statement Dim x as Chart and step through the declaration before entering statements in the Immediate window.

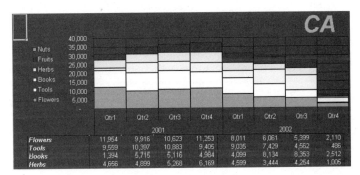

The name of the state should be just over the top of the plot area, and the lines around the horizontal labels should just barely touch the PivotTable lines. The grids don't match perfectly on the left, but because the alignment changes whenever the value scale changes, you'll create a macro later to fix the vertical alignment.

You can also change the colors of the chart to be evenly spaced shades from black to turquoise. Excel uses the eight colors from 17 through 24 as fill colors in a chart. You have seven series in the chart. By changing the colors in the palette, you can change the colors on the chart. The color turquoise contains the maximum possible amount (255) of green and blue, but no red. By dividing 255 by 6, you can obtain seven evenly spaced shades of turquoise.

2 In the Immediate window, enter the following two lines:

```
set x = ActiveWorkbook
For i=0 To 6:x.Colors(17+i)=RGB(0,i*(255/6),i*(255/6)):Next
```

The colors change to shades of turquoise.

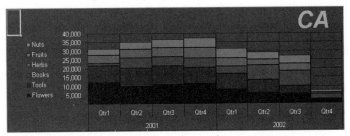

3 Switch back to Excel, and save the Chapter12 workbook.

The chart now blends in almost perfectly with the background. Next you can add some simple macros to control both the PivotTable and the PivotChart.

Controlling the Report with Macros

The users of your PivotTable and PivotChart will use the map to change states. You'll need to create a macro that both changes the state and adjusts the width of the chart to make it match the PivotTable grid. In addition, you'll need to create a macro that refreshes the PivotTable so that new data appears as changes are made to the database.

Make a Macro Change the PivotTable

If you create a macro that takes an argument giving the state code, you can use that one macro for any state. First create a macro that changes the PivotTable to display orders for an arbitrary state, and then add the argument to generalize the macro.

Run Macro

1 On the Visual Basic toolbar, click the Run Macro button. Type **SetPivot** as the macro name, and click Create.

The Visual Basic Editor opens with a new macro named SetPivot.

2 Enter these statements as the body of the SetPivot macro:

```
Worksheets("Data").Select
ActiveSheet.PivotTables(1).PageFields(1).CurrentPage = "OR"
Worksheets("ChartData").PivotTables(1).PageFields(1).CurrentPage = "OR"
```

This macro changes the PivotTable to display the orders for Oregon. The first statement selects the Data sheet, just in case it wasn't already the active sheet. The second statement changes the value of the CurrentPage property for the one page field of the one PivotTable on the sheet. The third statement makes the same change to the one PivotTable on the Chart sheet. For now, the new state (OR for *Oregon*) is a constant.

3 Press F5 to run the macro, which now changes the state to Oregon. Change the state code in the macro (in both places) to **NV** (for *Nevada*), and try it again.

4 Next you can change the macro to accept an argument for the state code. Insert **NewState** between the parentheses after the name of the macro. Then replace both occurrences of *NV* with **NewState**.

5 Press Ctrl+G to display the Immediate window, and in that window, type **SetPivot "ID"** and then press the Enter key. The state changes to Idaho. The SetPivot macro is ready to change both the PivotTable and the chart to any state.

6 Save the Chapter12 workbook.

A state with few orders, such as Idaho, has narrower labels than some of the larger states. The macro needs to adjust the horizontal position of the chart whenever you or another user changes the state.

Make a Macro Adjust a Chart

A stepped area chart looks best if it doesn't have borders around each area. Unfortunately, even if you remove the borders, each time you change the PivotTable, the borders reappear. Fortunately, you can write a simple macro to remove the borders each time the PivotTable changes. Also, the size of the value labels affects how the chart label gridlines align with the PivotTable gridlines. That's also something you can fix with a macro whenever the state changes.

1 Activate the Visual Basic Editor, and click below the SetPivot macro. From the Insert menu, click File, change to the folder containing the practice files for this book, and double-click the Code12a file. This AdjustChart macro appears in the module:

```
Sub AdjustChart()
    Dim myObject As ChartObject
    Dim myChart As Chart
    Dim myWidth As(?)
    Dim myLeft As(?)
    Dim mySeries As Series
    Set myObject = ActiveSheet.ChartObjects(1)
    Set myChart = myObject.Chart

    myWidth = myChart.PlotArea.Width _
        - myChart.PlotArea.InsideWidth
    myWidth = myChart.ChartArea.Left _
        + myChart.PlotArea.Left + myWidth
    myWidth = myWidth - 0.5

    myLeft = Range("C1").Left - myWidth
    myObject.Left = myLeft
    myObject.Width = Range("L1").Left - myLeft

    For Each mySeries In myChart.SeriesCollection
        mySeries.Border.LineStyle = xlNone
    Next mySeries
End Sub
```

This macro consists of four parts, separated by blank lines. The first part declares some variables and assigns references to both the chart's container object and the chart itself.

The second part of the macro calculates the width of the area from the left edge of the chart to the left edge of the plot area rectangle. A plot area on a chart has two definitions. The plot area you select on the chart is actually the inside plot area. The outer plot area includes the area with the axis labels. By subtracting the inside width of the plot area from the width, you get the size of the labels. Adding that to the starting position of the chart area and the outer plot area gives you the total width from the edge of the chart container to the edge of the inner plot area. Subtracting a half point from the width makes the grid line up better.

On a PivotChart, you can't adjust the positions of any of the objects within the chart. You can adjust only the location of the container. The third part of the macro calculates how much the chart needs to be shifted to the right and then subtracts that same amount from the width to keep the right side aligned.

The fourth and final part of the macro removes the border lines from each of the series in the chart. The On Error Resume Next statement is there because some of the charts contain *empty* series—series that are technically in the SeriesCollection collection but don't appear on the screen—and can't be modified.

2 Add the statement **AdjustChart** to the end of the SetPivot macro, and in the Immediate window, execute the statement that changes the report to Idaho.

3   Insert the statement **Application.ScreenUpdating = False** at the top of the SetPivot macro, and change the PivotTable to "WA".

4   Save the Chapter12 workbook.

The SetPivot macro is ready to use. Later you'll create a graphical interface that calls the SetPivot macro, passing the appropriate state code as an argument.

You've now created the core functionality of the application. The PivotTable retrieves the data from the external database, and the chart presents the data in a visually appealing way. Your next task is to create an effective mechanism for interacting with the application.

Creating a Graphical Interface

A graphical interface, such as a map, can be an effective way of presenting choices. Instead of selecting the name of a state from a list, the user can simply click within the state boundary.

Insert a Map

First you need to create a map on the worksheet. You can import pictures from Excel's clip art gallery or from a file in Windows. For this example, you'll import the picture from a file.

1   Select Sheet3 in the Chapter12 workbook. Rename the sheet as **Main**.

2   Press Ctrl+A to select all the cells, click the Fill Color button, and then change the color to Green (the fourth color on the second row in the color menu).

3   Select cell D3, and on the Insert menu, point to the Picture submenu and click From File.

4   Change to the folder containing the practice files for this book, select the Map.wmf file, and click Insert.

5   From the Format menu, click Picture, click the Size tab, set the height to 3.5 inches, and then click OK.

6   If necessary, click the Drawing button to activate the Drawing toolbar. Click the Draw menu on the Drawing toolbar, click the Ungroup command, and click Yes to convert the picture to a Microsoft Office drawing object.

7   Once again, click the Draw menu on the Drawing toolbar, and click the Ungroup command again.

This converts the group into separate objects, one for each state, plus a background.

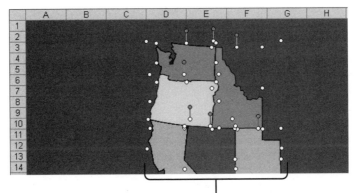

Ungrouping creates a separate
object for each state.

8 Press Esc to deselect the group. Then click in the vicinity of cell F4 to select the background shape, and press Delete.

9 Save the Chapter12 workbook.

The map is ready. You could have the user simply click on the state background, but adding the two-letter codes for the states will make things easier for people who get the states confused.

Add State Codes to the Map

You could use command buttons to add the state codes to the map, but buttons have limited formatting capabilities. Instead, try using WordArt text so that you can make the state codes look attractive. Because you will need to add a state code for each of seven states, you can record and modify a simple macro to make the task easier.

1 Select the map for Washington state.

2 On the Visual Basic toolbar, click the Record Macro button. Type **NameState** as the macro name, and click OK.

3 Click in the Name Box to the left of the formula bar, type **mapWA**, and press Enter.

Later you'll assign a macro to run when you click the state name. If you include the state code at the end of the name of each graphical object, you'll be able to use a single macro for all the states.

4 Click the arrow next to the Fill Color button, and click Fill Effects. Select One Color as the Colors option, select From Center as the Shading Styles option, and click OK.

This gives a shaded, 3-D effect to the background of the state.

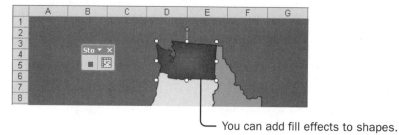

You can add fill effects to shapes.

WordArt

5 On the Drawing toolbar, click the Insert WordArt button. Select the silver text fourth style on the second row, and click OK.

Start with this WordArt style.

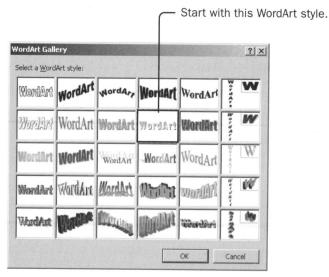

6 In the Edit WordArt Text dialog box, type **WA** as the text, and click OK.

Replace the default text with **WA**.

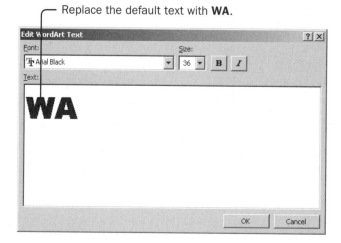

7 Click in the Name Box, type **lblWA**, and press Enter.

8 From the Format menu, choose Word Art. On the Size tab, specify 0.35 inch as the Height, 0.5 inch as the Width, and click OK.

9 Turn off the recorder, and then drag the label into the middle of the Washington state map. (If you accidentally drag the map for Utah instead of the label, you can press Ctrl+Z to put it back.)

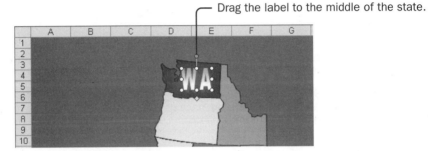

Drag the label to the middle of the state.

10 Click the Run Macro button, select NameState, and click Edit. The recorded macro should look like this:

```
Sub NameState()
    Selection.Name = "mapWA"
    Selection.ShapeRange.Fill.ForeColor.RGB = RGB(1, 128, 4)
    Selection.ShapeRange.Fill.Transparency = 0#
    Selection.ShapeRange.Fill.OneColorGradient _
        msoGradientFromCenter, 1, 0.23
    ActiveSheet.Shapes.AddTextEffect(msoTextEffect10, _
        "WA", "Arial Black", 36#, _
        msoFalse, msoFalse, 228.75, 134.25).Select
    Selection.Name = "lblWA"
    Selection.ShapeRange.LockAspectRatio = msoFalse
    Selection.ShapeRange.Height = 25.5
    Selection.ShapeRange.Width = 36#
    Selection.ShapeRange.Rotation = 0#
End Sub
```

The text string *WA* appears three times in the macro. Changing the state code to use an argument will make it easy to add the other six labels.

11 Between the parentheses, type **StateCode**. Replace "mapWA" with **"map" & StateCode**, replace "WA" with StateCode, and replace "lblWA" with **"lbl" & StateCode**. The modified macro should look like this:

```
Sub NameState(StateCode)
    Selection.Name = "map" & StateCode
    Selection.ShapeRange.Fill.ForeColor.RGB = RGB(1, 128, 4)
    Selection.ShapeRange.Fill.Transparency = 0#
    Selection.ShapeRange.Fill.OneColorGradient _
        msoGradientFromCenter, 1, 0.23
    ActiveSheet.Shapes.AddTextEffect(msoTextEffect10, _
```

(continued)

continued

```
        StateCode, "Arial Black", 36#, _
        msoFalse, msoFalse, 228.75, 134.25).Select
    Selection.Name = "lbl" & StateCode
    Selection.ShapeRange.LockAspectRatio = msoFalse
    Selection.ShapeRange.Height = 25.5
    Selection.ShapeRange.Width = 36#
    Selection.ShapeRange.Rotation = 0#
End Sub
```

12 In Excel, select the map for Oregon. In the Visual Basic Immediate window, type **NameState "OR"** and press Enter. In Excel, drag the new OR label to the middle of the Oregon state map.

13 Repeat for each of the remaining states using the appropriate state codes (ID, CA, NV, UT, and AZ). When you've finished, each object will have the state code as the last two letters of the name.

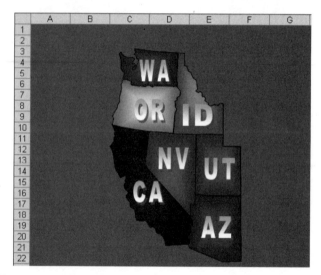

14 Save the Chapter12 workbook.

By assigning names ending in the two-letter state code to both the WordArt object and the map for each state, you can streamline the macro that enables a user to click either the letters or the background to run the macro.

Link a Macro to the Graphical Objects

Earlier in the chapter, you created a SetPivot macro. That macro can display any state, provided that you pass it the appropriate state code. Coincidentally, the state code is the last two letters of the name of each object for each state. You therefore need to create a macro that can retrieve the name from the object and extract the code for whichever state the user clicks.

In a macro, the Excel Application object has a property named Caller. The Caller property gives you the name of the object that the user clicked to run the macro. Visual Basic has a function named Right that extracts letters from the right side of a word. You can use the Right function to extract the state code from the name that the Caller property returns. Even if you group the states, the Caller property still returns the name of the specific item that you click.

Select Objects

1 On the Drawing toolbar, click the Select Objects button. Then drag a rectangle around the entire map.

You should see sizing handles around each of the seven states.

2 On the Drawing toolbar, click the Draw menu and then click Group.

This creates a single group out of all the selected objects.

3 Click in the Name Box, type **shpMap** as the name of the group, and press Enter. Then click the Select Objects button to turn it off.

4 Right-click on the map, and choose the Assign Macro command.

When you assign a macro to a grouped object, you actually assign the macro to each object within the group.

5 In the Assign Macro dialog box, type **ShowMe** as the macro name, and click New.

6 Enter these statements as the body of the ShowMe macro:

```
Dim myName As String
Dim myCode As String

myName = Application.Caller
myCode = Right(myName, 2)
SetPivot myCode
```

7 Save the Chapter12 workbook, and click anywhere inside the border of Nevada. The Data sheet should appear and display the orders for Nevada.

The Application.Caller property is a convenient tool for making a single macro handle any of several objects.

Tip

When you use the Control Toolbox to add an object such as a command button, you create an ActiveX control. Multiple ActiveX controls can't share a single macro because they use event handler procedures, and an event handler can link to only one object.

Add a Background Logo

You can also use WordArt to add an attractive logo for the EIS application. Later in the chapter, you'll animate the logo.

Insert WordArt

1 Activate the Main worksheet, and click the Drawing toolbar's Insert WordArt button.

2 Select the silver text (the fourth style on the second row), and click OK. Type **Garden** and press the Enter key, type **The** and press the Enter key again, type **Company**, and then click OK.

Start with a built-in format.

WordArt Shape

3 The new WordArt object has the appropriate colors, but it has a strange shape. You can easily adjust the shape. On the WordArt toolbar, click the WordArt Shape button and select the Button (Pour) shape (the rightmost shape on the second row).

WordArt Same Letter Heights

4 On the WordArt toolbar, click the WordArt Same Letter Heights button. Then click the WordArt Alignment button, and choose the Stretch Justify option.

5 Drag the upper left sizing handle to the upper left corner of cell C3, and drag the lower right sizing handle to the middle of the bottom of cell H22. Then center the map within the new WordArt shape.

WordArt Alignment

Many shapes have an adjustment marker that allows you to modify the shape. It appears as a yellow diamond to the left of center in the WordArt object. Later in the chapter, you'll see how a macro can change the adjustment.

6 Select the WordArt shape, and drag the adjustment marker to the left until it's about a quarter of an inch from the outside circle.

Drag the Adjustment handle to change the shape.

7 Click in the Name Box, type **shpLogo**, and press Enter.

8 Turn off the row and column headings. (From the Tools menu, click Options, click the View tab, and then clear the Row And Column Headers check box.)

9 Press the Esc key to deselect the logo, and then save the Chapter12 workbook.

The logo looks good, but you can make it even more attractive by animating it.

Animate the Logo

Animating a WordArt object is easy. You use a macro that simply makes many small changes to the adjustment values that are available. When you adjust shapes in a macro, however, Windows doesn't refresh the screen until the macro has completed. In many cases, you'll be glad that Windows doesn't refresh the screen because your macro runs faster that way. When you're animating a shape, however, you want the screen to refresh each time the macro adjusts the shape. As part of the animation, you can initially hide the map and then gradually display it.

1 On the Drawing toolbar, click the Rectangle button, and drag a rectangle large enough to completely cover the map.

2 Click the Draw menu on the Drawing toolbar. Click Order, and click Send Backward.

This moves the rectangle behind the logo, but leaves it in front of the map. The rectangle serves as a mask to hide the map.

3 Click in the Name Box, type **shpMask**, and press Enter.

4 Click the arrow next to the Line Color box, and select No Line.

5 Click the arrow next to the Fill Color box, and select Green (the fourth color on the second row—the same color as the worksheet background).

6 Click the arrow next to the Fill Color box, and select More Fill Colors. At the bottom of the dialog box, drag the Transparency slider to show approximately 50%. Then click OK.

The animation macro will gradually increase the transparency of the mask to reveal the map.

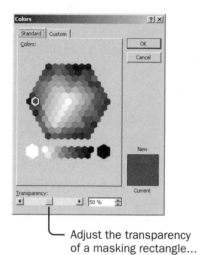

Adjust the transparency
of a masking rectangle...

...to gradually
reveal the map.

7 Activate the Visual Basic Editor, and click at the bottom of the module. From the Insert menu, click File, change to the folder containing the practice files for this book, and double-click the Code12b file.

This StartUpAnimation macro appears in the module:

```
Sub StartUpAnimation()
    Dim myLogo As Shape
    Dim myMap As Shape
    Dim myMask As Shape
    Dim i As Double
    Set myLogo = Worksheets("Main").Shapes("shpLogo")
    Set myMap = Worksheets("Main").Shapes("shpMap")
    Set myMask = Worksheets("Main").Shapes("shpMask")

    Application.EnableCancelKey = xlErrorHandler
    On Error GoTo StartUpAnimation_EndErrorHandler

    Application.ScreenUpdating = False
    myMap.Visible = msoFalse
    myLogo.Adjustments(1) = 91
    myLogo.Adjustments(2) = 0.49
    myLogo.TextEffect.Tracking = 0.1
    Worksheets("Main").Select
    Application.ScreenUpdating = True

    For i = 91 To 176 Step 5
        myLogo.Adjustments(1) = i
        DoEvents
    Next i
    For i = 0.48 To 0.18 Step -0.04
        myLogo.Adjustments(2) = i
        DoEvents
    Next i
```

```
    For i = 0.1 To 1.41 Step 0.2
        myLogo.TextEffect.Tracking = i
        DoEvents
    Next i
    For i = 0.2 To 0.45 Step 0.02
        myLogo.Adjustments(2) = i
        DoEvents
    Next i
    myMap.ZOrder msoSendToBack
    myMask.Fill.Transparency = 0
    myMap.Visible = msoTrue
    For i = 0 To 1 Step 0.2
        myMask.Fill.Transparency = i
        DoEvents
    Next i

StartUpAnimation_EndErrorHandler:
    myLogo.Adjustments(1) = 176
    myLogo.Adjustments(2) = 0.44
    myLogo.TextEffect.Tracking = 1.3
    myLogo.Visible = msoTrue
    myMap.ZOrder msoBringToFront
    myMap.Visible = msoTrue
End Sub
```

This macro consists of five parts, separated by blank lines. The first part simply declares some variables and assigns references to the three shapes on the worksheet.

The second part and the fifth part work together to allow you to skip the animation by pressing Ctrl+Break. The On Error Goto ErrorHandler statement tells the macro to jump to the ErrorHandler label if there's an error. The EnableCancelKey property tells Excel to consider it an error if the user presses Ctrl+Break. The statements in the final part (after the label) simply set the shape adjustments to their final values and display both shapes.

The third part of the macro sets the logo shape adjustments to their initial values, hides the map, and makes sure that screen updating hasn't been turned off by an earlier procedure. It then activates the Main worksheet, ready to show the animation. The Tracking property controls how much WordArt letters overlap.

Tip

The constants *msoTrue* and *msoFalse* are identical to the ordinary Visual Basic constants *True* and *False*. The *mso-* prefix stands for "Microsoft Office"; for some unknown reason, the designer of the Shape objects decided to create *True* and *False* values that are unique to Microsoft Office. You can use the *True* and *False* constants with Shape objects, but when you enter a statement using a Shape object, the Auto List offers only *msoTrue* and *msoFalse*.

The fourth part of the macro does the real animation. It consists of five loops, four of which change three different settings of the logo shape. The fifth loop changes the transparency of the mask. You can find appropriate start and end values for an animation by turning on the recorder and making manual changes to the adjustments for a shape. Much of the process is simply trial and error. The DoEvents statement is the secret to making an animation work. This statement tells Windows to refresh the screen (refreshing is an action that Windows should perform), without waiting for the macro to end.

8 Save the Chapter12 workbook, click in the StartUpAnimation macro, and press F5 to test the macro. You might want to set breakpoints in the macro and step through parts of the macro.

Your application now has both functionality and an effective user interface; however, it's still obviously part of Excel. Now is the time to package the application by removing any distracting toolbars, window features, and menu commands and by making the macros run automatically.

Packaging the Application

Packaging the application consists of bending the appearance and behavior of the Excel workspace to match your wishes. Many of the settings you'll need to change—such as the window size and the appearance of the toolbars—can also be customized by the user. Excel stores changes to those settings. For example, after a user changes which toolbars are visible, Excel saves the settings when the program closes and restores them the next time the program starts.

If your application changes customization settings, it must restore them to the original state when the application closes. For example, if your application hides all the toolbars when it opens, it should redisplay the toolbars when it closes.

Replace and Restore the Menu Bar

A Windows application can have many toolbars but only one menu bar. The way to remove the Excel menu bar is to replace it with a custom menu bar. When the application closes, removing the custom menu bar automatically restores the standard Excel menu bar. A menu bar is simply a command bar—just like a toolbar—that you designate as a menu bar. You give the menu bar a name when you create it, and you can then use that name to delete it. For this application, name the menu bar EIS.

1 In the Visual Basic Editor, add this procedure to the module:

```
Sub ZapMenu()
    On Error Resume Next
    CommandBars("EIS").Delete
End Sub
```

The On Error Resume Next statement allows you to use this macro to ensure that the custom menu is deleted, without worrying about whether it was ever created or not. When the application is working perfectly, the menu bar should never exist when the macro creates it, and it should always exist when the macro deletes it; but while you're developing and testing the application, you might sometimes run the ZapMenu macro when the menu has already been deleted. In that case, having the macro ignore the error makes your life simpler.

The menu bar for this application will have two commands: Exit and Return To Main. Before creating the macro that adds the custom menu bar, you can create the Sub procedures the commands will need.

2 Add this procedure to the module:

```
Sub ExitEIS()
    ZapMenu
    ActiveWorkbook.Close
End Sub
```

This procedure closes the active workbook. This is the macro that the Exit button will run.

3 Add this procedure to the module:

```
Sub ReturnToMain()
    Worksheets("Main").Select
End Sub
```

This procedure activates the Main worksheet. This is the macro that the Return To Main button will run.

4 Now you're ready to add the macro that adds the custom menu bar. Click at the bottom of the module, and from the Insert menu, click File and double-click the Code12c file to add this procedure to the module:

```
Sub SetMenu()
    Dim myBar As CommandBar
    Dim myButton As CommandBarButton

    ZapMenu
    Set myBar = CommandBars.Add(Name:="EIS", _
        Position:=msoBarBottom, _
        MenuBar:=True)

    Set myButton = myBar.Controls.Add(msoControlButton)
    myButton.Style = msoButtonCaption
    myButton.Caption = "E&xit"
    myButton.OnAction = "ExitEIS"

    Set myButton = myBar.Controls.Add(msoControlButton)
    myButton.Style = msoButtonCaption
    myButton.Caption = "&Return to Main"
    myButton.OnAction = "ReturnToMain"
    myButton.Visible = False

    myBar.Protection = msoBarNoMove    msoBarNoCustomize
    myBar.Visible = True
End Sub
```

This macro consists of five parts separated by blank lines. The first part simply declares a couple of variables.

The second part of the macro runs the ZapMenu macro to make sure the EIS menu bar doesn't already exist, and then it creates a new EIS menu bar. Passing *True* as the value of the *MenuBar* argument is what makes this new command bar into a menu bar. Putting the menu bar at the bottom of the screen makes it look less like a conventional menu bar.

The third and fourth parts of the macro add the two commands to the menu bar. Initially, the Return To Main command is invisible.

The fifth and final part of the macro protects the new menu bar. This property has an enumerated list of values that you can assign to it to control what you will and will not allow users to do to the menu bar. You can add values together to further control what you will allow. This macro doesn't allow the user to move or customize the new menu bar.

5 Save the Chapter12 workbook, and run the SetMenu macro and the ZapMenu macro.

In summary, replacing the Excel menu bar is easy—you just create a new one of your own. Restoring the Excel menu bar is even easier—you just delete the one you created.

Show and Hide a Menu Command

You still need to make the Return To Menu command visible whenever the Data worksheet becomes active, and to make it invisible whenever the Data worksheet becomes inactive. This looks like a job for event handler procedures—one to hide the command and one to show it. You can create a single procedure with an argument, and then you have the event handlers call that procedure.

1 Insert this procedure into the module:

```
Sub CommandVisible(IsVisible)
    On Error Resume Next
    CommandBars("EIS").Controls(2).Visible = IsVisible
End Sub
```

The On Error Resume Next statement again allows you to avoid inconveniences while building and testing the application—in case this procedure runs when the menu hasn't been created. The other statement makes the command visible or invisible, depending on the value of the argument.

Project Explorer

2 Click the Project Explorer button, and double-click the entry for the Data worksheet.

3 Insert these two event handler procedures:

```
Private Sub Worksheet_Activate()
    CommandVisible True
End Sub
Private Sub Worksheet_Deactivate()
    CommandVisible False
End Sub
```

Whenever the Data worksheet becomes active, the Return To Menu command will become visible. Whenever the worksheet becomes inactive, the command will disappear.

4 Reactivate the module, close the Project window, save the Chapter12 workbook, and run the SetMenu macro.

5 Activate Excel, and switch back and forth between the Data and Main worksheets. Watch to see the command appear and disappear.

6 Run the ZapMenu macro.

Change and Restore Windows

You can create a pleasant-looking package for the application by creating a window that's precisely the right size for the table and chart. When the application closes, however, you should restore the window to its previous state. Restoring the window is harder than restoring the Excel menu bar because you must make the macro remember the original size of the window.

You can store the size of the window in a variable, but when you use Dim to declare a variable inside a procedure, the variable lasts only as long as the procedure is running. You can keep a variable from disappearing by using the word Static to declare the variable.

1 Insert this partial procedure into the module:

```
Sub SetWindow(State)
    Const myWidth = 540
    Const myHeight = 340
    Static myOldWidth
    Static myOldHeight
    Static myOldState


End Sub
```

You'll use this same procedure to change the window and to restore it. The *State* argument will determine which task the procedure will carry out. By using a single procedure for both tasks, you can store the old values right here in the *SetWindow* procedure using the Static keyword. The Const statements give the new custom values for the height and width. A Const is a constant value. You can use it like a read-only variable. Giving the width and height new values at the top like this makes them easy to change if you want to adjust your application later.

2 Click in the blank line before the End Sub statement of the SetWindow procedure, and from the Insert menu, click File and then double-click the file Code12d to insert the following part of the macro:

```
If State = xlOn Then
    myOldWidth = Application.Width
    myOldHeight = Application.Height
    myOldState = Application.WindowState
    Application.WindowState = xlNormal
    Application.Width = myWidth
    Application.Height = myHeight
    Application.Caption = "The Garden Company EIS"

    ActiveWorkbook.Unprotect
    ActiveWindow.WindowState = xlMaximized
    ActiveWindow.Caption = ""
    ActiveWorkbook.Protect , True, True

    ProtectSheet xlOn, "Main"
    ProtectSheet xlOn, "Data"
    Application.DisplayFormulaBar = False
```

(continued)

continued

```
    Application.DisplayStatusBar = False
    ActiveWindow.DisplayHorizontalScrollBar = False
    ActiveWindow.DisplayVerticalScrollBar = False
    ActiveWindow.DisplayWorkbookTabs = False
```

This is the first half of an If...Else...End If structure. It runs if the value of the *State* argument is *xlOn*. The value *xlOn* is a built-in Excel constant. Using the constant makes the macro easier to read than using an arbitrary number, and using a built-in constant is easier than creating a custom constant.

Setting the window consists of three parts. The first part stores the old height, width, and window states of the Excel application window in the static variables. It then assigns new values to those properties. When you resize the application window, you should always set the WindowState property to *xlNormal* first because if the application is maximized, you can't change the width or the height. This part also customizes the Excel application caption.

The second part of setting the window makes sure that the workbook window is maximized and protected. You must unprotect it before attempting to maximize it. Setting the caption to an empty text string keeps the workbook name from appearing in the caption bar. The final statement of this part of the structure protects both the structure and the windows of the workbook. ProtectSheet is a procedure you'll create shortly that protects or unprotects a sheet. You give it the sheet name and specify whether protection should be on or off.

The third part of setting the window is mostly for your convenience as you develop the application. You could protect the worksheets interactively, but then you'd always have to unprotect them interactively to make any changes. Likewise, you could hide the scroll bars, the sheet tabs, the formula bar, and the status bar interactively, but sometimes they're useful while you're developing the application.

3 Click before the End Sub statement of the SetWindow procedure, and insert the file Code12e to add the remainder of the procedure:

```
Else
    Application.Caption = Empty
    If Not IsEmpty(myOldWidth) Then
        Application.Width = myOldWidth
        Application.Height = myOldHeight
        Application.Top = myOldTop
        Application.Left = myOldLeft
        Application.WindowState = myOldState
    End If
    ProtectSheet xlOff, "Main"
    ProtectSheet xlOff, "Data"
    ActiveWorkbook.Unprotect
    Application.DisplayFormulaBar = False
    Application.DisplayStatusBar = False
    Application.DisplayFormulaBar = True
    Application.DisplayStatusBar = True
    ActiveWindow.DisplayHorizontalScrollBar = True
    ActiveWindow.DisplayVerticalScrollBar = True
    ActiveWindow.DisplayWorkbookTabs = True
End If
```

These statements are the second half of the *If...Else...End If* structure. Basically, they undo everything the statements in the first half did. Again, checking whether the *myOld-Width* variable is empty is for your convenience while you're developing the macro. When you make certain changes in Visual Basic for Applications—such as adding or deleting a procedure—the value of static variables can be lost, effectively replacing the value with zero. Checking to see whether the *myOldWidth* variable is empty keeps the macro from shrinking the application window to a tiny block on the screen if you happen to do something that resets the static variables.

4 Click at the bottom of the module, and insert the file Code12f to add the ProtectSheet procedure:

```
Sub ProtectSheet(State, SheetItem)
    If State = xlOn Then
        Worksheets(SheetItem).EnableSelection = xlNoSelection
        Worksheets(SheetItem).Protect , True, True, True, True
    Else
        Worksheets(SheetItem).Unprotect
    End If
End Sub
```

This is the macro that the SetWindow macro calls to protect a worksheet. Setting the EnableSelection property to *xlNoSelection* prevents the user from selecting any cells when the worksheet is protected.

5 You need a way to run the SetWindow macro with the appropriate arguments. Insert these two macros in the module:

```
Sub InitView()
    SetMenu
    SetWindow xlOn
End Sub

Sub ExitView()
    ZapMenu
    SetWindow xlOff
End Sub
```

6 Save the Chapter12 workbook, and test the InitView and ExitView procedures.

7 Activate the Main sheet and click WA. The macro stops with an error when it attempts to hide the border lines on the chart. Even though the current protection for the worksheet should allow macro commands to execute, you do need to completely unprotect the worksheet in order to change the border of the chart. Fortunately, you can take advantage of the ProtectSheet procedure you created.

8 Click Debug and type the statement **ProtectSheet xlOff "Data"** before the loop and **ProtectSheet xlOn "Data"** after the loop. The final code section of code should look like this:

```
ProtectSheet xlOff "Data"
For Each mySeries In myChart.SeriesCollection
    mySeries.Border.LineStyle = xlNone
Next mySeries
ProtectSheet xlOn "Data"
```

9 Save the workbook, initialize the view, and click OR.

Effectively protecting a workbook always requires a lot of testing and often requires minor adjustments to the code.

Remove and Restore Toolbars

The procedure for removing and restoring toolbars is very similar to that for changing and restoring windows. Store the old values before making changes, and then use the stored values to restore the workspace. Storing toolbars, however, adds a new twist. Storing the size of the window always requires exactly three static variables for three and only three values (height, width, and state), but storing the list of visible toolbars can involve an unknown and varying number of toolbars.

As you know, Excel organizes multiple objects into collections. In fact, the toolbars themselves are in a collection. Visual Basic will actually allow you to create your own custom collection; you can make a collection of only those toolbars that need to be restored. Collections are powerful tools, and this example shows only a very simple (but extremely useful) way to take advantage of them.

1 Click at the bottom of the module, and insert the file Code12g to create this procedure:

```
Sub SetBars(State)
    Static myOldBars As New Collection
    Dim myBar

    If State = xlOn Then
        For Each myBar In Application.CommandBars
            If myBar.Type <> 1 And myBar.Visible Then
                myOldBars.Add myBar
                myBar.Visible = False
            End If
        Next myBar
    Else
        For Each myBar In myOldBars
            myBar.Visible = True
        Next
    End If
End Sub
```

Once again, a single procedure handles both the changing and the restoring so that a static variable can store the old values. This time, however, the static variable is declared as a *New Collection*. Declaring a variable as a *New Collection* tells Visual Basic that you want to create a collection of your own.

The first half of the *If...Else...End If* structure loops through each of the items in the application's CommandBars collection. If the command bar is a menu bar, its Type property is *1* and you should not hide or restore it. Otherwise, if the command bar is visible, you want to add it to your custom collection and then make it invisible. To add an item to a custom collection, you use the Add method followed by a reference to the item you want to add. The second half of the *If...Else...End If* structure simply loops through the custom collection, unhiding every toolbar in it.

2 You can launch SetBars from the InitView and ExitView macros, the same as you did with SetWindow. Insert the statement **SetBars xlOn** before the End Sub statement of the Init-View macro.

3 Insert the statement **SetBars xlOff** before the End Sub statement of the ExitView macro.

4 Save the Chapter12 workbook, and test the InitView and ExitView procedures.

This section didn't give details about all the ways you can use a custom collection, but even if you use a custom collection only for storing items from a standard collection—essentially copying the code from this chapter—you'll find it a valuable tool.

Complete the Package

All the pieces are in place for the finished application. You just need to make it happen automatically when the workbook opens.

1 Activate the Project Explorer window, and double-click ThisWorkbook.

2 Insert this event handler for when the workbook opens:

```
Private Sub Workbook_Open()
    Application.ScreenUpdating = False
    ProtectSheet xlOff, "Data"
    ActiveWorkbook.PivotCaches(1).Refresh
    InitView
    StartUpAnimation
End Sub
```

Every time the workbook opens, you want to check for new data in the database, customize the environment, and play the initial animation. To check for new data, you refresh the PivotCache that stores the data for the PivotTable. There is only one PivotTable in the workbook, so you can simply specify the first item in the PivotCache collection. You do, however, need to be sure that the worksheet containing the PivotTable is unprotected before refreshing the PivotCache. Fortunately, the *ProtectSheet* procedure you previously created is easy to use. Setting ScreenUpdating to *False* restricts the amount of flashing you see on the screen.

3 Insert this event handler for when the workbook closes:

```
Private Sub Workbook_BeforeClose(Cancel As Boolean)
    ExitView
    ActiveWorkbook.Saved = True
End Sub
```

Every time the workbook closes, you want to restore the environment. You also want to keep Excel from asking whether to save changes. Setting the Saved property of the active workbook to *True* makes Excel believe that it has been saved, so it doesn't ask.

4 In the ExitEIS macro, insert the statement **ExitView** before the ActiveWorksheet.Close statement. The *Workbook_BeforeClose* event handler needs to run ExitView in case the user closes the workbook by clicking the Excel Close Window button.

Tip

Theoretically, the ExitEIS macro shouldn't have to run ExitView. ExitEIS closes the window, and the event handler should run when the window closes regardless of what causes it to close. For some reason, however, the event handler doesn't run the ExitView macro if the ExitEIS macro triggered the event. It's just another reminder that Visual Basic for Applications was created by humans.

5   If you have a digital signature, sign the Visual Basic for Applications project to avoid the warning message when you open it.

6   In Excel, hide the ChartData sheet. (On the Format menu, point to the Sheet submenu and click the Hide command.)

7   Add a new sheet if necessary and name it **Blank**. Turn off the row and column headers. Select a cell several rows and columns away from cell A1. Save the workbook while the Blank sheet is active so that the user won't see anything when the workbook first opens.

8   Close the workbook, and reopen it. Test the application, and close the workbook.

The application is beautiful. It has functionality. It has an effective user interface. It's well packaged. Congratulations!

Index

Send feedback about this index to mspindex@microsoft.com.

F

N

About the Author

Reed Jacobson is a consulting manager with Aspirity, a company that specializes in Business Intelligence solutions with a focus on Microsoft SQL Server 2000 Analysis Services. Reed received a B.A. degree in Japanese and Linguistics, an MBA from Brigham Young University, and a graduate fellowship in Linguistics from Cornell University. He worked as a Software Applications Specialist for Hewlitt-Packard for 10 years and ran his own consulting firm for 5 years. Reed is the author of *Excel Trade Secrets for Windows*, *Microsoft Excel Advanced Topics Step by Step*, *Office 2000 Expert Companion*, and *Microsoft SQL Server Analysis Services Step by Step*. He has given presentations on Excel at TechEd and other Microsoft conferences and seminars. He has also created training video tapes for Excel, Access, and Visual Basic.

Work smarter
as you experience
Office XP
inside out!

You know your way around the Office suite. Now dig into Microsoft Office XP applications and *really* put your PC to work! These supremely organized references pack hundreds of timesaving solutions, trouble-shooting tips and tricks, and handy workarounds in concise, fast-answer format. All of this comprehensive information goes deep into the nooks and crannies of each Office application and accessory. Discover the best and fastest ways to perform everyday tasks, and challenge yourself to new levels of Office mastery with INSIDE OUT titles!

- MICROSOFT® OFFICE XP INSIDE OUT
- MICROSOFT WORD VERSION 2002 INSIDE OUT
- MICROSOFT EXCEL VERSION 2002 INSIDE OUT
- MICROSOFT OUTLOOK® VERSION 2002 INSIDE OUT
- MICROSOFT ACCESS VERSION 2002 INSIDE OUT
- MICROSOFT FRONTPAGE® VERSION 2002 INSIDE OUT
- MICROSOFT VISIO® VERSION 2002 INSIDE OUT

Microsoft®

mspress.microsoft.com

Get developer-to-developer *insights*
for building
and customizing Office XP solutions!

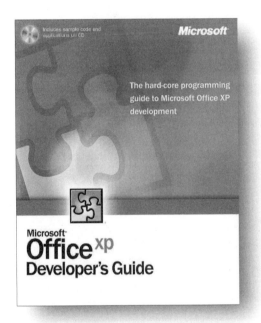

The hard-core programming guide to Microsoft Office XP development

Microsoft
Office XP
Developer's Guide

U.S.A.	**$49.99**
Canada	$72.99

ISBN: 0-7356-1242-0

Exploit the powerful programmability in Microsoft® Office XP with authoritative information straight from the Office XP development team. This hard-core programming reference comes packed with practical resources to help you maximize your productivity with Microsoft Office Developer. You get both design and coding examples that take advantage of the COM interfaces exposed by Office XP. Use this incisive coverage to build on what you know and to accomplish everything from automating simple tasks to creating complex vertical-market applications. And the companion CD-ROM contains procedure code you can use right now—helping you to focus your creativity on designing solutions, rather than on building rudimentary code. It's everything you need to create better business solutions, faster!

mspress.microsoft.com

Get a **Free**
e-mail newsletter, updates,
special offers, links to related books,
and more when you

register on line!

Register your Microsoft Press® title on our Web site and you'll get a FREE subscription to our e-mail newsletter, *Microsoft Press Book Connections.* You'll find out about newly released and upcoming books and learning tools, online events, software downloads, special offers and coupons for Microsoft Press customers, and information about major Microsoft® product releases. You can also read useful additional information about all the titles we publish, such as detailed book descriptions, tables of contents and indexes, sample chapters, links to related books and book series, author biographies, and reviews by other customers.

Registration is easy. Just visit this Web page and fill in your information:

http://www.microsoft.com/mspress/register

Microsoft®

MICROSOFT LICENSE AGREEMENT
Book Companion CD

IMPORTANT—READ CAREFULLY: This Microsoft End-User License Agreement ("EULA") is a legal agreement between you (either an individual or an entity) and Microsoft Corporation for the Microsoft product identified above, which includes computer software and may include associated media, printed materials, and "online" or electronic documentation ("SOFTWARE PRODUCT"). Any component included within the SOFTWARE PRODUCT that is accompanied by a separate End-User License Agreement shall be governed by such agreement and not the terms set forth below. By installing, copying, or otherwise using the SOFTWARE PRODUCT, you agree to be bound by the terms of this EULA. If you do not agree to the terms of this EULA, you are not authorized to install, copy, or otherwise use the SOFTWARE PRODUCT; you may, however, return the SOFTWARE PRODUCT, along with all printed materials and other items that form a part of the Microsoft product that includes the SOFTWARE PRODUCT, to the place you obtained them for a full refund.

SOFTWARE PRODUCT LICENSE

The SOFTWARE PRODUCT is protected by United States copyright laws and international copyright treaties, as well as other intellectual property laws and treaties. The SOFTWARE PRODUCT is licensed, not sold.

1. **GRANT OF LICENSE.** This EULA grants you the following rights:

   a. **Software Product.** You may install and use one copy of the SOFTWARE PRODUCT on a single computer. The primary user of the computer on which the SOFTWARE PRODUCT is installed may make a second copy for his or her exclusive use on a portable computer.

   b. **Storage/Network Use.** You may also store or install a copy of the SOFTWARE PRODUCT on a storage device, such as a network server, used only to install or run the SOFTWARE PRODUCT on your other computers over an internal network; however, you must acquire and dedicate a license for each separate computer on which the SOFTWARE PRODUCT is installed or run from the storage device. A license for the SOFTWARE PRODUCT may not be shared or used concurrently on different computers.

   c. **License Pak.** If you have acquired this EULA in a Microsoft License Pak, you may make the number of additional copies of the computer software portion of the SOFTWARE PRODUCT authorized on the printed copy of this EULA, and you may use each copy in the manner specified above. You are also entitled to make a corresponding number of secondary copies for portable computer use as specified above.

   d. **Sample Code.** Solely with respect to portions, if any, of the SOFTWARE PRODUCT that are identified within the SOFTWARE PRODUCT as sample code (the "SAMPLE CODE"):

      i. **Use and Modification.** Microsoft grants you the right to use and modify the source code version of the SAMPLE CODE, *provided* you comply with subsection (d)(iii) below. You may not distribute the SAMPLE CODE, or any modified version of the SAMPLE CODE, in source code form.

      ii. **Redistributable Files.** Provided you comply with subsection (d)(iii) below, Microsoft grants you a nonexclusive, royalty-free right to reproduce and distribute the object code version of the SAMPLE CODE and of any modified SAMPLE CODE, other than SAMPLE CODE, or any modified version thereof, designated as not redistributable in the Readme file that forms a part of the SOFTWARE PRODUCT (the "Non-Redistributable Sample Code"). All SAMPLE CODE other than the Non-Redistributable Sample Code is collectively referred to as the "REDISTRIBUTABLES."

      iii. **Redistribution Requirements.** If you redistribute the REDISTRIBUTABLES, you agree to: (i) distribute the REDISTRIBUTABLES in object code form only in conjunction with and as a part of your software application product; (ii) not use Microsoft's name, logo, or trademarks to market your software application product; (iii) include a valid copyright notice on your software application product; (iv) indemnify, hold harmless, and defend Microsoft from and against any claims or lawsuits, including attorney's fees, that arise or result from the use or distribution of your software application product; and (v) not permit further distribution of the REDISTRIBUTABLES by your end user. Contact Microsoft for the applicable royalties due and other licensing terms for all other uses and/or distribution of the REDISTRIBUTABLES.

2. **DESCRIPTION OF OTHER RIGHTS AND LIMITATIONS.**

   - **Limitations on Reverse Engineering, Decompilation, and Disassembly.** You may not reverse engineer, decompile, or disassemble the SOFTWARE PRODUCT, except and only to the extent that such activity is expressly permitted by applicable law notwithstanding this limitation.

   - **Separation of Components.** The SOFTWARE PRODUCT is licensed as a single product. Its component parts may not be separated for use on more than one computer.

   - **Rental.** You may not rent, lease, or lend the SOFTWARE PRODUCT.

   - **Support Services.** Microsoft may, but is not obligated to, provide you with support services related to the SOFTWARE PRODUCT ("Support Services"). Use of Support Services is governed by the Microsoft policies and programs described in the user manual, in "online" documentation, and/or in other Microsoft-provided materials. Any supplemental software code provided to you as part of the Support Services shall be considered part of the SOFTWARE PRODUCT and subject to the terms and conditions of this EULA. With respect to technical information you provide to Microsoft as part of the Support Services, Microsoft may use such information for its business purposes, including for product support and development. Microsoft will not utilize such technical information in a form that personally identifies you.

- **Software Transfer.** You may permanently transfer all of your rights under this EULA, provided you retain no copies, you transfer all of the SOFTWARE PRODUCT (including all component parts, the media and printed materials, any upgrades, this EULA, and, if applicable, the Certificate of Authenticity), **and** the recipient agrees to the terms of this EULA.

- **Termination.** Without prejudice to any other rights, Microsoft may terminate this EULA if you fail to comply with the terms and conditions of this EULA. In such event, you must destroy all copies of the SOFTWARE PRODUCT and all of its component parts.

3. COPYRIGHT. All title and copyrights in and to the SOFTWARE PRODUCT (including but not limited to any images, photographs, animations, video, audio, music, text, SAMPLE CODE, REDISTRIBUTABLES, and "applets" incorporated into the SOFTWARE PRODUCT) and any copies of the SOFTWARE PRODUCT are owned by Microsoft or its suppliers. The SOFTWARE PRODUCT is protected by copyright laws and international treaty provisions. Therefore, you must treat the SOFTWARE PRODUCT like any other copyrighted material **except** that you may install the SOFTWARE PRODUCT on a single computer provided you keep the original solely for backup or archival purposes. You may not copy the printed materials accompanying the SOFTWARE PRODUCT.

4. U.S. GOVERNMENT RESTRICTED RIGHTS. The SOFTWARE PRODUCT and documentation are provided with RESTRICTED RIGHTS. Use, duplication, or disclosure by the Government is subject to restrictions as set forth in subparagraph (c)(1)(ii) of the Rights in Technical Data and Computer Software clause at DFARS 252.227-7013 or subparagraphs (c)(1) and (2) of the Commercial Computer Software—Restricted Rights at 48 CFR 52.227-19, as applicable. Manufacturer is Microsoft Corporation/One Microsoft Way/Redmond, WA 98052-6399.

5. EXPORT RESTRICTIONS. You agree that you will not export or re-export the SOFTWARE PRODUCT, any part thereof, or any process or service that is the direct product of the SOFTWARE PRODUCT (the foregoing collectively referred to as the "Restricted Components"), to any country, person, entity, or end user subject to U.S. export restrictions. You specifically agree not to export or re-export any of the Restricted Components (i) to any country to which the U.S. has embargoed or restricted the export of goods or services, which currently include, but are not necessarily limited to, Cuba, Iran, Iraq, Libya, North Korea, Sudan, and Syria, or to any national of any such country, wherever located, who intends to transmit or transport the Restricted Components back to such country; (ii) to any end user who you know or have reason to know will utilize the Restricted Components in the design, development, or production of nuclear, chemical, or biological weapons; or (iii) to any end user who has been prohibited from participating in U.S. export transactions by any federal agency of the U.S. government. You warrant and represent that neither the BXA nor any other U.S. federal agency has suspended, revoked, or denied your export privileges.

DISCLAIMER OF WARRANTY

NO WARRANTIES OR CONDITIONS. MICROSOFT EXPRESSLY DISCLAIMS ANY WARRANTY OR CONDITION FOR THE SOFTWARE PRODUCT. THE SOFTWARE PRODUCT AND ANY RELATED DOCUMENTATION ARE PROVIDED "AS IS" WITHOUT WARRANTY OR CONDITION OF ANY KIND, EITHER EXPRESS OR IMPLIED, INCLUDING, WITHOUT LIMITATION, THE IMPLIED WARRANTIES OF MERCHANTABILITY, FITNESS FOR A PARTICULAR PURPOSE, OR NONINFRINGEMENT. THE ENTIRE RISK ARISING OUT OF USE OR PERFORMANCE OF THE SOFTWARE PRODUCT REMAINS WITH YOU.

LIMITATION OF LIABILITY. TO THE MAXIMUM EXTENT PERMITTED BY APPLICABLE LAW, IN NO EVENT SHALL MICROSOFT OR ITS SUPPLIERS BE LIABLE FOR ANY SPECIAL, INCIDENTAL, INDIRECT, OR CONSEQUENTIAL DAMAGES WHATSOEVER (INCLUDING, WITHOUT LIMITATION, DAMAGES FOR LOSS OF BUSINESS PROFITS, BUSINESS INTERRUPTION, LOSS OF BUSINESS INFORMATION, OR ANY OTHER PECUNIARY LOSS) ARISING OUT OF THE USE OF OR INABILITY TO USE THE SOFTWARE PRODUCT OR THE PROVISION OF OR FAILURE TO PROVIDE SUPPORT SERVICES, EVEN IF MICROSOFT HAS BEEN ADVISED OF THE POSSIBILITY OF SUCH DAMAGES. IN ANY CASE, MICROSOFT'S ENTIRE LIABILITY UNDER ANY PROVISION OF THIS EULA SHALL BE LIMITED TO THE GREATER OF THE AMOUNT ACTUALLY PAID BY YOU FOR THE SOFTWARE PRODUCT OR US$5.00; PROVIDED, HOWEVER, IF YOU HAVE ENTERED INTO A MICROSOFT SUPPORT SERVICES AGREEMENT, MICROSOFT'S ENTIRE LIABILITY REGARDING SUPPORT SERVICES SHALL BE GOVERNED BY THE TERMS OF THAT AGREEMENT. BECAUSE SOME STATES AND JURISDICTIONS DO NOT ALLOW THE EXCLUSION OR LIMITATION OF LIABILITY, THE ABOVE LIMITATION MAY NOT APPLY TO YOU.

MISCELLANEOUS

This EULA is governed by the laws of the State of Washington USA, except and only to the extent that applicable law mandates governing law of a different jurisdiction.

Should you have any questions concerning this EULA, or if you desire to contact Microsoft for any reason, please contact the Microsoft subsidiary serving your country, or write: Microsoft Sales Information Center/One Microsoft Way/Redmond, WA 98052-6399.

PN 097-0002296